Augustine and Catholic Christianization

PATRISTIC STUDIES

Gerald Bray
General Editor

Vol. 10

PETER LANG
New York • Washington, D.C./Baltimore • Bern
Frankfurt • Berlin • Brussels • Vienna • Oxford

Horace E. Six-Means

Augustine and Catholic Christianization

The Catholicization of Roman Africa, 391–408

PETER LANG
New York • Washington, D.C./Baltimore • Bern
Frankfurt • Berlin • Brussels • Vienna • Oxford

Library of Congress Cataloging-in-Publication Data

Six-Means, Horace E.
Augustine and Catholic Christianization:
the Catholicization of Roman Africa, 391–408 /
Horace Six-Means.
p. cm. — (Patristic studies; v. 10)
Includes bibliographical references and index.
1. Augustine, Saint, Bishop of Hippo. 2. Catholic Church—Africa
(Roman province). 3. Africa (Roman province)—Church history.
4. Augustine, Saint, Bishop of Hippo—Sermons—History
and criticism. I. Title.
BR65.A9S59   270.2092—dc22   2011007676
ISBN 978-1-4331-0804-4
ISSN 1094-6217

Bibliographic information published by **Die Deutsche Nationalbibliothek**.
Die Deutsche Nationalbibliothek lists this publication in the "Deutsche
Nationalbibliografie"; detailed bibliographic data is available
on the Internet at http://dnb.d-nb.de/.

The paper in this book meets the guidelines for permanence and durability
of the Committee on Production Guidelines for Book Longevity
of the Council of Library Resources.

© 2011 Peter Lang Publishing, Inc., New York
29 Broadway, 18th floor, New York, NY 10006
www.peterlang.com

Printed in Germany

Table of Contents

Acknowledgments

For their support through different stages of this work I owe thanks to so many, only a few of which can be named here. Foremost are three mentors of whom I am particularly appreciative: Professors Kathleen McVey, Peter Brown, and James F. Ross. Kathleen McVey was my advisor from my days as a Master of Divinity student at Princeton Seminary, through the completion of my dissertation. I have appreciated the breadth and depth of her critical vision, her wisdom and encouragement, and especially her sense of humor. Peter Brown of Princeton University, graciously welcomed me, a student from the school across the street, and helped me to explore the richness of the texts and textures of Augustine and the Roman world of late antiquity. James Ross, first introduced me to Augustine as an undergraduate at the University of Pennsylvania and encouraged me to pursue further study. For their contributions at various stages, I also thank Professors Scott Hendrix, Paul Rorem, and Andrew Walls

During the writing of the dissertation and the process of revision into the present book I benefited greatly from access to many libraries especially, the Princeton Theological Seminary Speer and Luce Libraries, the Firestone Library at Princeton University, the Z. Smith Reynolds Library of Wake Forest University, The Rowan County Public Library, and the Library of Hood Theological Seminary. Many thanks to the staff of those institutions for their gracious service. I would like to acknowledge with particular gratitude the help of Kate Skrebutenas, David Stewart, and Donald Vorp of Princeton Seminary and Cynthia Keever of Hood for their help in locating and acquiring the sources that were crucial to my research. Thanks also to Patout Burns, Mike Gaddis, and Elizabeth Johnson; each of these scholars allowed me to use work then unpublished.

Many friends and colleagues helped shape my thinking. Chief among those I wish to credit here is Marianne Delaporte, who along with being a valued conversation partner edited the final version of the dissertation. Thanks also to Sword and Spoon, Felix Asiedu, Kossi Ayedze, Chad Mullet Bauman, Joe Coker, Arun Jones, Jackie Maxwell, Glory and Jim Thomas, Jenny Reese, Austra Reines, and Haruko Ward.

I am grateful to those who helped make it financially possible for me to pursue doctoral studies. Thanks to Princeton Seminary and particularly those in Ph.D. Studies, the Office of Financial Aid, ARAMARK, Facilities, and the Theological Book Agency. Thanks also to the administration of Hood Seminary and my colleagues there. Thanks to the people I have had the pleasure of working with at Peter Lang Publishers: Heidi Burns, Nicole Grazioso, Alexandra Leach, Sarah Stack, Izmail Eyg, and Gerald Bray. Thanks also to the many patient and skilled people who worked on this book but who I do not know by name.

Family has been vitally important to seeing me through. There are too many aunts, uncles, and cousins from the Means and Cannon branches of the family to name them all here. However, I would like to particularly thank my sister Nadine, her husband Victor Valentine, and their family; my cousin who has been like a brother to me, William Howell III; and my uncle Alfred Means, his wife Constella, and their family. I also want to express my appreciation to and for my loving and long-suffering wife, Amy, who gave everything from encouragement to editing skills and appreciation to and for our son, David Augustine, who, as he grew with the dissertation, and then the book, served as a living beacon of hope spurring me on. Lastly, my deepest thanks to my parents, Constance Means and Rev. Horace Means Sr. I dedicate this book to them. Sadly, my father passed away on July 1, 2010, after a long struggle with cancer and was not able to see the completion of this work.

Thematic Foundations

CHAPTER ONE

Introduction

Since at least the latter part of the twentieth century, Christianization has been a topic of great interest in the study of the late Roman Empire, and Augustine of Hippo has featured prominently in a number of these studies. This research mainly focuses on the power struggles of Christians and non-Christians,[1] with limited reference to struggles between Christian groups. The evidence, at least in the case of Roman Africa of the fourth and fifth centuries, however, points to a more complex picture. I will argue in this book that Augustine wanted Africa to be Christian rather than part of what he called "paganism,"[2] but more significantly, he wanted people to adopt Catholic Christianity as opposed to Donatist, Manichean, Arian,

---

1. Ramsay MacMullen's *Christianizing the Roman Empire A.D. 100–400* (New Haven: Yale University Press, 1984), and *Christianity and Paganism in the Fourth to Eighth Centuries* (New Haven: Yale University Press, 1997) are good examples of this tendency.

2. This term "pagan" is used by Augustine and other Christian writers of the period to refer to all those who do not fit into the Christian or Jewish category. This term also has often been used by scholars across the centuries, but recently some scholars have opted to use "polytheism" as a more descriptive and less polemically based term. Compare MacMullen's works, mentioned above, with Garth Fowden's article "Polytheist Religion and Philosophy," in *Cambridge Ancient History*, vol. XIII: *The Late Empire, A.D.*, 3rd ed., edited by Averil Cameron and Peter Garnsey (Cambridge: Cambridge University Press, 1998), 538–560. Despite the use of the term "pagan," however, MacMullen does avoid the pitfall of giving it monolithic meaning.

or any other form of Christianity. The process whereby he works for this end I call Catholicization.[3] While this entails the preaching and writing of Augustine at its forefront, it also involves the concerted activity of his fellow bishops as well.

Specifically, with respect to Augustine, I argue that at the end of the fourth and beginning of the fifth centuries, Augustine emerged as the African Catholic Church's key articulator and "spin doctor" in a comprehensive, multivalent campaign to Catholicize Roman Africa through a twofold plan. On the one hand, there were strategies for internal reform of the African Catholic Church; on the other hand, there were strategies for combating religious rivals.

In this book, I will be examining the strategies of appeal that Augustine developed for various audiences, from his ordination as a priest in 391 until the fall of Stilicho in 408. I shall focus on sermons given between August 403 and June 404. Particularly of interest are a few sermons from the recently discovered Dolbeau collection.[4] However, as needed, I shall refer to other sermons, letters, and treatises,

3. "Catholicization" is a term that has been used by scholars before. I was directed by Kathleen McVey to a couple of interesting examples that deal with the period between Jesus and Augustine. They are Gillis Pison Wetter, "La catholicisation du Christianisme primitive," *Revue d'Histoire et de Philosophie Religieuses* (1927): 17–33; and Damien Casey, "Irenaeus: Touchstone of Catholicity," *Australian eJournal of Theology* 1 (2003), http://dlibrary.acu.edu. au/research/theology/ejournal/aet_1/Casey.htm, accessed May 8, 2004. Wetter argues that the Catholic Church neither fell from heaven nor departed from the teaching of the apostles. His concern is to reject the claims that some make that the Hellenism equated with the development of the Catholic Church as an institution tainted the original purity of the Church. Casey argues that "[t]he Irenaean catholicisation of the sacred is at odds with the sacrificial logic of closure and exclusion." Casey's overarching project is to understand Ireneaus's catholicity on its own terms without distorting his thought to support post-second-century constructions of "Roman" Catholicism. To do that he situates Ireneaus's theology of the Eucharist in his second-century struggles with the Gnostics and argues for an openness in the sacrament against their particularity. These authors, and others, do generally use the term to refer to the process of making Catholic but without reference to the program that I argue was developed by Augustine and his colleagues in Roman Africa.

4. François Dolbeau discovered twenty-six "new" sermons of Augustine in 1990. For his Latin editions with an introduction and notes in French, see François Dolbeau, *Augustin D'Hippone Vingt-Six Sermons au Peuple D'Afrique: Retrouvés à Mayence*, édités et commentés par François Dolbeau, Collection des Études Augustiniennes, Séries Antiquité 147 (Paris: Institut d'Études Augustiniennes, 1996). This is a compilation of the various articles wherein Dolbeau previously published editions of the Latin text of the sermons with commentary in French. These articles can be found in *Revue Bénédictine* 101–104 and in *Revue des Études Augustiniennes* 37–40. English translations of the sermons can be found in *The Works of Saint Augustine: A Translation for the 21st Century: Part III, Sermons*, Vol. 11: *New Sermons*, translated and notes by Edmund Hill, O.P.; and edited by John E. Rotelle, O.S.A. (Hyde Park, NY: New City Press, 1998). These sermons will be discussed in greater detail in Chapter 5.

placing them all in relationship to the African Catholic Bishops' Councils[5] and imperial legislation,[6] especially the Edict of Unity of 405.[7]

There are four areas of contribution that I see this study making. To begin with, this study refocuses research both on Christianization in Roman Africa and on Augustine's doctrine of the Church. Aside from works on Christianization, there has been much written on Augustine's doctrine of the Church.[8] However, none of these works deal with the sociohistorical development of Augustine's thinking about the Church in relationship to both pagans and those whom he comes to label as schismatics or heretics. This study will consider the process of Christianization's local manifestation in Roman Africa of the late fourth and early fifth centuries through the thought and action of Augustine. It posits Catholicization as a better term to describe the process uncovered there, whereby Augustine and colleagues sought to establish the legalized dominance of the Catholic Church and win adherence to the Catholic Christian faith from the population across the broad range of socioeconomic strata.

Second, it seeks to study this process primarily from Augustine's perspective. It will describe the development of what he thought and did as the chief theorist and articulator of, and agitator for, this particular ecclesiology.

Third, although Augustine is the pivotal person in the process of Catholicization, it will be shown that he did not act alone. Augustine was at the forefront of a phalanx of bishops, priests, and monks, some of whom he recruited, who sought to establish the true faith against paganism, heresy, and schism.[9] Most notable

---

5. See *Concilia Africae A. 345–525*, vol. 149 of *Corpus Christianorum: Series Latina*, edited by Charles Munier (Turnhout, Belgium: Brepols, 1974).

6. See *The Theodosian Code [Codex Theodosianus; CT] and Novels and the Sirmondian Constitutions*, translated, with commentary, glossary, and bibliography, by Clyde Pharr in collaboration with Theresa Sherrer Davidson and Mary Brown Pharr, introduction by C. Dickerman Williams (Princeton: Princeton University Press, 1952).

7. *CT* 16.5.38.

8. Important starting points on Augustine's ecclesiology have been Agostino Trapè's discussion of Augustine's doctrine of the Church and the bibliography that he gives: *Patrology*, vol. 4, edited by Angelo Di Berardino, introduction by Johannes Quasten, translated by Placid Solari (Westminster MD: Christian Classics, Inc., 1994), 445–449. Some works of particular interest are Pierre Battifol, *Le catholicisme de st. Augustin*, 4th ed. (Paris: Librairie Lecoffre, 1928); P. Bogomeo, *L'Église de ces temps dans la prédication de Saint Augustin* (Paris, 1962); Robert Evans, *One and Holy: The Church in Latin Patristic Thought* (London: SPCK, 1972); Stanislaus Grabowski, *The Church: An Introduction to the Theology of St. Augustine* (St. Louis: Herder, 1957).

9. This is brought out to some degree in the aforementioned works that either have the ecclesiological focus or the Christianization focus. But there is not a work that deals with the subject of the relationship to the issues on which I am concentrating here, nor do they have the benefit of the evidence provided by the new sermons. Jane Merdinger's book, *Rome and the African Church*

among this group is Aurelius, Bishop of Carthage, the first city of Roman Africa, and the contested See, which gave rise to the division of the African Church into Catholic and Donatist parties.

Lastly, this study will be examining material little studied in English. Most important, canons of the African Catholic Bishops' Councils, Augustine's treatise *Contra Cresconium*, and recently discovered sermons will be analyzed. They provide key pieces of evidence from Augustine's early episcopate that, when placed alongside existing evidence, will lead to adjustments in our understanding of Augustine and his context. It is as if we are seeking to restore a mosaic that has been damaged by the passage of time and travelers. Many scenes are quite familiar to us, but these new tesserae cause us to look with a more careful eye at a familiar picture to reconsider what we thought we had already seen.

The book is written in two sections. The first section presents the theoretical framework of our understanding Augustine's role in the process of Catholicization. Then, using the frames developed in Section I, in Section II we look at some key works that support my thesis.

In Section I, Chapters 2, 3, and 4, titled "Self-Understanding," "Social Order," and "Rhetoric," respectively, I explore Augustine's self-understanding, or the role he thinks he is performing. Then, I consider the objective in mind, or what he hopes to produce in his hearers and those for and to whom he writes. Finally, I illustrate the varied rhetorical strategies that he used.

These themes emerged from my reading of Augustine's texts, in particular the sermons. I found Augustine understanding himself as a bishop and shepherd of souls. The chief responsibilities of the bishop are preaching and dispensing the sacraments; it is through these activities that he, as God's servant and imitator of Christ, guides people on the path to salvation. Consistent with what we find in *On Christian Doctrine*, Augustine avoids speaking or preaching for mere delight; rather, delight is subordinate to teaching and moving his hearers to action in accord with what they have learned.[10]

To articulate my understanding of these themes, and to turn these themes into analytical tools, I have needed to engage a number of different methodological disciplines. I have striven to achieve eclectic simplicity without superficiality. Specialists in the various disciplines I engage may think otherwise.

---

in the Time of Augustine (New Haven: Yale University Press, 1997), based on her dissertation, is a good example of how Augustine can be viewed as a leader amongst a cadre of bishops. However, Merdinger focuses on cases of appeal to explain the development of the African Church in relationship to Roman primacy, whereas I will explore the Catholic Church's rise in Africa and Augustine's role in it as my central purpose rather than as an incidental item.

10. *On Christian Doctrine (De Doctrina Christina)* 4.12.

Chapter 2 traces the development of Augustine's self-understanding as he moved through various social roles from rhetor to bishop. This is viewed principally from the vantage point of the *Confessions*, with references to other works as well. It is shown that by the time he wrote the *Confessions*, Augustine had linked identity and self-understanding in a way that provided motivation for action. Augustine had become a bishop by 396; this identity obliged him to fulfill certain responsibilities in society. These obligations were akin to those he had as a rhetor, but with a different fundamental motivation and a different authority to whom he was accountable. As a bishop, Augustine would strive to be the humble and faithful servant of God and God's people, and not the prideful servant of his own passions.

Augustine's self-understanding as a bishop committed him to a broad vision of social order, discussed in Chapter 3. The identity of the rhetor fit in a version of social order that was of the temporal age or temporal world. The identity of the bishop fit with an eternal perspective in Augustine's mind. That eternal perspective was the reconciliation of souls to God. Following Cyprian, to a certain degree, Augustine would claim that if one would have God as Father, then the Catholic Church must be mother. Chapter 3 first discusses the development of the recognition and favoring of the Catholic Church in imperial legislation in the late fourth century. It then moves to tracking the development of Augustine's understanding of Catholicity[11] while also tracking the development of a plan to make the Catholic Church in Africa the dominant religious institution. The earliest expression we have of this plan is found in Augustine's *Epistle* 22, which is discussed in Chapter 3 as "the charter of Catholicization." In that letter we see Augustine encouraging his friend Aurelius, the bishop of Carthage, to lead the way in pursuing moral reform in the Catholic churches of Africa so that they can better guide people in imitation of Christ and actively confront a range of external opponents.

The last chapter in the first section, Chapter 4, tackles the chief means by which Augustine was personally active in promoting Catholicization, his rhetoric. In this chapter, Augustine's rhetorical strategies are examined both from the perspective of the classical traditions of rhetoric in which he was trained and from the perspective of modern rhetorical analysis drawn principally from literary and political theory. Augustine's *De Doctrina Christiana* is a key source that is examined in this chapter. It provides explicit testimony from Augustine about how he approached persuasive discourse. I argue that *De Doctrina Christiana* also shows

---

11. I pay particular attention to Augustine's use of Ambrose, Optatus of Milevis, Tyconius, and Cyprian. Augustine returned to Africa having been primarily influenced by Ambrose. But over the first decade of his episcopate, Optatus, Tyconius, and Cyprian became sources on whom Augustine increasingly relied.

how Augustine hoped to train Catholic clergy through this handbook to be more skilled in persuasion as part of his plan of Catholicization.

Section II, "The Road to Unity and Its Aftermath," revolves around the Edict of Unity and accompanying legislation issued from Ravenna by Emperor Honorius. Chapter 5, "Catholicization and the Preaching Tours of Augustine: August 403– June 404," focuses on some of Augustine's preaching between the African Catholic Bishops' Councils of August 403 and June 404. Augustine's preaching displays a hardening of the Catholic position that results in the June 404 council sending representatives to Ravenna to ask for a more supportive posture from the government for the Catholic Church. Two groups of sermons are discussed as examples of Augustine's deployment of rhetorical strategies targeted to audiences outside Hippo, and mainly in Carthage, for the purpose of winning people to the Catholic faith and delegitimizing the positions of opponents.

The last substantive chapter of the book, Chapter 6, deals with Honorius's Edict of Unity of February 405 and its aftermath through the lenses of Augustine's work *Contra Cresconium* and his *Epistle* 93 to Vincentius. Augustine's work against Cresconius is particularly interesting because the attacks that Cresconius levels against Augustine can be seen as one of three challenges: to Augustine's self-understanding, to the execution of his program of social order (Catholicization), or to the means by which Augustine is personally engaged and implicated in Catholicization through his rhetoric. And, finally, I summarize my conclusions in Chapter 7.

CHAPTER TWO

Self-Understanding: From Rhetor to Bishop

Self-Understanding and Self-Presentation

Is it possible to know what Augustine's understanding of himself was, or do we merely encounter his presentation of himself? What is the difference between the two, and, for the purposes of this study, if there is a difference, how much does it matter? All authors, all people, present themselves in ways that possibly do not correspond to the person they perceive themselves to be. The reasons for the distance between the two selves, the self-known self and the presented self, can be placed on a spectrum falling between intentional deceit and innocent limits of intended communication. Also complicating this picture is the degree to which the self-knowledge of a person can be flawed. It is possible for someone to be deceived about themselves.

What, then, are we to make of Augustine? In arguing for the reality of the program of social order that I am calling Catholicization, I claim that Augustine's understanding of himself was crucial in the development of that program. During the years we are considering Augustine's activities, Augustine consistently presents himself as acutely concerned with knowledge and understanding of himself. As early as the *Soliloquies* (*Soliloquia*), begun at Cassiaciacum in 386[1] but perhaps finished in the

---

1. On dating and for a good brief introduction and overview, see Allan Fitzgerald, ed., *Augustine through the Ages: An Encyclopedia* (Grand Rapids, MI: Wm. B. Eerdmans, 1999), s.v.

winter of 387 after returning to Milan, we see Augustine taking up investigation of the self. *Soliloquium* (*Soliloquia*), "talking to one's self"[2] in fact, is a term invented by Augustine to describe his novel project of holding a dialogue between Augustine and Reason (*Ratio*). There in the opening lines he says:

> For a long time I had been turning over in my mind many various thoughts. For many days I had been earnestly seeking to know myself and my chief good and what evil was to be shunned. Suddenly someone spoke to me, whether it was myself or someone else from without or from within I know not. Indeed, to know that is my main endeavor.[3]

Reason instructs Augustine to present the goals of his search to God in the form of a prayer, saying: "Pray for health and for aid to attain what you desire; and write this down that you may become more spirited in your quest." Then Reason asks him to summarize his prayer and Augustine replies: "I desire to know God and the soul" (*Deum et animam scire cupio*).[4] Thus, the *Soliloquies* clearly establishes Augustine's interest in self-understanding. Pursuit of this interest is part of his overall pursuit of truth and wisdom.

If we doubt Augustine's commitment to truth telling, we do it in the face of his general orientation and his particular commitment as demonstrated throughout his works and presented explicitly in his work *On Lying* (*De Mendacio*) of 395. Augustine there defines the person who lies as follows: "Wherefore, that man lies, who has one thing in his mind and utters another in words, or by signs of whatever kind."[5] He proceeds to argue that even though there are kinds of lies of varying degrees, no circumstance justifies an intentional effort to deceive, even for such noble reasons as to spare someone pain or even death.[6] This pursuit of an honest vision of himself Augustine constantly presents before other people and before God. In the

---

"*Soliloquia,*" by Joanne McWilliam. See also the introduction to the *Soliloquies*, edited by John H. S. Burleigh, *Soliloquies*, in *Augustine: Earlier Writings*, Library of Christian Classics (Philadelphia: Westminster Press, 1953), 19–22.

2. Lewis and Short's *A Latin Dictionary*, 1984 ed., "*Soliloquium.*"

3. Augustine, *Soliloquies* 1.1. "Volventi mihi multa ac varia mecum diu, ac per multos dies sedulo quaerenti memetipsum ac bonum meum, quidve mali evitandum esset; ait mihi subito, sive ego ipse, sive alius quis extrinsecus, sive intrinsecus, nescio: nam hoc ipsum est quod magnopere scire molior."

4. Ibid., 1.2.7.

5. Augustine, *De Mendacio* 3.3. "Quapropter ille mentitur, qui aliud habet in animo, et aliud verbis vel quibuslibet significationibus enuntiat." For discussion of this work compared to his later work *Contra Mendacium* (420), see *Augustine through the Ages: An Encyclopedia*, 1999 ed., s.v. "*Mendacio, De/ Contra Mendacium,*" by Boniface Ramsey.

6. Augustine, *De Mendacio* 18.25ff.

Confessions, about a decade after the *Soliloquies,* Augustine addresses the questions that readers may have about the reliability of the self-understanding that he presents, as it goes right to the heart of whether he is making an honest confession or not.

> Why then should I be concerned for human readers to hear my confessions? It is not they who are going "heal my sicknesses" (Ps. 102:3). The human race is inquisitive about other people's lives, but negligent to correct their own. Why do they demand to hear from me what I am when they refuse to hear from you what they are? And when they hear me talking about myself how can they know if I am telling the truth, when no one "knows what is going on in a person except the human spirit which is within" (1 Cor. 2:11)? But if they were to hear about themselves from you, they could not say "The Lord is lying." To hear you speaking about oneself is to know oneself. Moreover, anyone who knows himself and says "That is false" must be a liar. But "love believes all things" (1 Cor. 13:7), at least among those that love has bonded to itself and made one. I also, Lord, so make my confession to you that I may be heard by people to whom I cannot prove that my confession is true. But those whose ears are opened by love believe me.[7]

There are three observations that I want to make about Augustine's comments here in particular and his approach to self-understanding in general.

1. He wants to be humble and honest[8] before God.
2. He believes self-knowledge is only received from God.
3. Love is the basis for the reception of knowledge either immediately from God, or mediated through other people.

It may be too much to ask that we love him, yet his interest in the self and in communicating about himself is compelling and should at least warrant our respect. For many scholars it has done as much. With particular reference to the *Confessions,*

7. Augustine, *Confessions,* translated by Henry Chadwick (New York: Oxford, 1991), 10.3.3. "Quid mihi ergo est cum hominibus, ut audiant confessiones meas, quasi ipsi sanaturi sint omnes languores meos? Curiosum genus ad cognoscendam vitam alienam, desidiosum ad corrigendam suam. Quid a me quaerunt audire qui sim, qui nolunt a te audire qui sint? Et unde sciunt, cum a me ipso de me ipso audiunt, an verum dicam, quandoquidem nemo scit hominum, quid agatur in homine, nisi spiritus hominis, qui in ipso est? Si autem a te audiant de se ipsis, non poterunt dicere: 'Mentitur Dominus.' Quid est enim a te audire de se nisi cognoscere se? Quis porro cognoscit et dicit: 'Falsum est,' nisi ipse mentiatur? Sed quia caritas omnia credit, inter eos utique, quos connexos sibimet unum facit, ego quoque, Domine, etiam sic tibi confiteor, ut audiant homines, quibus demonstrare non possum, an vera confitear; sed credunt mihi, quorum mihi aures caritas aperit."

8. Given his statements in general and his work *De Mendacio* in particular, it is clear that Augustine was passionately seeking truth and he understood the difference between truth telling and falsity.

scholars have been drawn to Augustine with varying methods of approach and equally varying interpretations.

Literarily, Gian Biagio Conte proclaims Augustine to be "the richest and most gifted of the Latin thinkers and at the same time a writer of great elegance." Yet he frankly admits that:

> To give even an approximate idea of the vast literary writings produced by a man who could illuminate the most obscure and disturbing aspects of his own soul and could write about them using all the formal artifices of rhetoric in magisterial fashion is a disheartening enterprise. Augustine always has some surprise, makes some unexpected leap, making all systematizations precarious and questionable. His introspection is at its greatest in the *Confessions,* where he reaches levels of psychological analysis never reached before and difficult to find again in later periods.[9]

Indeed there is a consensus that attributes to Augustine greatness and originality, particularly where introspection is concerned. In some of these views, the *Confessions* is, as Conte says, "the first autobiography in the modern sense of the term."[10] While recognizing his notable originality, some other scholars have sought to link Augustine with other examples of self-understanding in antiquity. William Babcock, for example, compares Marcus Aurelius's *Meditations* with Augustine's *Confessions,* and argues that:

> Augustine found a better solution to the problem of the self in its alienation from a world that seemed to render trivial and senseless all human action and ambition— better in the sense that it established more and more links between the self and both its own history and its human and natural environment.[11]

Later in this chapter we shall see some of the ways in which Augustine's self-understanding develops from one that was more insular to one that emphasized the connectedness of which Babcock speaks.

Another example of recognizing the significance of Augustine's *Confessions,* while seeing it in relationship to antecedents, is Pierre Courcelle's massive *Les Confessions de S. Augustin dans la tradition littéraire* (1962),[12] a sequel of sorts to his *Recherches sur les Confessions de S. Augustin* (1950, 1968). This study on the literary tradition takes up antecedents and posterity. In the sections on antecedents,

9. Gian Biagio Conte, *Latin Literature,* translated by Joseph B. Solodow, revised by Don Fowler and Glenn W. Most (Baltimore: Johns Hopkins University Press, 1994), 688.

10. Ibid., 690.

11. William Babcock, "Patterns of Roman Selfhood: Marcus Aurelius and Augustine of Hippo," *Perkins School of Theology Journal* 29, no. 6 (Winter 1976): 19.

12. Pierre Courcelle, *Les Confessions de S. Augustin dans la tradition littéraire* (Paris: Études Augustiniennes, 1962).

Courcelle focuses in Part 1, Section 1 on the books of the Platonists, referred to in the *Confessions*.[13] Part 1, Section 2 considers Augustine's account of his conversion and the myriad of potentially influential predecessors, from pagan sources, such as Augustine's fellow African, the second-century author Apuleius,[14] to Christian sources, such as Gregory of Nazianzus, the fourth-century Cappadocian.[15] The comparisons of Babcock, Courcelle, and others serve to highlight the literary significance of self-understanding in antiquity, with Augustine being, if not unique, at least paradigmatic and perhaps most revolutionary in developing a profoundly psychological mode of writing.

It stands to reason then that Augustine's concern for self-understanding would not be neglected by philosophers and psychologists. Philip Cary's *Augustine's Invention of the Inner Self*[16] claims that Augustine, following a particularly Neoplatonic tradition, establishes the self as a philosophic category for reflection. Sandra Lee Dixon begins her *Augustine: The Gathered and the Scattered Self*[17] with a discussion of the rich tradition of applying psychological categories of analysis to Augustine over the past fifty years. After highlighting some profitable studies and dead-ends, she offers what she sees as some advances in using psychology to read Augustine and his *Confessions*. Her work is particularly helpful because the discipline of psychology as it has developed can bring into sharper focus the difficulty in making sense of a person's self-understanding. With authors in general, and Augustine in particular, we can recognize that there are some inconsistencies and discordances, but overall the picture that emerges from examining his letters, sermons, and treatises displays a coherent wholeness. Viewed diachronically, the evidence points to developments and changes in Augustine's self-understanding as he moves from rhetor to bishop, with many turns along a winding road from one to the other. Viewed synchronically, inconsistency shown in the sources can largely be explained as rhetorical adjustments called for by differences in genre and/or audience. In any case, because Augustine makes his self-understanding a central part of his writings and a key factor in motivating his actions, and because we presume truth telling unless there is countermanding evidence, we will trace the development of his self-understanding, as he presents it, from his youth through his first decade or so as a bishop.

13. Augustine, *Confessions* 7.9.13.

14. Courcelle, 101–109.

15. Ibid., 134–136.

16. Philip Cary, *Augustine's Invention of the Inner Self* (New York: Oxford, 2000). See also Edward Booth, *Saint Augustine and the Western Tradition of Self-Knowing* (Villanova, PA: Villanova University Press, 1989).

17. Sandra Lee Dixon, *Augustine: The Gathered and the Scattered Self* (St. Louis: Chalice, 1999).

The *Confessions* (397–401)[18] offers the most famous and inviting starting place for all who come to know Augustine.[19] It is indeed a literary milestone and master-piece that tells us much about Augustine. However, given that the autobiographical narrative from Books 1–9 covers only his life from birth (354) to just after his baptism (387), beginning with the *Confessions* would seem to be of little value for considering Augustine's self-understanding from 391, the year of his ordination to the priesthood, onward. Nevertheless, we will begin with the *Confessions* for two reasons. First, his self-understanding as it developed in those early years before his ordination in 391 provides important contrasting background for what happens after his ordination. Second, in Book 10 of the *Confessions*, having finished discussion of his past, Augustine speaks of his present.

> See the long story I have told to the best of my ability and will respond to your prior will that I should make confession to you, my Lord God. For "you are good, for your mercy is for ever" (Ps. 117:1).
>
> But when shall I be capable of proclaiming by "the tongue of my pen" (Ps. 44:2) all your exhortations and all your terrors and consolations and directives, by which you brought me to preach your word and dispense your sacrament to your people (*quibus me perduxisti praedicare verbum et sacramentum tuum dispensare populo tuo?*)? And if I have the capacity to proclaim this in an orderly narrative, yet the drops of time are too precious to me.[20]

Augustine tantalizingly wishes for time to give an account of how God brought (him) to preach and dispense the sacraments, but we do not get that account in the *Confessions*. We need to piece that story together from his letters, treatises, sermons, and the biography of his disciple Possidius. We shall come to those pieces of evidence in due time. But with the passage above, we have a key phrase, "you brought

---

18. The dating I am using is James O'Donnell's. See his discussion in his very thorough three-volume commentary on the Latin text of the *Confessions*. James O'Donnell, ed., *Augustine: Confessions* (New York: Oxford University Press, 1992), 1:xli–xlii.

19. There are numerous works written about Augustine's life and works. Some of the most helpful in English are Peter Brown, *Augustine of Hippo*; James O'Donnell, *Augustine*; Van Der Meer, *Augustine the Bishop*; John Burnaby, *Amor Dei*; Gerald Bonner, *Augustine Life and Controversies*; and Henry Chadwick, *Augustine*. We learn a great deal about Augustine's life through his *Confessions*, which gives a biographical spiritual journey until his baptism. For life from that point on, our early sources are his letters, sermons, and other writings. We are guided through many of these works by Augustine himself in his *Retractations*, a catalogue of sorts wherein Augustine orders many of his works chronologically and gives his opinion of them in his mature years. We are also fortunate enough to have an early biography from Possidius, a younger disciple of Augustine.

20. Augustine, *Confessions* 11.1.1–11.2.2.

me to preach your word and dispense your sacrament to your people (*quibus me perduxisti praedicare verbum et sacramentum tuum dispensare populo tuo*)," which James O'Donnell says "epitomizes the demands of ordained ministry, demands whose burdens he (Augustine) always felt."[21] Thus, we can see the *Confessions* as the story of a bishop reflecting on his pre-ecclesial life, and thus, indirectly telling us about his ecclesial life. So now let us examine Augustine's self-understanding as it developed before he was made a bishop, and for that, yes, first we turn to the *Confessions*.

Despite being hailed as such by scholars like Conte, the *Confessions* is not straightforward autobiography in our modern sense. The first nine books are the roughly autobiographical account of how Augustine came to be a baptized Catholic. The last four are somewhat puzzling to scholars as to how they fit with the autobiographical narrative. Augustine himself, however, says that "the first ten books were written about myself; the last three about Holy Scripture, from the words: 'In the beginning God created heaven and earth' as far as the Sabbath rest (Genesis 1.1–2.2)."[22] In the face of Augustine's characterization of his *Confessions*, scholars have struggled to understand to what degree the *Confessions* is a work with a coherent intentional plan. Some, like John O'Meara and Courcelle, have argued that the work lacks a coherent plan and exemplifies Augustine's haphazard practice of composition.[23] Others, like R. D. Crouse, Robert McMahon, and C. J. Starnes, have claimed various forms of rationality that tie together all thirteen books.[24] These coherency views often focus on some spiritual meaning found in the text, such as ascent of the mind or conversion. McMahon, interestingly, has argued that incoherency is part of Augustine's plan. According to McMahon, in recognizing the commonly accepted self-presentation of the *Confessions* as a conversation with God, one must realize the following:

> Like all genuine dialogue, it does not develop according to some rigid, preconceived plan.
> Though the *Confessions* traces the course of Augustine's life up to the death of Monica

---

21. See commentary on *Confessions* 11.1.1–11.2.2 by James O'Donnell in *Augustine: Confessions*, vol 3:255–256.] 255–256. See also the paper by Thomas F. Martin, "*Clericatus sarcina* (ep.126.3): Augustine and the Care of the Clergy," http://people.vanderbilt.edu/~james.p.burns/chroma/clergy/Martinorders.html accessed November 24, 2010.

22. *Retractations* 2.32.1, translated by Sister Mary Inez Bogan (Washington D.C.: Catholic University of America Press, 1968).

23. John J. O'Meara, *The Young Augustine* (London: Longmans, 1954; repr., Alba House, 1965); and Pierre Courcelle, *Recherches sur les Confessions de S. Augustin* (Paris: Boccard, 1950; 2nd ed., 1968).

24. R. D. Crouse, "'Recurrens in te unum' The Pattern of Saint Augustine's *Confessions*," *Studia Patristica* XIV (1976): 389–392; Robert McMahon, *Augustine's Prayerful Ascent: An Essay on the Literary Form of the Confessions* (Athens, GA: Georgia University Press, 1989); C. J. Starnes, "The Unity of the Confessions" *Studia Patristica* XVIII, no. 4 (1990): 105–111.

and scrutinizes the text of Genesis I more or less verse by verse, it does so with frequent shifts and unexpected moves. In his prayerful dialogue with God, the writer is moved now to narrate some past act, now to meditate upon it, to speak at length of Alypius here and Monica there, to accuse himself and to praise God by sudden turns. Such turns are part of every genuine dialogue. Neither party alone completely controls its course.[25]

There are indeed many turns in the story, and often in the literature on the *Confessions,* one finds discussion of the conversion or conversions of Augustine. The conversion described in Book 8 is the culmination of the narrative. There in the famous garden scene Augustine tells of his pivotal surrender to God brought about by a confluence of providential movements.[26] It has also been noted, however, that there are other key turns, conversions, or shifts in Augustine's identity.[27] First, there was Augustine's encounter with the *Hortensius*;[28] then his cleavage to a group, the Manichees;[29] and then he becomes persuaded by the books of the Platonists.[30] Finally, on April 24–25, 387, in Milan, he is baptized as a Christian.[31] But it is not just any kind of Christian he becomes; under the influence of Ambrose and Simplicianus, Augustine becomes a Catholic. Let us now look at these various turns and identity shifts in greater detail.

Pre-baptismal Identity Shifts

Rhetor[32]

Augustine was born to Monica and Patricius in November 354. Monica was a Catholic Christian, probably of Berber background, and Patricius was a pagan,

---

25. McMahon, 9.

26. Augustine, *Confessions* 8.12.28–30.

27. On Augustine's conversions, see particularly Leo Ferrari, *The Conversions of Saint Augustine* (Villanova, PA: Villanova University Press, 1984), and Robert Markus, *Conversion and Disenchantment in Augustine's Spiritual Career* (Villanova, PA: Villanova University Press, 1989).

28. Augustine *Confessions,* 3.4.7.

29. Ibid., 3.6.10.

30. Ibid., 7.9.13.

31. This baptism took place approximately nine months after his decision in the garden in 386. O'Donnell argues that the importance of the baptism as the decisive act of Augustine to identify himself with the Catholic Christian community has often been underestimated. See O'Donnell, *Augustine: Confessions* 1:xxviii.

32. I have chosen to deal with Augustine as rhetor under a heading separate from Manichee and Seeker of Truth, even though he was employed as rhetor when he was a Manichee and a

probably of mixed Numidian/Roman descent.[33] Augustine was instructed in the religion of Monica as he was growing up, but he did not receive baptism until he was an adult.[34] This is after his famed and exaggerated prodigal wanderings.[35] Although his mother wanted Augustine to be a baptized Christian, she did not follow through with a planned baptism during a childhood illness. According to Augustine, the religious concern for him was solely his mother's. Both his mother and father, however, were united in their desire to see their son become successful. Patricius was a *curiales*, a minor civic official.[36] He had some status and enough wealth to own some slaves, but he and his family were far from rich. They could be seen as solidly middle class. Their desires for their son were for greater status and wealth. This ambition became Augustine's as well. His intelligence and skill with language became the ticket to that success. But from the first book of the *Confessions* on, he declares that the gift of intelligence that God

philosopher, because the rhetorician identity or self-understanding is presented first and foundationally in the *Confessions*, and the other personae are built upon it.

33. These are educated guesses based on what is known about society in Roman Africa at this time. W. H. C. Frend, for example, argues that Monica's name indicates a tie to Berber culture and would be uncommon for someone of Latin lineage. Frend, "A Note on the Berber Background in the Life of Augustine," *Journal of Theological Studies* XLIII, nos. 171/172 (July–October 1942): 230. Patricius, though, is a fine Latin name and Possidius says that he was a *curiales* (*Life of Augustine* 1.1). So, as O'Meara claims, he most likely comes from a mixed Numidian/Roman background (O'Meara, 25). Understanding the details of Augustine's life begins with the *Confessions* and *The Life of Augustine* by Augustine's disciple Possidius. As for modern scholarship, there were a number of important works in the last half of the twentieth century. The classic biography by Peter Brown has now been published in a new edition by University of California Press (2000). This edition reprints the classic of 1967 but adds new material in a new two-chapter epilogue. These new chapters present both Brown's reflections on the original and his wrestling with the more than two decades of progress in the study of Augustine and his age. Of particular interest is Brown's treatment of the Divjak letters and the Dolbeau sermons. Other biographical works of note are Serge Lancel, *Saint Augustin*; F. Van Der Meer, *Augustine the Bishop*; and Bonner, *Saint Augustine of Hippo, Life and Controversies*.

34. Augustine, *Confessions* 1.11.17. Augustine was signed with the cross as an infant to mark him as a catechumen. He was slated for baptism when he was struck with a serious illness. When he unexpectedly recovered, however, his mother postponed baptism for fear that the years he had ahead of him would present an opportunity for him to fall into a sin that penance could not expunge. This was a common practice in fourth-century Africa.

35. Augustine himself says that he was faithful to one woman, the unnamed woman of the *Confessions*. This relationship lasted for about fifteen years, before, thanks to the urging of Augustine's mother, the woman was sent back to Africa. *Confessions* 4.2.2.

36. Ibid., 2.3.5; Possidius, *V. Augustini* 1.1, in *Augustine Through the Ages: An Encyclopedia*, 1999 ed., s.v. "Patricius," by Allan Fitzgerald.

gave him "was wasted on follies."[37] As a student in Carthage, around nineteen years of age, Augustine describes himself as already at the top of his class in the rhetor's school. He describes the course of study in the following way: "My studies, which were deemed respectable had the objective of leading me to distinction as an advocate in the law courts where one's reputation is high in proportion to one's success in deceiving people."[38] In a section where he compares himself to the prodigal son of Luke 15:11–32, Augustine reflects on his early attraction to the life of garnering honors that a rhetorician pursues. He says: "When one considers the men proposed to me as models for my imitation, it is no wonder that in this way I was swept along by vanities and traveled right away from you, my God."[39]

Augustine began his education in Thagaste, and continued it in Madura and Carthage.[40] With his parents investing beyond their means in his education, and with the financial help of a wealthy benefactor by the name of Romanianus, Augustine received some of the finest education that the Latin part of the empire had to offer.[41] With this education Augustine began a promising career that took him from Thagaste to Carthage to Rome and, finally, to Milan. This movement was a progression upward in terms of careers of the late Roman Empire. Augustine went to Milan, in fact, having been appointed as professor of rhetoric there by Symmachus, Prefect of Rome.[42] The up and comer had arrived. There had been turns in the road of various sorts and there were some major ones on the way that would take Augustine from the path of being a well-known and respected Latin rhetorician to being a Christian bishop. The change in path was accompanied by a change in desires and self-understanding as well. Augustine's career as a rhetor was a promising one. From the age of nineteen, he built an impressive résumé that included delivering panegyrics for the emperor Valentinian II in 384 and the consul Bauto in 385.[43] But in that nineteenth year,

---

37. Augustine, *Confessions* 1.17.27.

38. Ibid., 3.3.6.

39. Ibid., 1.18.28.

40. For descriptions of these cities in Augustine's time, as can best be determined from archaeological remains, see Claude Lepelley, *Les Cites de L'afrique romaine au bas-empire, Tomes I et II* (Paris: Études Augustiniennes, 1979), Thagaste, 175; Madura 127; and Carthage 11.

41. Augustine, *Confessions* 2.2.6.

42. Ibid., 5.13.23.

43. For the mention of the panegyric on Valentinian, see *Confessions* 6.6.9; and for the one on Bauto, see *Contra litteras Petiliani* 3.30. See also Chadwick's discussion of these two in his translation of the *Confessions* 6.6.9, p. 97n10.

he would make an inward turn that would increase tension between his inner and outer selves.

Seeker of Truth

"Following the usual curriculum"[44] as a student, Augustine came across Cicero's *Hortensius*. This book, an appeal calling for men to take up the life of a philosopher, had a profound impact on Augustine. He says in the *Confessions* that it kindled in him a desire to become a lover of wisdom. Philosophers in the Roman world were those who took up not just a point of view about the world but also a way of life to live in the world.[45] Harald Hagendahl argues that: "The bent towards philosophical thinking, which lasted all his life, and the familiarity with ancient philosophy, of which the earliest writings give evidence, are the final outcome of the stimulus that the first reading of the *Hortensius* meant to him."[46] Hagendahl notes the prominence of references to the *Hortensius* in Augustine's writings in general, and in the Cassiaciacum dialogues of 386 in particular.[47] He goes on to argue convincingly that the first book of the *Contra Academicos* is an exhortation to take up the philosophical Christian life modeled on the *Hortensius*.[48]

Augustine also says, in the *Confessions*, that the *Hortensius* was instrumental in bringing him back to God.

> The book changed my feelings. It altered my prayers, Lord, to be towards yourself.
> It gave me different values and priorities. Suddenly every vain hope became empty to

44. Augustine, *Confessions* 3.4.7. More will be said about Augustine and his education in Chapter 4. A comprehensive history is given by Henri Irénée Marrou in his *A History of Education in Antiquity*, translated by George Lamb (Madison: University of Wisconsin Press, 1982).

45. Carol Harrison, *Augustine: Christian Truth and Fractured Humanity* (New York: Oxford, 2000), 6–7. See also O'Donnell's discussion of the scholarship on the influence of the *Hortensius*, 2:162ff.

46. Harald Hagendahl, *Augustine and the Latin Classics* (Göteborg: Studia Graeca et Latina Gothoburgensia 20, 1967), 2:488.

47. In the fall of 386, after the garden conversion and before his baptism in the spring of 387, Augustine, his mother, son, and a few friends retired to the estate of his friend Verecundus near Milan. Augustine, *Confessions* 9.5. This estate at Cassiaciacum is the setting for a group of writings dating from this period: the *Soliloquies, Contra Academicos, De Beata Vita*, and *De ordine*. Some modern scholars have called into question whether the dialogues record actual conversations, asserting that Augustine composed the texts using the persons present at Cassiaciacum. However, in spite of the historicity question, McWilliam claims "those dialogues themselves are historical in reflecting the mind of Augustine in 386 as faithfully as the *Confessions* do for his more mature mind more than a decade later." *Augustine Through the Ages: An Encyclopedia*, 1999 ed., s.v. "Cassiaciacum Dialogues," by Joanne McWilliam.

48. Hagendahl, 489–490.

me, and I longed for the immortality of wisdom with an incredible ardour in my heart. I began to rise up to return to you.[49]

The *Hortensius*'s call had an appeal for Augustine, but he writes: "One thing alone put a brake on my intense enthusiasm—that the name of Christ was not contained in the book."[50] This quest for truth ironically leads Augustine both to and from the Manichees.

Manichee[51]

Hagendahl claims that the "*Hortensius* did not pave the way to Christianity for him [Augustine], as his words suggest."[52] He goes on to argue that it led him to Manicheism, taking for granted that Christianity and Manicheism are clearly entirely different things. I differ with this assessment. The view that Christianity and Manicheism are entirely different seems be supported by a theological assumption about the nature of true Christianity. That distinction is one Augustine himself was unable to make when he was drawn to the Manichees. He only makes it after he becomes converted to what he will believe is the only true form of Christianity, Catholic Christianity. We should accept Augustine's report about his self-understanding at the time he was becoming a Manichee. From the passage above and the one quoted below, he seems to suggest that he found Christianity in its truest form when he became a Manichee. Augustine was led to the Manichees because even though Cicero's *Hortensius* made him burn "with longing to leave earthly things and fly back to [God],"[53] it did not reconnect him with his Christian roots, whereas Manicheism seemingly did. He says about the importance of the name of Christ:

> [T]his name, by your mercy Lord (Ps. 24:7), this name of my Savior your Son, my infant heart had piously drunk in with my mother's milk, and at a deep level retained the memory. Any book which lacked this name, however well written or polished or true, could not entirely grip me. Therefore decided to give attention to the holy scriptures and to find out what they were like.

49. Augustine, *Confessions*. 3.4.7.
50. Ibid., 3.4.8.
51. For a good brief introduction to Mani and the highly dualistic and gnostic form of Christianity that was Manicheism, see Allan Fitzgerald, ed., *Augustine Through the Ages: An Encyclopedia*, 1999 ed., s.v. "Mani, Manicheism," by J. Kevin Coyle. An important thorough history of the movement can be found in Samuel N. C. Lieu, *Manichaeism in the Later Roman Empire and Medieval China* (Manchester, 1985; 2nd, rev. ed., Tübingen: J. C. B. Mohr, 1992).
52. Hagendahl, 487.
53. Augustine, *Confessions*, 3.4.8.

When Augustine consulted the Scriptures, he found "something neither open to the proud nor laid bare to mere children, a text lowly to the beginner but, on further reading, of mountainous difficulty and enveloped in mysteries." Seeing it "unworthy of the dignity of Cicero," he was ripe prey for the Manichees, who were able to present questions that troubled him with regard to what he thought Catholic teaching was as well as answers that persuasively appealed to his intellect.[54] Following the Manichees is something that Augustine claims was motivated by pride and facilitated by their use of doctrine that referred to Christ and other religious terms with which he was familiar from his Catholic upbringing. "In their mouths were the devil's traps and a birdlime compound of a mixture of the syllables of your name, and that of the Lord Jesus Christ, and that of the Holy Spirit. These names were never absent from their lips; but it was no more than sound and noise with their tongue. Otherwise their heart was empty of truth."[55]

As Henry Chadwick points out, the Manichees were a religious group who saw themselves as Christians who had the true understanding of God, creation, good and evil, Christ, and the Holy Spirit.[56] Augustine says that at the time he was drawn into the Manichee faith, he was unable to think about spiritual or nonmaterial categories. Thus, the answers to the questions "where does evil come from?" and "is God confined within a corporeal form?"—provided by the Manichees— gave Augustine seemingly sounder religious doctrine than what he perceived to be coming from the Catholics.[57]

He says that he was content to be a Manichee hearer for nine years not just because of the intellectual attraction, but also because the Manichees provided a means through which he could ignore his failings. "I liked to excuse myself and to accuse some unidentifiable power which was with me and not yet I."[58] Cicero had directed Augustine to chastely seek truth; instead, he could not master his fleshly desires, and, as a rhetorician, he belonged to a profession that held truth to be irrelevant.[59] About his time as a Manichee in his twenties, he also says: "Publicly I was

54. According to Richard Lim, these "aporetic questions" were part of standard Manichee evangelical strategy "as a means of securing their listeners' attention and preparing the way for their preaching." Richard Lim, *Public Disputation, Power and Social Order in Late Antiquity* (Berkeley: University of California Press, 1995), 70.

55. Augustine, *Confessions*. 3.5.9–3.6.10.

56. Ibid., 3.5.10.

57. Ibid., 3.7.12.

58. Ibid., 5.10.18.

59. There are traditions going back at least to Plato's Socrates that criticize rhetoric for being concerned with persuasion without regard for truth. See Stanley Porter, *Handbook of Classical Rhetoric in the Hellenistic Period, 330 B.C.–A.D. 400* (Boston: Brill Academic Publishers, 2001), xiii.

a teacher of the arts which they call liberal; privately I professed a false religion—in the former role arrogant, in the latter superstitious, in everything vain."[60] The tension between his inward feelings and his outward appearance would increase. His break from the Manichees, however, did not require the resolution of this tension. Ironically, it was the intellectual pull of Manicheism that weakened and set him adrift.

Over the years, questions about Manicheism arose for Augustine. But it was not until 383 that he became so disillusioned that he decided he had no hope with the Manichee doctrine. In response to his increasing questions, the elect in Carthage said that the Manichee bishop Faustus would be able to give Augustine satisfaction. When Faustus came, and Augustine was able finally to speak with him, Augustine found him likeable and entertaining, but unable to give intellectually persuasive arguments to support the edifice of doctrine crumbling in Augustine's mind. Augustine, in fact, became the teacher of the one from whom he hoped to learn.

> [M]y entire effort on which I had resolved, to advance higher in that sect was totally abandoned, once I had met that man. My position was that I had not found anything more satisfactory than that into which I had somehow fallen. I decided to be content for the time being unless perhaps something preferable should come to light. So the renowned Faustus, who had been for many "a snare of death" (Ps. 17:6), without his will or knowledge had begun to loosen the bond by which I had been captured.[61]

Later, after his conversion, Augustine would respond to a work written by Faustus against him with his own treatise *Contra Faustum Manicheum* (398).[62] Symbolic of his internal departure from the Manichee faith was his departure from Carthage for Rome. He recalls, however, that the key factor for his leaving was pursuit of his career. He said that he wanted better, less rowdy, students.[63] Having been forced to let go intellectually of the Manichees, he did not know what he could lay hold of for sure, so he adopted the skeptical position of the Academics.[64]

60. Augustine, *Confessions*. 4.1.1.

61. Ibid., 5.7.13.

62. *Augustine Through the Ages: An Encyclopedia*, 1999 ed., s.v. *"Faustum Manicheum, Contra,"* by J. Kevin Coyle, and "Faustus of Milevus," by Allan Fitzgerald.

63. Augustine, *Confessions*. 5.8.14.

64. The Academics were the successors of Plato who adopted a position of skepticism as the appropriate philosophical position of the wise man. Augustine was led to this position by another of the works of Cicero, the *Academica*. Augustine's passage into the Catholic truth led to a retracing of his intellectual journey at Cassiaciacum to establish firmly the conviction that finding truth, or being led to truth, was possible. For a brief essential introduction to the Academic skepticism with which Augustine wrestled, see *Augustine Through the Ages: An*

Augustine says that their rejection of certitude was something that once again served his pride.[65] Psycho-spiritually, under the surface, the tension grew. Socially, he maintained the close circle of friends and contacts that he had cultivated for nearly a decade, and was thus still in large measure Manichee.

Skeptic

The *Confessions* can be described as a story of procession and return.[66] Given the prominent roles played by themes of the prodigal son, on the one hand, and Plotinus's philosophy, on the other, this is surely intentional.[67] Book 5 can be seen as the place where Augustine hits bottom and begins to return. In one sense, Augustine becomes better off in having been freed from active pursuit of advancing in Manicheism, but, in another sense, he is worse off given that he chooses to take up skepticism. His time as a skeptic would not be long, for soon after he goes to Rome he makes another career move to Milan, where he will have an intellectual revolution and eventually a conversion to Catholic Christianity.

While he had taken up the Academics' position, of withholding judgment, as his intellectual position, this time of transition was, for him, a time of increased anxiety and tension in psycho-spiritual terms. Sociopolitically, he maintained his connections with the Manichee hearers and elect of Rome. It seems that they, although officially outlawed,[68] provided the connections useful for career advancement. For a

---

Encyclopedia, 1999 ed., s.v. "Academics" and "Skeptics, Skepticism," by Philip Carey. For a discussion of Augustine's attempts to respond to skepticism, particularly in the first decade and a half following his conversion, see John M. Rist, *Augustine: Ancient Thought Rebaptized* (New York: Cambridge, 1994), 41–91.

65. Augustine, *Confessions.* 5.10.19.

66. See the following for variations on this idea: Crouse, "'Recurrens in te unum': The Pattern of Saint Augustine's *Confessions.*" *Studia Patristica* XIV (1976):389–392; David J. Leigh, "Augustine's *Confessions* as a Circular Journey." *Thought* 60 (1985): 73–87; Carl Avren Levenson, "Distance and Presence in Augustine's *Confessions.*" *The Journal of Religion* 65 (1985): 500–512; and C. J. Starnes, "The Unity of the *Confessions,*" *Studia Patristica* 18, no. 4 (1990): 105–111.

67. See, particularly, *Confessions* 1.18.28. I am indebted to Peter Brown for drawing my attention in a graduate seminar to the significance of the thematic conversion between Plotinus and Jesus's parable. See also O'Donnell's commentary, 1:92–98.

68. Legislation against Manichees went back to the reign of Diocletian. But recent laws included one from 372 that forbade Manichee assemblies and declared that "the habitations in which the profane doctrine is taught shall undoubtedly be appropriated to the resources of the fisc" (*Codex Theodosianus* 16.5.3). Other laws before Augustine's conversion were issued in 381 (16.5.7); 382 (16.5.9); and 383 (16.5.11). Peter Brown claims that the repression of Manicheism in the Christian empire was the spearhead of religious intolerance (94). Later in the essay, he goes on to say, "This rigidity increases notably at the end of the fourth century: the laws against

rhetor this also could mean political advancement. Augustine even developed hopes of a provincial governorship later in life. It may even be the case that his involvement in Manichee circles led Symmachus,[69] then Prefect of Rome, to recommend him for the chair of Rhetoric at Milan. Some scholars suggest that Symmachus did this to put a thorn in the side of his Catholic cousin Ambrose, Bishop of Milan,[70] who was a former provincial governor, and who still carried significant political influence.[71] As an old Roman polytheist, Symmachus looked to check the rising power of the Catholic elite at whatever occasion possible. So, from Symmachus's perspective, to have a non-Catholic (while not a pagan but, rather, a Manichee Christian) in the Chair of Rhetoric of Milan would block the further advancement of the Catholics in the important city of imperial residence. Unwittingly, however, Symmachus's recommendation of Augustine not only did not weaken Ambrose's position, it gave Ambrose a convert and disciple. As Augustine describes their relationship, they were not close, but Ambrose had an overwhelming impression on Augustine. Ambrose provided the model for Augustine of what it meant to be Catholic and what it meant to be a bishop.[72]

---

the Manichees are repeated with increasing severity form Valentinian I onwards" because of "the fusing of Roman prejudice with Christian doctrinal intolerance" (106) Peter Brown, "The Diffusion of Manichaeism," *Religion and Society in the Age of Saint Augustine* (London: Faber and Faber, 1972), 94–118. Originally published in *Journal of Roman Studies* 59 (1969): 92–103. See also Peter Brown.

69. For background on Symmachus, see *Augustine Through the Ages: An Encyclopedia*, 1999 ed., s.v. "Symmachus," by Neil McLynn.

70. On Ambrose, see Neil B. McLynn, *Ambrose of Milan: Church and Court in a Christian Capital* (Berkeley: University of California Press, 1994).

71. Augustine, *Confessions* 5.11. See also Peter Brown, *Augustine of Hippo*, 58ff, for discussion of this appointment that presents the political intrigue and the irony of Ambrose's ultimate influence on Augustine. Timothy Barnes presents a very different view that sees little intrigue and no major career move to be "Minister of Propaganda," in his article "Augustine, Symmachus and Ambrose," in *Augustine from Rhetor to Theologian*, edited by Joanne McWilliams (Waterloo, Ontario: Wilfred Laurier University Press, 1992), 7–13. A reconciliation of the positions of Brown and Barnes can be found in Neil McLynn's comparison of Augustine in the Milanese court to Claudian's career a decade later. According to McLynn, in *Ambrose of Milan*, for both Augustine and Claudian the Valentinian court was "makeshift." But Augustine went without a great reputation like the one Claudian had established when he went to Milan (McLynn, 169–170).

72. Before Augustine met Ambrose, he had a favorable Catholic episcopal example in the person of Elpidius. In Carthage, before he left for Rome, he apparently was the first Catholic bishop who was able to present reasoned arguments from the canonical scriptures that were more convincing than what the Manichees taught. Augustine, *Confessions* 5.11.21.

Neoplatonist

When Augustine got to Milan, he went to hear Ambrose out of professional curiosity, for Ambrose's reputation as an orator was great. Augustine says that although his manner of speech was not as entertaining as Faustus's, the content of what he said was far more profound. With Ambrose's preaching Augustine heard Catholic doctrine in a form that he says was then unfamiliar to him. He heard those problematic texts on which the Manichees focused, particularly from the Old Testament, read not literally but spiritually or allegorically. This preaching was steeped in Neoplatonic philosophy in a Christianized form. At around this same time, Augustine encounters this system in its non-Christian form through the books of the Platonists. Patout Burns, following Courcelle, distinguishes two stages of Augustine's listening to Ambrose's sermons. First, from the fall of 384 to the spring of 385, Augustine listened occasionally out of rhetorical interest. Second, from the spring of 385 on, his mother, Monica, was in Milan and successfully urged Augustine to regularly hear Ambrose.[73]

Post-baptismal Identity Shifts

Monk

Augustine had nearly been baptized as a child when terribly sick, but his mother forbade it once he recovered, fearing that he would grow up to sin, so as to make post-baptismal penance difficult if not impossible.[74] Augustine indeed struggled with sin and the acceptance of the Catholic Christianity of his mother. He tried to get away from her and her faith, in a literal journey from Africa that symbolized his spiritual journey.[75] Now, after having received baptism into the Catholic Church at the hands of Ambrose, Bishop of Milan, at Easter 387, Augustine soon left his prestigious teaching position, left Milan, and went back to Africa. By 388, he had established a monastic community in Thagaste, and by 391, he was well set on the path of a Christian ascetic. As Peter Brown shows, many like Augustine in the Roman Empire were renouncing the world and becoming "Slaves of God (*servi Dei*)."[76] Augustine's return to Africa was a return to the church of his

---

73. Patout Burns, "Ambrose Preaching to Augustine: The Shaping of Faith," in *Collectanea Augustiniana*, edited by J. C. Schnaubelt and F. Van Fleteren (New York: Peter Lang, 1990), 373–386.

74. Augustine, *Confessions*, 1.11.17.

75. Ibid., 5.8. He deceives his mother and sails from Carthage to Ostia, Rome's port city.

76. See Peter Brown's discussion of this phenomenon in *Augustine of Hippo*, chap. 13, 125–130.

mother.[77] He entered the Catholic Church as a devout lay ascetic, a monk. This was where he began; but, within half a decade, he would be drawn from the insular life of a monk to become a priest and then a bishop. As one of these "Slaves of God," he was determined to live as a contemplative ascetic, pursuing knowledge of "God and the soul," as he writes in the *Soliloquies*.[78] As a priest and bishop, he would realize the need for a Christian faith more deeply rooted in scripture, and the rhythms of the people he was bound to serve.[79] His involvement in controversies, most importantly the Donatists, would demand this.[80]

Polemics in Augustine's writings from 386 to 391, the year he was made a priest, were not of the public controversial nature. *Against the Academics* (*Contra Academicos*), for example, from a group of writings done at Cassiaciacum, after his garden conversion and before his baptism, reflects an effort on his part to articulate a re-thought out understanding of truth through conversation with a select few like-minded seekers. It was an exercise in self-understanding that reflected his rejection of skepticism. It was done without the added component of greater service to the Church, thus, it was work that was personal, rather than Catholic, in nature. Other writings from Cassiaciacum and his pre-ordination period also show this attitude.[81] Once he was made a priest, however, service to God became increasingly other-centered and Catholic, as well as personal, in nature.

77. Augustine, *Confessions* 9.8.36. Brown argues that Monica, Augustine's biological mother, was for him the symbol of the Christian Church. Also, Brown notes the importance of the Church as mother for African Christians. "In a land which to judge from Monica, had a fair share of formidable mothers, the *Catholica*, the Catholic Church was The Mother." Then quoting Cyprian, whose legacy Augustine wrestled over with the Donatists, he adds, "One Mother prolific with Offspring: of her we are born, by her milk we are nourished, by her spirit we are made alive" (Cyprian, *de unitate*, 5). See Brown, *Augustine of Hippo*, chap. 13, "*Ubi Ecclesia.*"

78. Augustine, *Soliloquies* 1.27.

79. We note here a particularly interesting example of Augustine's concern to speak to his congregation, his *Psalmus contra partem Donati*. In the *Retractations*, Augustine writes the following about this psalm: "[B]ecause I wished, too, to familiarize the most lowly people, and especially the ignorant and uneducated, with the cause of the Donatists and to impress on their memory to the best of my ability, I composed a psalm to be sung by them, arranged according to the Latin alphabet. . . . Further I did not want this psalm composed in any form of metrical verse lest the metrical requirement force me [to use] some words which are not familiar to common people." *Retractations* 1.19. See also the discussion given by Gerald Bonner in *St. Augustine of Hippo: Life and Controversies*, 253–258. Another example of Augustine's interest in communicating to the common folk is his *Catechizandis Rudibus* (*On Catechizing the Uninstructed*) (399–405), a response to a request from Deogratis, a Catholic deacon in Carthage, for guidance in teaching the basics of the Christian faith to those who did not have the benefit of a classical education.

80. Brown, *Augustine of Hippo*, chap. 15.

81. The other writings from that fall/winter are *De Beata Vita, De Ordine*, and *Soliloquia*. Other pre-ordination writings include *De immortalitate animae, De Musica, De Libero Arbitrio*

Priest

If his self-understanding as monk was that of a *servus Dei*, then his self-understanding as a priest and as a bishop was that of a *servus Dei et servus populum Dei*. Examining Augustine's writings, we will see that he developed the conviction that being a priest meant not just devotion to God but also devotion to God's people. Certainly his understanding of the monastic life contained some of this other-oriented understanding, but the priesthood presented challenges to serve in a much greater and sustained degree. The levels and kinds of attention to others were not in Augustine's plans. If the move from outside the Catholic Church to a place inside it involved a revolutionary shift in Augustine's self-understanding, then the move from laity to ordained clergy was as revolutionary, or perhaps even more so.

In 391, he went from Thagaste to Hippo to recruit a member for his community, when he himself was unexpectedly recruited for a different kind of service. Augustine knew that he could end up like Ambrose, drafted into the episcopacy, so he attempted to guard against that possibility.[82] Years after the fact, in *Sermon* 355 of 425/6,[83] on the anniversary of his ordination, Augustine tells his congregation that he was in the habit of avoiding cities and towns without bishops. Knowing that Hippo already had a bishop caused him to feel comfortable worshipping there without being dragged up to the altar to be consecrated.[84] Augustine, however, did not count on the vision and the shrewdness of the present bishop. In 391, Valerius orchestrated the ordination of Augustine as priest.[85] Pushing him into the priesthood was the first step in grooming Augustine for the *cathedra*. Soon he took the irregular action of making Augustine the co-adjutor bishop in 395.[86] Thus, at the

---

(Book 1), *De moribus ecclesiae catholicae et de moribus Manichaeorum, De Genesi contra Manichaeos, De Magistro,* and *De Vera Religione. De Libero Arbitrio* was not finished until 395, and *De Diversis Questionibus* was begun in 388 but was not finished until 396. For the chronology of this period, see Brown, *Augustine of Hippo,* 2nd ed., 64.

82. If we are to believe Paulinus, an early biographer, Ambrose went to great lengths to avoid becoming bishop of Milan. Paulinus says that Ambrose as governor of the region came to the cathedral to calm the unrest surrounding the need to elect a new bishop. Having been proclaimed bishop by a little child and then by the entire crowd, Ambrose had some criminals tortured, invited some prostitutes over to his house, and, finally, he left town. He was captured, baptized, and consecrated bishop of Milan. Paulinus of Milan, *The Life of Saint Ambrose* 7–9, in Boniface Ramsey, *Ambrose.* London: Routledge 1997. For discussion see McLynn, 44ff.

83. Unless otherwise noted, I use the dating for sermons provided by Eric Rebillard in his article "*Sermones,*" in *Augustine Through the Ages: An Encyclopedia,* 1999 ed.

84. Brown, *Augustine of Hippo,* 131–132.

85. Possidius, *Life of Saint Augustine,* introduction by Michele Pellegrino (Villanova, PA: Augustinian Press, 1988), 4.

86. Ibid., 8. See also Brown, *Augustine of Hippo,* 133.

death of Valerius in 396, Augustine would become the head shepherd of the flock of Hippo.[87]

The new life with new responsibilities was unlike what Augustine expected the Christian life to be, and it was unwanted. Nevertheless, he accepted this change of plans, taking it as God's will, saying: "A slave may not contradict his Lord."[88] To deal with this change, Augustine asked his bishop, Valerius, for time to study. This was not a short request. It was an appeal worthy of his former profession. It is a "confession" of sorts, in which he reveals a shift in his self-understanding. Instead of a rhetor, a seeker of truth, or monk, he now sees himself as a priest, charged to serve God and God's people. He begins his letter by giving his understanding of service that is pleasing to God and service that is not.

> 1. Before all things I ask your pious wisdom to take into consideration that, on the one hand, if the duties of the office of a bishop, or presbyter, or deacon, be discharged in a perfunctory and time-serving manner, no work can be in this life more easy, agreeable, and likely to secure the favour of men, especially in our day, but none at the same time more miserable, deplorable, and worthy of condemnation in the sight of God; and, on the other hand, that if in the office of bishop, or presbyter, or deacon, the orders of the Captain of our salvation be observed, there is no work in this life more difficult, toilsome, and hazardous, especially in our day, but none at the same time more blessed in the sight of God. But what the proper mode of discharging these duties is, I did not learn either in boyhood or in the earlier years of manhood; and at the time when I was beginning to learn it, I was constrained as a just correction for my sins (for I know not what else to think) to accept the second place at the helm, when as yet I knew not how to handle an oar.[89]

Let us note the concern to carry out the orders of "the Captain of our salvation (*noster imperator*)" in spite of the fact that it is "difficult (*difficilius*)," "toil-

---

87. See F. Van Der Meer, *Augustine the Bishop* (New York: Sheed and Ward, 1961), 3–9, for a vivid account of the intricacies of Augustine's early ecclesial career.

88. *Sermon* 355.2. "Sed, ut dixi, Domino servus contradicere non debet." Quoted and discussed in Brown, *Augustine of Hippo*, 131.

89. Augustine, *Epistle* 21.1 (*NPNF* Series 1, vol. 1, translated by J. G. Cunningham). "Ante omnia peto, ut cogitet religiosa prudentia tua, nihil esse in hac vita, et maxime hoc tempore, facilius et laetius, et hominibus acceptabilius episcopi, aut presbiteri, aut diaconi officio si perfunctorie atque adulatorie res agatur: sed nihil apud Deum miserius, et tristius, et damnabilius. Item nihil esse in hac vita, et maxime hoc tempore difficilius, laboriosius, periculosius episcopi, aut presbiteri, aut diaconi officio; sed apud Deum nihil beatius, si eo modo militetur quo noster imperator iubet Quis autem iste sit modus, nec a pueritia, nec ab adolescentia mea didici: et eo tempore quo discere coeperam, vis mihi facta est, merito peccatorum meorum (nam quid aliud existimem nescio), ut secundus locus gubernaculorum mihi traderetur, qui remum tenere non noveram."

some (*laboriosius*)," and "hazardous (*periculosius*)."[90] Confronted with this new life, Augustine realized that he needed new learning; his old Neoplatonic categories, which characterized the spiritual life as the individual ascent of the soul by disciplined intellectual, contemplative reflection, failed him. So, following his nautical theme, he surmises that the Lord was rebuking him because:

> I presumed, as if entitled by superior knowledge and excellence, to reprove the faults of many sailors before I had learned by experience the nature of their work. Therefore, after I had been sent in among them to share their labours, then I began to feel the rashness of my censures; although even before that time I judged this office to be beset with many dangers. And hence the tears which some of my brethren perceived me shedding in the city at the time of my ordination, and because of which they did their utmost with the best intentions to console me, but with words which, through their not knowing the causes of my sorrow, did not reach my case at all. But my experience has made me realize these things much more both in degree and in measure than I had done in merely thinking of them: not that I have now seen any new waves or storms of which I had not previous knowledge by observation, or report, or reading, or meditation; but because I had not known my own skill or strength for avoiding or encountering them, and had estimated it to be of some value instead of none. The Lord, however, laughed at me, and was pleased to show me by actual experience what I am.[91]

Thus, now realizing his deficiencies, and understanding "what is necessary for a man who ministers to a people in the divine sacraments and word," he hopes that Valerius will grant him time away to study the Scriptures. He concludes his letter with an impassioned plea.

> Consider all these things, aged Valerius; consider them, I beseech you, by the goodness and severity of Christ, by His mercy and judgment, by Him who has inspired you

90. Another word Augustine often uses to describe ministry is *sarcina* (burden). For a discussion of this language for describing the ministry, see, for example, the paper by Thomas F. Martin, "*Clericatus sarcina* (*ep.* 126.3): Augustine and the Care of the Clergy."

91. Augustine, *Epistle* 21.2. "Sed arbitror Dominum meum propterea me sic emendare voluisse, quod multorum peccata nautarum, antequam expertus essem quid illic agitur, quasi doctior et melior reprehendere audebam. Itaque posteaquam missus sum in medium, tunc sentire coepi temeritates reprehensionum mearum; quamquam et antea periculosissimum iudicarem hoc ministerium. Et hinc erant lacrymae illae quas me fundere in civitate, ordinationis meae tempore, nonnulli fratres animadverterunt, et nescientes causas doloris mei, quibus potuerunt sermonibus, qui omnino ad vulnus meum non pertinerent, tamen bono animo consolati sunt. Sed multo valde ac multo amplius expertus sum, quam putabam: non quia novos aliquos fluctus aut tempestates vidi quas ante non noveram, vel non audieram, vel non legeram, vel non cogitaveram; sed ad eas evitandas aut perferendas solertiam et vires meas omnino non noveram, et alicuiusmomenti arbitrabar. Dominus autem irrisit me, et rebus ipsis ostendere voluit meipsum mihi."

with such love for me that I dare not displease you, even when the advantage of my soul is at stake. You, moreover, appeal to God and to Christ to bear witness to me concerning your innocence and charity, and the sincere love which you bear to me, just as if all these were not things about which I may myself willingly take my oath. I therefore appeal to the love and affection which you have thus avouched. Have pity on me, and grant me, for the purpose for which I have asked it, the time which I have asked; and help me with your prayers, that my desire may not be in vain, and that my absence may not be without fruit to the Church of Christ, and to the profit of my brethren and fellow-servants. I know that the Lord will not despise your love interceding for me, especially in such a cause as this; and accepting it as a sacrifice of sweet saviour, He will restore me to you, perhaps, within a period shorter than I have craved, thoroughly furnished for His service by the profitable counsels of His written word.[92]

Valerius granted him the leave, and Augustine began attentive re-evaluation of the Scriptures with a view to becoming a dutiful priest. Augustine described how humbling an experience he was finding the ordained ministry, and, thus, as he studies the Scriptures, humility becomes increasingly recognized as the virtue necessary for conduct of the ministry. For Augustine this need for humility confirmed in the Scriptures, and linked with other qualities like obedience, unselfishness, and love, led him to personal reformation and ecclesiastical service.[93]

Over a short span of time, Augustine developed an acute sense of his responsibility for his congregation, and even for people outside of his congregation. In 392, for example, Augustine, the new priest, had the boldness and naiveté to write a letter to Maximin, a Donatist bishop, about that bishop's possible practice of rebaptism. He hopes that the reports that Maximin has rebaptized a Catholic deacon who was brought into the Donatist Church are untrue. If the reports are

92. Augustine, *Epistle* 21.6. "Attende omnia ista, senex Valeri, obsecro te per bonitatem et severitatem Christi, per misericordiam et iudicium eius, per eum qui tantam tibi inspiravit erga noscaritatem, ut ne te, nec pro lucro animae nostrae, audeamus offendere. Sic autem mihi Deum et Christum testem facis innocentiae et caritatis, et sinceri affectus quem circa nos habes, quasi ego non de his iurare omnibus possim. Ipsam ergo caritatem et affectum imploro, ut miserearis mei, et concedas mihi, ad hoc quod rogavi, tempus quantum rogavi, atque adiuves me orationibus tuis, ut non sit inane desiderium meum, necinfructuosa Ecclesiae Christi atque utilitati fratrum et conservorum meorum absentia mea. Scio quod illam caritatem pro me orantem, maxime in tali causa, non despicit Dominus; et eam sicut sacrificium suavitatis accipiens, fortassis breviore tempore quam postulavi, me saluberrimis consiliis de Scripturis suis reddet instructum."

93. Lee F. Bacchi, "A Ministry Characterized by and Exercised in Humility: The Theology of Ordained Ministry in the Letters of Augustine of Hippo," in *Presbyter Factus Sum*, edited by Joseph T. Lienhard, Earl C. Muller, and Roland J. Teske (New York: Peter Lang, 1993); Pellegrino, *The True Priest*.

false, he hopes that Maximin will publicly set the record straight.[94] Considering that the reports might be true, Augustine reveals the depths of his shift in self-understanding by presenting his anxious concern to Maximin:

> I could not pass over in silence the rebaptizing of our deacon; for I know how much harm my silence might do to myself. For I do not propose to spend my time in the empty enjoyment of ecclesiastical dignity; but I propose to act as mindful of this, that to the one Chief Shepherd I must give account of the sheep committed unto me. If you would rather that I should not thus write to you, you must, my brother, excuse me on the ground of my fears; for I do fear greatly, lest, if I were silent and concealed my sentiments, others might be rebaptized by you. I have resolved, therefore, with such strength and opportunity as the Lord may grant, so to manage this discussion, that by our peaceful conferences, all who belong to our communion may know how far apart from heresy and schism is the position of the Catholic Church, and with what care they should guard against the destruction which awaits the tares and the branches cut off from the Lord's vine. If you willingly accede to such conference with me, by consenting to the public reading of the letters of both, I shall unspeakably rejoice. If this proposal is displeasing to you, what can I do, my brother, but read our letters, even without your consent, to the Catholic congregation, with a view to its instruction? But if you do not condescend to write me a reply, I am resolved at least to read my own letter, that, when your misgivings as to your procedure are known, others may be ashamed to be rebaptized.[95]

This pastoral sentiment was expressed as a priest, to a rival bishop, in a district that was not even Augustine's! Once he became a bishop, this sense of accountability would only increase. Accountability and responsibility were evidently encouraged by Valerius. On the one hand, there is no evidence that survives, if there ever was any, of there being any resentment of Augustine's zeal. On the other hand, to the

---

94. Augustine, *Epistle* 23.3.

95. Augustine, *Epistle* 23.6. "Ego de rebaptizato diacono nostro silere non possum: scio enim quam mihi silentium perniciosum sit. Non enim cogito in ecclesiasticis honoribus tempora ventosa transigere, sed cogito me principi pastorum omnium rationem de commissis ovibus redditurum. Si forte nolles ut haec tibi scriberem, oportet te, frater, ignoscere timori meo. Multum enim timeo ne me tacente etdissimulante, alii quoque rebaptizentur a vobis. Decrevi ergo, quantum vires et facultatem Dominuspraebere dignatur, causam istam sic agere, ut pacificis collationibus nostris omnes qui nobis communicant, noverint ab haeresibus aut schismatibus quantum catholica distet Ecclesia, et quantum sit cavenda pernicies vel zizaniorum vel praecisorum de vite Domini sarmentorum. Quam collationem mecum si libenti animo susceperis, ut concordibus nobis amborum litterae populis recitentur, ineffabilis exultabo laetitia. Si autem id aequo animo non accipis, quid faciam, frater, nisi ut te quoque invito epistolas nostras populo catholico legam, quo esse possit instructior? Quod si rescribere dignatus non fueris, vel meas legere decrevi, ut saltem diffidentia vestra cognita rebaptizari erubescant."

contrary, Valerius gave him significant responsibilities. For example, preaching was usually, in North Africa, reserved for bishops; but, soon after naming him a priest, Valerius had Augustine preach.[96] In 393, Augustine was even asked to teach at the African Catholic Bishops' Councils assembled in Hippo. This teaching session comes down to us as *De Fide et Symbolo* (*On Faith and the Creed*). This council, and Augustine's role in it, are key parts of the early stages of Catholicization as a plan of social formation, and will, therefore, be discussed in greater detail in the next chapter. Perhaps an even greater sign of Valerius's confidence in Augustine was having him named Co-adjutor Bishop in 395, effectively preventing any other town or city from claiming his priest as their bishop.[97] Along with these tasks, Augustine still guided a monastic community and began to write in the service of the Catholic Church.

In the years after being made a priest, and before being ordained a bishop, aside from *De Fide et Symbolo*, Augustine wrote a few exegetical and polemical works. The main inspiration for these works was the way in which the Manichees haunted Augustine's mind. His first works as a priest had been *De utilitate credendi* (*On the Usefulness of Belief*), *De duabus animabus contra Manichaeos* (*On the Two Souls Against the Manichees*), and *De libero arbitrio* (*On the Freedom of the Will*), all from 391. In these works Augustine is concerned with undoing the damage of his adherence to Manicheism. His intent is, partially, to cast off his Manicheist teaching and adopt views more consistent with Catholic teaching. But, even more, particularly in *De utilitate credendi*, he is also attempting to draw out of Manicheism someone he drew in, namely Honoratus.

Galatians, along with Romans and Genesis, were three biblical texts on which Augustine commented during this period. He first wrote *De Genesi contra Manichaeos* in 388–389, an allegorical commentary. Then he attempted a literal interpretation that he did not complete, *De Genesi ad litteram, imperfectus liber* of 393–394. In 394–395, he wrote *Epistulae ad Galatas exposito* (*Commentary on the Letter to the Galatians*), a literal commentary; *Epistulae ad Romanos expositio inchoato* (*Unfinished Commentary on the Letter to the Romans*), an incomplete attempt at a literal commentary like the Galatians text; and *Expositio quarumdam Epistulae ad Romanos* (*Commentary on Statements from the Letter of the Apostle to the Romans*), an exposition of some selected propositions on Romans focusing on grace.

Bishop

In light of Valerius's treatment of Augustine, it is understandable, then, that his sense of self-understanding as a priest would not change a great deal once he be-

---

96. Possidius, 5. This led to other priests being allowed to preach in the Catholic churches.
97. Ibid., 8.

came a bishop. The most significant way that the offices of priest and bishop are distinguished is by rank, not the fundamental nature of the ministry. Recalling *Epistle* 21, where Augustine, as a priest, requested from Valerius time for study, it is clear that Augustine understood that priests ranked lower than, and were accountable to, bishops. Yet in light of his lament in *Confessions* Book 10, mentioned earlier, it is also clear that he believed that they had the same responsibility to be slaves of God and slaves of the people of God, principally through the administration of the sacraments and the preaching of the word.[98]

In contrast to his ordination as a priest, Augustine does not offer us a clear account of his elevation to the episcopacy. We must chiefly rely on Possidius to tell of Valerius's maneuverings to secure the election of Augustine as his co-adjutor. According to Possidius, Valerius consulted with Aurelius as Primate of Africa, but not Megalius, the primate of Numidia, nor Augustine himself. Thus, when it came time to ordain Augustine Megalius, Augustine, and a number of bishops, were caught by surprise. Augustine, according to Possidius, "refused to go against the practice of the Church and accept the episcopate while his own bishop was still living."[99] But after examples of the practice in "[c]hurches abroad and in Africa" were cited, Augustine yielded.[100] Later, however, Augustine would discover that the practice ran contrary to one of the canons of Nicaea, and lamented the unusual measures of his election. So convinced was he of the error in procedure of his ordination, he refused to have his successor, Eraclius, similarly elevated.[101] Augustine named him some time before his own death, but Eraclius was not ordained and consecrated until after Augustine died.

---

98. Augustine, *Confessions* 11.1.1–11.2.2. "But when shall I be capable of proclaiming by 'the tongue of my pen' (Ps. 44:2) all your exhortations and all your terrors and consolations and directives, by which you brought me to preach your word and dispense your sacrament to your people (*quibus me perduxisti praedicare verbum et sacramentum tuum dispensare populo tuo?*)? And if I have the capacity to proclaim this in an orderly narrative, yet the drops of time are too precious to me."

99. Possidius, 8.3.

100. Ibid., 8.4.

101. Augustine, *Epistle* 213.4. "I approve of that of which you also express your approval, but I do not wish that to be done in regard to him which was done in my own case. What was done many of you know; in fact, all of you, excepting only those who at that time were not born, or had not attained to the years of understanding. When my father and bishop, the aged Valerius, of blessed memory, was still living, I was ordained bishop and occupied the episcopal see along with him which I did not know to have been forbidden by the Council of Nice; and he was equally ignorant of the prohibition. I do not wish to have my son here exposed to the same censure as was incurred in my own case." Where Possidius in 8.5 describes Augustine's ordination, Pellegrino offers a helpful note (n5) that directs the reader to the letter quoted above.

Conclusion

Peter Brown has persuasively argued that as a bishop, Augustine's sense of responsibility deepened as he continued to reflect on the Scriptures. As an early ascetic Christian, he had greater confidence in his ability to gain the happy life through a disciplined life. Neither the life of *otium* at Cassiaciacum nor the community at Thagaste provided the safe passage of withdrawal. Public ministry had led Augustine to invest himself in the study of the Scriptures. Provoked by the understanding of sin he develops from the early chapters of Genesis, and also the Pauline material, he was forced to wrestle with the linked problems of habit and pride. Confronting habit, Augustine came to realize change and lasting attainment of the vision of God were rendered impossible by human sin, chiefly manifest in pride. Thus, the solution was humility. Humans had to be humble enough to accept the way made by Jesus, the humble mediator.[102] These opinions would be shaped throughout the 390s and were clearly expressed in the *Confessions*. In making his case, Brown cites this passage where, about habit, Augustine writes:

> And sometimes you fill me with a feeling quite unlike my normal state, an inward sense of delight, which were it to reach fulfillment in me, would be something entirely different from my present life. But my heavy burden drags me back: I am sucked back by my habits, and find myself held fast; I weep greatly, but I am firmly held. The load of habit is a force to be reckoned with!"[103]

The intractability of sin was a major question that the Manichees had put forth to advance their cause.[104] To better deal with these challenges from his own experience and from the Manichees, Augustine had taken up focused study of Paul's letters. This actually began in his years as a priest and continued into his episcopate. Brown points out that this was not a discovery of Paul, rather it was seeing him anew.[105] Around 395 Augustine's thinking about Paul gels when he

---

102. For more on the idea of pride versus humility with respect to mediation, see Brian Daley, "A Humble Mediator: The Distinctive Elements in St. Augustine's Christology," in *Word and Spirit: A Monastic Review 9* (Petersham, MA: St. Bede's Publications, 1987), 100–117. He notes the longevity of this idea in Augustine's writings, placing its first appearance as early as 394 in *Epistolae ad Galatas expositio* (394/5), 24. See also *De catechizandis rudibus* (399), 4.8.

103. Augustine, *Confessions* 10.40.65. Quoted in Brown, *Augustine of Hippo*, 143.

104. Ibid., 142. They used this fact to suggest their view of human nature was correct. There were in fact two warring forces at work in the person and in the cosmos. Aside from the experiential evidence, they appealed to Paul, citing passages such as "the flesh lusteth against the spirit and that which you wish not you do." *Acta contra Forunatum manichaeum* (392).

105. Ibid., 151.

is asked by Simplicianus of Milan to answer questions about predestination and free will. Working with Paul, Augustine sees for the first time "man as utterly dependent on God, even for his first initiative in believing in Him: '[w]ork out your salvation in fear and trembling: for it is God who works in you, both that you should wish and act with a good will.'"[106]

In response to his search for truth, Augustine found "the most healthy council" of the Scripturesleading him to the humility of Christ to heal his sinfulness. This would mean for Augustine humbling himself to not just the authority of Christ but the authority of Christ's church. Beyond merely being a lesson for his personal spiritual reflection, this advice, or counsel, according to Brown,

> will eventually crystallize into an ideal of ecclesiastical authority that will dominate Augustine's life until his death. Plainly, what he absorbed at this time were the lessons of the active life of S. Paul. He will identify himself passionately with the ideal of authority shown in the letters of Paul to his wayward communities: "insisting in season and out of season," committed to impinge constantly on his flock and its enemies, driven by the objective "terror" of the Holy Scriptures.[107]

Thus, Augustine's views on habit, pride, and humility begin with self-understanding, but ultimately translate to a project of social order. By the waning years of the fourth century and the dawning years of the fifth, Augustine had come to see himself as having moved from a self-serving ambition to a God-and-other-serving ambition. In these years he often described the base essentials of his role as a bishop as preaching the word and dispensing the sacraments. Over the years, many other specific duties and actions would either grow organically from or be grafted on to this basic self-understanding. The varied nature of the duties is attached to typical roles such as the "shepherd (*pastor*)" and "guardian (*custos*)."[108] Though these signify positions of power, Augustine is always careful to subordinate the role of the bishop to the rule of Jesus Christ. He will call for obedience

---

106. Ibid., 154. *De diversis quaestionibus VII ad Simplicianum* (396), I, qu. ii, 12. It is interesting to note that although Paul is figuring prominently in the development of Augustine's self-undertanding, Augustine's style of introspection was most likely foreign to Paul. Krister Stendahl has argued persuasively that modern Western ways of reading Paul derive from the influence of Augustine through Luther. The interpretive lenses of Augustinian introspection are thus used on Paul because Augustine had discovered what the apostle was intending to communicate. Stendahl shows that this is inconsistent with Paul's self-understanding as shown in his self-presentation. Krister Stendahl, "The Apostle Paul and the Introspective Conscience of the West," *Harvard Theological Review* 56 (1963): 199–215.

107. Brown, *Augustine of Hippo*, 201–202.

108. See Grabowski, 107–108, for discussion of these and other roles used by Augustine to characterize the ministry.

from his congregants at the same time that he is calling all clergy to be obedient to their superior, Jesus; this is the proper order of things as he sees it. But Jesus is not only seen as Lord above, he is also seen as the mediator and model.

In the Galatians commentary, Augustine gives his first extended treatment of the image of Christ as mediator.[109] He takes his cue principally from Gal. 3:19–20, and links this passage to 1 Tim. 2:5.[110] Later, in the *Confessions*, we find the following:

> The true Mediator you showed to humanity in your secret mercy. You sent him so that from his example they should learn humility. He is the "mediator between God and men the Man Christ Jesus." He appeared among mortal sinners as the immortal righteous one; mortal like humanity, righteous like God.[111]

Jesus is mediator between God and humans to effect the atonement, but he is model in that all should follow his example of humility in order to be pleasing to God.

For Augustine, as he understands his role as a bishop, he becomes anxious to see that his life is pleasing to God, and to lead others so that their lives can be as well. This other-centered desire becomes part of a plan that appears in the 390s and goes on till the end of his life. The concern in this book is to describe what I argue can be seen as an intentional process of Catholicization, focusing on the years of Augustine's early episcopate till the fall of Stilicho in 408. Augustine's self-understanding, and the program of Catholicization, did not become frozen at that time; however, developments beyond that time are beyond the limits I have set for this study. It is to this project of social order that we will turn in the next chapter.

109. For more on Augustine's understanding of Christ as mediator, see Daley. See also Goulven Madec, *Le Patrie et La Voie: Le Christ dans la vie et la pensée de saint Augustin* (Paris: Desclée, 1989); and G. Remy, *Le Christ mediateur dans l'oeuvre de saint Augustin* (These de Strasbourg: Faculté de Theologie catholique, 1977; Lille-Paris, 1979).

110. See Augustine, *Epistolae ad Galatas expositio* (394/5) *CSEL 84*, 86.24–94.28; and 140.63. For a brief discussion, see Remy, 46–48.

111. Augustine, *Confessions* 10.43.68.

CHAPTER THREE

Social Order

Imperial Legislation: Christianization versus Catholicization

Constantine is the icon of Christianization. His dream, his edict, and his support of the Christian institutions, exemplified in his sponsoring the Council of Nicaea, serve to mark him as the key figure in a great reversal of fortune for Christians in the Roman Empire. Narratives of Christian triumph over paganism feature him prominently. They generally tell of a community experiencing its fiercest persecution under Diocletian, which is then favored by a Constantine. The narratives continue to tell of the decline of paganism and the empire-wide triumph of Christianity by the fifth century. This narrative is not the construction of modern historians; on the contrary, Eusebius, Socrates, Sozomen, Theodoret, and Evagrius, historians of the fourth and fifth centuries, writing with clear commitment to a Christian point of view, lay out this narrative in its basic form.[1]

---

1. For a description of the relationship between these historians and an argument for how, despite some differences, they embrace the idea of a Christian empire in a way that has significant commonalities, especially over and against an Augustinian historiographic tradition, see Glenn F. Chestnut, *The First Christian Histories: Eusebius, Socrates, Sozomen, Theodoret, and Evagrius*, 2nd ed. (Macon, GA: Mercer University Press, 1986).

In the latter part of the twentieth century, this narrative began to be called into question. Ramsay MacMullen's work, for example, has been among the most influential in challenging this narrative. In his *Christianizing the Roman Empire A.D. 100–400* (1984), he proclaims: "My object is history. It might be, but it isn't, theology."[2] MacMullen's book presents wide and varied evidence to support his general claim that Christianization, as it typically had been presented by earlier historians, even back to Eusebius, was not as swift or thorough as they had claimed. Nevertheless, MacMullen does acknowledge that he is concerned with "the period . . . that saw the church become dominant and Europe Christian."[3] In a sequel of sorts, *Christianity and Paganism in the Fourth to Eighth Centuries*, he extends his argument across time to the dawn of the Middle Ages.

Whereas MacMullen provides a challenge from the outside by considering evidence from those who were being Christianized, Peter Brown has developed an inside challenge. Taking into account the work of MacMullen and others, Brown has presented challenges to the historical narratives constructed by Eusebius, Rufinus, Theodoret, and Socrates in *Authority and the Sacred* as well as in an article in *Cambridge Ancient History*.[4] Augustine, although not usually seen as a church historian, as are Eusebius et al., does present a historical perspective. In his treatises, but I think more interestingly in his sermons, we have Augustine presenting a kind of triumphal narrative. This narrative, as presented before Alaric's sack of Rome, was modified in the wake of those events. In *City of God (De Civitate Dei)*, Augustine presents a narrative where expansion of the Christian community and spread of the Christian message are not equated with the extent, stability, and prosperity of the Roman Empire.

The rest of this chapter will move from general consideration of Christianization to the specific example of Augustine in Roman Africa. As was said at the end of the last chapter, Augustine's self-understanding as a bishop committed him to a particular worldview. This in turn led to his development of a plan of social order. Instead of taking up the perspective of the historians, I will begin with the laws of the empire and describe the ways in which these laws intersected with the African context and Augustine's experience and emerging program.

Some important legislation for the late empire can be found in the Theodosian Code, a collection of laws from Constantine to 437. The collection was commissioned

2. MacMullen, *Christianizing the Roman Empire*, 1.

3. Ibid., vii.

4. Peter Brown, "Christianization and Religious Conflict," in *Cambridge Ancient History*, vol. XIII: *The Late Empire, A.D.*, 3rd ed., edited by Averil Cameron and Peter Garnsey (Cambridge: Cambridge University Press, 1998), 337–425.

by Theodosius II in 429, and finally promulgated in October 437.[5] The code provides a rich resource for scholars, but, as John Matthews has recently argued, it also provides some hazards. In his book *Laying Down the Law,* he discusses how the laws of the empire were composed and promulgated, but also how the Theodosian Code does not always provide a clear indication of the timing and range of the application of a law.[6] Looking in the Theodosian Code, one can find in the legislation of the latter half of the fourth century a distinct favoring of the Christian churches. An even more careful look, particularly at the laws of the emperor Theodosius I, shows a favoring of the Catholic brand of Christianity. Consider, for example, the following law of 380:

> It is Our Will that all the peoples who are ruled by the administration of Our Clemency shall practise that religion which the divine Peter the Apostle transmitted to the Romans, as the religion which he introduced makes clear even unto this day. It is evident that this is the religion that is followed by the Pontiff Damasus and by Peter, bishop of Alexandria, a man of apostolic sanctity; that is, according to the apostolic discipline and the evangelic doctrine, we shall believe in the single Deity of the Father, the Son, and the Holy Spirit, under the concept of equal majesty and of the Holy Trinity. We command that those persons who follow this rule shall embrace the name of Catholic Christians. The rest, however, whom We adjudge demented and insane, shall sustain the infamy of heretical dogmas, their meeting places shall not receive the name of churches, and they shall be smitten first by divine vengeance and secondly by the retribution of Our own initiative, which We shall assume in accordance with divine judgement.[7]

Let us note that in this law, there is a clear presentation of "Catholic" Christianity as the exclusive Christian option. The law should be viewed against the historical backdrop of controversies after the Council of Nicaea. The principal reason for Constantine calling the Council of Nicaea was the controversy that had arisen in the east surrounding the Alexandrian priest Arius (256–336).[8] Arius was a presbyter, and the

---

5. In January 438, Theodosius ordered that only the laws of Constantine and his successors, including himself, included in the code would have legal force. See Timothy Barnes, "Theodosian Code," in *Late Antiquity: A Guide to the Post Classical World* (Cambridge: Harvard University Press, 1999).

6. See John Matthews, *Laying Down the Law: A Study of the Theodosian Code* (New Haven: Yale University Press, 2000).

7. *Codex Theodosianus* (*CT*) 16.1.2. See also *CT* 16.5.2.1.

8. For background on Arius and his writings, see Johannes Quasten's introduction in *Patrology*, 3:7–13. For a readable account that integrates the history of the Council of Nicea and after with the sociopolitical history in general, see W. H. C. Frend, *The Rise of Christianity* (Philadelphia: Fortress Press, 1984), 498–650. For a focus on the west and the immediate background of how Augustine encountered Arianism in Milan, see Daniel H. Williams, *Ambrose and the End of the Nicene–Arian Conflicts* (New York: Oxford University Press, 1995).

controversy is said to have broken out after Alexander (d. 328), Bishop of Alexandria, had asked his presbyters to give an account of Proverbs 8:22–31, which begins: "The Lord created me at the beginning of his work" (NRSV). Perhaps in response to what he perceived as Sabellian teachings of Alexander,[9] Arius presented a radical monotheism that subordinated the being of the Son to the Father.[10] Theodosius's concern seems to have been to establish the Nicene theological position as "Catholic" and legal, while pronouncing all other positions as "heretical" and illegal.

Although this law of 380 only explicitly deals with internal Christian definition, there were other laws from Theodosius that addressed religion external to the Christian movement. A law of 391 limits public sacrifice, for example.

> No person shall pollute himself with sacrificial animals; no person shall slaughter an innocent victim; no person shall approach the shrines, shall wander through the temples, or revere the images formed by mortal labour, lest he become guilty by divine and human laws. Judges also shall be bound by the general rule that if any of them should be devoted to profane rites and should enter a temple for the purpose of worship anywhere, either on a journey or in the city, he shall immediately be compelled to pay fifteen pounds of gold, and his office staff shall pay a like sum with similar haste, unless they resist the judge and immediately report him by a public attestation. Governors and the rank of consular shall pay six pounds of gold each, their office staffs a like amount; those with the rank of corrector or of praeses shall pay four pounds each, and their apparitors, by equal lot, a like amount.[11]

In January 381, in the wake of the Council at Constantinople, Theodosius again upholds the Nicene orthodoxy,[12] and in 388, he legislates against diverse sects.[13] Certain laws of 399 and 405 are also very important. In August 399, Honorius and Arcadius sent two laws to the proconsul of Africa. The first reiterated prohibition of "profane rites" and allowed the continuance of public "amusements . . . but without any sacrifice or any accursed superstition."[14] The other law

9. See Frend, *The Rise of Christianity*, 495.

10. Jaroslav Pelikan, *The Christian Tradition: A History of the Development of Doctrine*, Vol. 1: *The Emergence of the Catholic Tradition* (100–600) (Chicago: University of Chicago Press, 1971), 193.

11. *CT* 16.10.10.

12. Ibid., 16.5.6.

13. Ibid., 16.5.15. For a discussion of these and other laws, see David Hunt, "Christianising the Roman Empire: The Evidence of the Code," in *The Theodosian Code: Studies in the Imperial Law of Late Antiquity*, edited by Jill Harries and Ian Wood (New York: Duckworth, 1993), 143–158.

14. *CT* 16.10.17.

sought to remove idols from the public space while maintaining temple buildings devoid of religious imagery and practice.

> No man by the benefit of our sanctions shall attempt to destroy temples which are empty of illicit things. For We decree that the condition of the buildings shall remain unimpaired; but if any person should be apprehended while performing a sacrifice, he shall be punished according to laws. Idols shall be taken down under the direction of the office staff after an investigation has been held, since it is evident that even now the worship of a vain superstition is being paid to idols.[15]

Later in his career, Augustine tells us that also in that year, 399, the temples of Carthage were ordered closed.

> But, as we know, in the most noted and eminent city, Carthage, in Africa, Gaudentius and Jovius, officers of the Emperor Honorius, on the fourteenth day before the kalends of April, overthrew the temples and broke the images of the false gods. And from that time to the present, during almost thirty years, who does not see how much the worship of the name of Christ has increased, especially after many of those became Christians who had been kept back from the faith by thinking that divination true, but saw when that same number of years was completed that it was empty and ridiculous?[16]

With respect to heresy, in 405 Honorius gave the following prohibition of Manicheism and Donatism known as the Edict of Unity.

> No one shall recall to memory a Manichean, no one a Donatist[17], who especially, as we have learned, do not cease their madness. There should be one Catholic worship, there should be one salvation, the Trinity's sanctity, equal and harmonious within itself, should be sought. But if any person should dare to participate in practices that are interdicted and unlawful, he shall not escape the toils of innumerable previous constitutions and of the law that was recently issued by Our Clemency. If perchance seditious mobs should assemble, he shall not doubt that the sharp goads of a more severe punishment will be applied to him.[18]

---

15. Ibid., 16.10.18.

16. Augustine, *City of God (De Civitate Dei)* 18:54 (*NPNF* vol. 1).

17. The Manichees were a dualistic Christian tradition that clearly diverged from Nicene definitions of the Trinity, while the Donatists, although accepting the Nicene formula, differed from Catholics on the nature of the Church, its sacraments, and ordained ministry. The division grew out of a dispute during the Diocletianic persecution and led to two substantially parallel church hierarchies in Roman Africa. A good introduction to Augustine's relationship to these two groups can be found in the relevant articles in *Augustine Through the Ages* and in Gerald Bonner's *Saint Augustine of Hippo, Life and Controversies*.

18. *CT* 16.5.38.

Being "Catholic" is the key element defining Christianity in these laws. Yet these laws are but the foreground of the picture showing the movement of Catholic institutions and lifeways into prominence, and even dominance, in late antique society. As David Hunt says: "In the case of the laws on Christian orthodoxy, the background is a network of episcopal politics and church councils, aided and abetted by the emperor and his officials."[19] In the rest of this chapter, we shall examine that background and Augustine's role in it.

The Rhetor in Society and the Challenge of the Christian Bishop

By the time he writes the *Confessions*, Augustine has accepted his shift of societal roles from rhetor to bishop. There are ways that these roles served similar social functions in late antique society, but there are important differences as well. In terms of similarity, rhetors and bishops were both looked upon as wielders of the spoken word. Perhaps the main difference between the two, for Augustine, was the motivation for speech. The rhetor spoke on his own, motivated by pride. The bishop spoke for God, motivated by humility. This contrast extended beyond these specific roles to embrace a general class defined by those motivations. Thus, a rhetor, or those rhetorically trained who used their gifts under their own direction, was prideful and to be unfavorably compared with bishops, priests, and holy men, as well as women of all sorts, who, whether rhetorically trained or not, spoke for God, as they embraced the virtue of humility.

In the latter part of the twentieth century, a great deal of attention was given to describing the way in which these two roles, rhetor and bishop, were at odds, and how the latter supplanted the former. In particular, from Peter Brown and Averil Cameron, we have clear demonstrations of the important role that people with rhetorical skill played in society.[20] They also clearly show how Christian leaders came to take over this key role across the empire. There are regional differences as to how this was accomplished, but the result was essentially the same. In the east, bishops, abbots, and holy men not so closely tied to the ecclesiastical structure rivaled and then supplanted traditional pagan elites who were rooted in the ancient urban power structure like decurians and philosophers. In

19. Hunt, 148–149.

20. Peter Brown, *Power and Persuasion in Late Antiquity: Towards a Christian Empire* (Madison: University of Wisconsin Press, 1992); and Averil Cameron, *Christianity and the Rhetoric of Empire: The Development of Christian Discourse* (Berkeley: University of California Press, 1991).

the west, it was mainly bishops who took up the struggle with these traditional pagan power wielders.[21]

Self-Understanding and Social Order

As we have seen, Augustine's self-understanding, by the time he finished the *Confessions*, had developed to the point where he sees himself as charged by God with affecting other people's lives. This was carried out through two ways: the preaching of the word and the dispensing of the sacraments (*Confessions* 11.2.2). These two ways are simple yet complex in that all episcopal activity can be reduced to, or summed up in, them. I believe that Augustine's concern for these two activities is at the core of his plan of social order that I call Catholicization. Proclamation of God's message and administering the sacramental rituals that ground that message were, at root, activities geared towards making people Catholic Christians.

It may seem that the focus on the term "Catholic" is a mere quibble. Is not Catholic a mere accidental adjective? For Augustine, I believe, the term is essential to the name Christian. In viewing the past, we can become persuaded by people like Augustine to accept Catholic as being equivalent to Christian. By the mere fact that we use terms like "Arian," "Donatist," "Manicheist," and "Pelagian" speaks to the success of people like Augustine in determining who can bear the name Christian. In a context where the use of the name Christian is being contested, Catholic emerges as the only legal equivalent by the late fourth and early fifth centuries.[22] In Roman Africa, in response to the question "who is Christian?" Augustine and his colleagues answer that "the Catholic is Christian." This, however, begs another question: "what does it mean to be Catholic?" In the remainder of this chapter, I shall explore the way in which Augustine develops his understanding of what it means to be Catholic, and then how he forms and carries out a plan to define, reform, and promote the Catholic Church in Africa.

---

21. Perhaps the most famous example of this is Ambrose's ongoing feud with Symmachus over the Altar of Victory. For treatment of the shrewdness of Ambrose in this controversy and in the whole struggle over Christianization or Catholicization in Milan, see Neil B. McLynn, *Ambrose of Milan: Church and Court in a Christian Capital* (Berkeley: University of California Press, 1994), 263–275. For general discussion of the significance of the bishop in late antiquity, see the papers collected in Henry Chadwick, *The Role of the Christian Bishop in Ancient Society*, Colloquy 35 (Berkeley: Center for Hermeneutical Studies in Hellenistic and Modern Culture, 1979).

22. *CT* 16.5.6, of 380 from Gratian, Valentinian II, and Theodosius I, which will be discussed in chapter 4 of this book.

What were the sources of Augustine's understanding of what it meant to be Catholic? As a new bishop, in the late 390s, writing in the *Confessions*, Augustine recalls that he had one idea of what it meant to be Catholic, which he became convinced was wrong based on his encounter with Ambrose and the Catholics of Milan.[23] We know that the dominant Christian community of Thagaste during Augustine's childhood was Catholic, but we do not have a sense of the form and content of the faith of that community. Based on Monica's contrasting experience with Ambrose's church, we know that celebrations at the tombs of the martyrs were practices that she, at least, saw as important in the Catholic.[24] We also know that Augustine found his understandings of the Catholic faith of his youth to be susceptible to Manichee criticism. The Manichees not only broke the religious bonds that tied people to Catholic and other communities but they broke the social bonds as well. All the while, they wove new bonds to intricate Manichee belief, but perhaps more importantly to Manichee social organization.[25] This alternative vision of social order holds Augustine for some nine years. "From my nineteenth to my twenty-eight year," Augustine says, "our life was one of being seduced and seducing, being deceived and deceiving" (2 Tim. 3:13).[26] Manichean evangelism, as Richard Lim points out, involved engaging people in a dispute in intimate settings and winning them over; the wider community was held together through these intimate cells. Augustine was won over this way and actively worked, successfully, to win others. By 382, in his late twenties, Augustine had come to questions that even the great Manichee bishop Faustus could not answer.[27] Although Augustine sought a new faith, interestingly, he maintains his Manichee social connections and they eventually take him to Milan, along with a new faith and a new vision of social order.[28]

Milan can thus be seen as the birthplace of Augustine's Catholicism. I will argue, however, that there are two significant cultural contexts that shape Augustine's Catholicism. Milan is important, but Africa is also important. After the initial formation of his ecclesiological ideas inspired by his Milan experience, Augustine, once back in Africa, reconnected with more indigenous resources. In the next section, I will discuss the Milanese contribution to Augustine's Catholicism. Then at the end of the chapter, after having discussed the early formulation and execution of Catholicization, I will come back to the African contribution to Augustine's understanding of Catholicity, and, thus, to Catholicization.

23. Augustine, *Confessions* bks. 5–7.
24. Ibid., 6.2.2.
25. Lim, 70–108.
26. Augustine, *Confessions* 4.1.1.
27. Ibid., 5.6.11–5.7.13.
28. Ibid., 5.10.18–19.

The Development of Augustine's Catholicism: Milan

After moving from Carthage to Rome, Augustine continues on to Milan, having won a recommendation for the chair of Rhetoric there by impressing Symmachus, the influential Prefect of Rome, with his oratory. In Book 5 of the *Confessions*, Augustine writes: "And so I came to Milan to Ambrose the bishop, known throughout the world as among the best of men, devout in your worship. . . . I was led to him by you, unaware that through him, in full awareness, I might be led to you." From the one who "received him like a father,"[29] Augustine was led to the Catholic Church, even though he listened to Ambrose at first, "only for his rhetorical technique." Step by step Augustine was drawn. First, he "did not think it impudent to assert the Catholic faith, which he thought defenseless against Manichee critics,"[30] yet he did not move to full assent. Instead, he took up the philosophical position of the Academics. Augustine says:

> I doubted everything, and in the fluctuating state of total suspense of judgement I decided I must leave the Manichees, thinking at that period of my skepticism that I should not remain a member of a sect to which I was now preferring certain philosophers. But to those philosophers, who were without Christ's saving name; I altogether refused to entrust the healing of my soul's sickness. I therefore decided to be a catechumen in the Catholic Church, which the precedent of my parents recommended to me, until some clear light should come by which could direct my course.[31]

That light came principally through continued exposure to Ambrose and through his readings of the books of the Platonists. Although Augustine yearned to "pour out" the inner anguish of his soul to Ambrose, he never found opportunity for such intimate conversation. Nevertheless, through Ambrose's example, and especially his preaching, Augustine says he heard practiced the principle of interpretation founded on (2 Cor. 3:6). "The letter kills, the spirit gives life"; Augustine was persuaded to give "preference to the Catholic faith." Through Ambrose, Augustine was moving from a position of skepticism to one of trust:

> I thought it more modest and not in the least misleading to be told by the Church to believe what could not be demonstrated—whether that was because a demonstration existed but could not be understood by all or whether the matter was not one open to rational proof—rather than from the Manichees to have a rash promise of knowledge with mockery of mere belief, and then afterwards to be ordered to believe

29. Ibid., 5.13.23.
30. Ibid., 5.14.24.
31. Ibid., 5.14.25.

many fabulous and absurd myths impossible to prove. Then little by little, Lord, with a most gentle and merciful hand you touched and calmed my heart. I considered the innumerable things I believed which I had not seen, events occurred when I was not present, such as many incidents in the history of the nations, many facts concerning places and cities which I had never seen, many things accepted on the word of friends, many from physicians, many from other people. Unless we believed what we were told, we would do nothing at all in this life.[32]

Thus, "little by little" Augustine turned from pride to humility by submitting himself to the authority of the Church. There was still to come the final move of assent described in the garden scene[33] and, of course, his baptism.[34] From assent to the authority of the Church to serving that authority involved the shift in self-understanding described in the previous chapter. What is being highlighted here is the way that this shift entailed a new view of social order. This view had a crucial stage of development in Milan. Clearly this seems to be the case from the vantage point of the *Confessions*. But how accurate is Augustine's hindsight? Does Augustine remember himself being more Catholic than he was?

One important thing to note is that, from what survives, we do not have evidence that Ambrose himself used "Catholic" as a distinguishing term in his writing or preaching.[35] Nevertheless, Ambrose was an important influence on Augustine. As a non-African, he both conveyed theological content that was a witness to true doctrine outside of Africa and he served as a living example of Catholicity.

Between his identity as a rhetor and that of a priest, as a young convert Augustine saw himself as a contemplative. The accompanying view of social order is narrower than that which he would develop as a priest and then bishop. This view is clearly demonstrated in the Cassiaciacum writings. In the autumn of 386, Augustine, his mother and son, a few students, and various friends retired to the villa of Verecundus. From this setting, Augustine produced the *Soliloques* (*Soliloquia*, 386–387) and three dialogues: *Against the Academics* (*Contra Academicos*, 386–387), *On the Happy Life* (*De beata vita*, 386–387), and *On Order* (*De ordine*, 386–387). Although these writings may not be verbatim records of the conversations at Cassiaciacum, they at least tell us about Augustine's understanding of Christianity at the time.[36] The topics

32. Ibid., 6.5.7.

33. Ibid., 8.8.19–8.12.30.

34. Ibid., 9.6.14.

35. Pierre Batiffol, *Le Catholicisme de Saint Augustin*, 5th ed., edited by J. Gabalda et Fils (Paris: Librairie Lecoffre, 1929), 212–213.

36. For an excellent summary of the state of research on the Cassiaciacum writings as well as for some interesting assertions to move discussion forward, see *Augustine Through the Ages*, 1999 ed., s.v. "Cassiaciacum Dialogues," by Joanne McWilliam.

of these writings, and the movement of the speakers in them, show Augustine pitting truths that he had recently come to embrace from the Catholic community of Milan against positions of communities, like the Manichees and the skeptics, which formerly held his allegiance. In spite of the obvious debt owed to the Catholic community of Milan, as represented in Ambrose, Augustine's recognition of Catholic institutional authority is weak. It is not until after baptism, with works like *On the Catholic and Manichean Ways of Life* (*De moribus ecclesiae catholicae et de moribus manichaeorum*, 388), *On True Religion* (*De vera religione*, 389–391), and *On the Usefulness of Belief* (*De utilitate credendi*, 391–392), that we see Augustine strongly promoting the authority of the institutional church. In *On True Religion*, for example, although Neoplatonic themes are still evident, particularly in defining true religion and modeling it as an ascent, Augustine is clear in his promotion of the Catholic Church as defined by its doctrine and sacraments. To Romanianus, he delivers this short treatise that admonishes him to "hold fast to the Christian religion of and the communion of the Church which is Catholic, and which is called Catholic not only by its own members but also by all its enemies."[37] A little earlier in the work he had just laid out the basis for distinguishing the Catholic Church from all other religious options.

However philosophers may boast, anyone can understand that religion is not to be sought from them. For they take part in the religious rites of their fellow-citizens, but in their schools teach divergent and contrary opinions of the nature of their gods and of the chief god, as the multitude can testify. If we could see this one great vice healed by Christian discipline, no one should deny that that would be an achievement worthy of all possible praise. Innumerable heresies that turn aside from the rule of Christianity testify that men not admitted to sacramental communion who think and endeavour to persuade others to think otherwise of God the Father, of his wisdom and of the divine gift [the Holy Spirit] than as the truth demands. So it is taught and believed as a chief point in man's salvation that philosophy, i.e., the pursuit of wisdom cannot be quite divorced from religion, for those whose doctrine we do not approve do not share in *our* sacramental rites.

There is little to be surprised at in this in the case of those who have chosen to have different religious rites from ours such as the Ophites whoever they may be, or the Manichaeans and others. It is more noticeable in the case of those who celebrate similar religious rites but differ from us in doctrine and are more vigorous in defending their errors than careful to have them corrected. These are excluded from Catholic

---

37. Augustine, *On True Religion* 7.12, in *Augustine: Earlier Writings*. For some background and analysis of *On True Religion*, see Frederick Van Fleteren's article "*Vera Religione, De*," in *Augustine Through the Ages*; and J. H. S. Burleigh's introduction to the translation in *Augustine: Earlier Writings*, 222–224.

communion and from participation in our rites in spite of their similarity. They have deserved to have names of their own and separate meetings, being different not only in matters of words, but also because of their superstition; like the Photinians, the Arians and many others. It is another matter with those who have caused schisms. The Lord's threshing-floor might have kept them as chaff until the time of the last winnowing, had they not in levity been carried off by the wind of pride, and separated from us of their own accord. The Jews, it is true, worship the one omnipotent God, but they expect from him only visible goods. Being too secure they were unwilling to observe their own Scriptures the indications of a new people of God arising out of humble estate, and so they remained in "the old man." This being so, religion is to be sought neither in the confusion of the pagans, nor in the offscourings of the heretics, nor in the insipidity of schismatics, nor in the blindness of the Jews, but only among those who are called Catholic or orthodox Christian, that is, guardians of truth and followers of right.[38]

The institutional church is the Catholic Church, whose authority is to be accepted over other groups who are set apart by the way they are constituted around different doctrines and rites, and are, thus, given a different name by Catholics. Still, this work was written before he was made a priest.

On the Usefulness of Belief, written shortly after his ordination in early 391, reflects further developments in Augustine's Catholicized thinking. In this book, the appeal is made to Honoratus to leave off the Manichee faith to which Augustine led him and come to the unity of the Catholic Church of whose institution Augustine is now a servant, agent, and priest.[39] This text shows Catholicization working on a one-on-one level. But, as time moves on and after he is made a priest, Catholicization also developed into a more programmatic approach to ordering society. This is evident in Augustine's *Epistle* 22 of 392.

Epistle 22: Charter of Catholicization

When Augustine returned to Africa, he wanted to be a monk, but, as we have seen, he was drafted into the priesthood by the congregation of Hippo. This would seem to have been done at the instigation of Valerius, who recognized his potential for leadership. Thus, it could be said that the first stage of Augustine's plan of Catholicization was not orchestrated by Augustine, but, rather, by Valerius. From *Epistle* 21, we can see that Augustine had developed some criticism of what he saw in the Catholic Church of Hippo, but had come to realize that any program of reform must begin with him. Accordingly, his request of Valerius for a study leave can be seen as

---

38. Augustine, *On True Religion* 5.8–9.
39. Augustine, *On the Usefulness of Belief* 1.1–2.4, in *Augustine: Earlier Writings.*

an effort to impose personal reform before he seriously embarks on social reform. Support for this contention can be found in his *Epistle* 22 to Aurelius.

Epistle 22, of 392, is a letter from the priest Augustine to the new Catholic bishop of Carthage, Aurelius. Augustine is responding to a lost letter of Aurelius of Carthage. He speaks of a "long hesitation *(diu hesitans)*" to reply to Aurelius's letter but says that he

> cast himself upon God that he might work in me according to my strength, so that I should reply to you as befitted our mutual zeal in the Lord and our care for His church, you in your exalted station and I in my subordinate post.[40]

Augustine can hardly contain himself in response to Aurelius's grant of permission for Alypius to stay with Augustine's community in Hippo. He thanks Aurelius for allowing Alypius to stay with his (Augustine's) community. Augustine assures Aurelius that:

> The whole company of brethren that has begun to form around them is therefore bound to you with great gratitude, for you looked after our interests as if very present in spirit, although our abode is so far removed from yours in space. So we devote our strength to praying that the Lord will deign to uphold with you the flock committed to your care that He will never leave you but be a present help in time of trouble, showing with His Church such mercy through your ministry as spiritual men implore Him with tears and groanings to show.[41]

> Let me assure you therefore, my Lord most revered, worthy of all devotion and of overflowing affection, that we are not without hope—nay, are rather strongly hopeful—that through the authority you bear, laid as we trust, not on your flesh, but on your spirit, our Lord and God may use the weighty sword of councils and your own weight for the healing of many carnal sores and disorders which the African Church is suffering in so many quarters and lamenting in so few (problem in the text)[42]

40. Augustine, *Epistle* 22:1, in *Augustine: Select Letters*, trans. J. H. Baxter, Loeb Series (Cambridge, MA: Harvard University Press, 1953). "Commisi me tamen deo, qui pro viribus meis operaretur in me, ut ea rescriberem, quae utrique nostrum studio in domino et cura ecclesiastica pro tua praestantia et mea obsecundatione congruerent."

41. Ibid. "Omnis itaque fratrum coetus, qui apud nos coepit coalescere, tanta tibi praerogativa obstrictus est, ut locis terrarum tantum longe disiunctis ita nobis consulueris tanquam praesentissimus spiritu. Quapropter precibus quantum valemus incumbimus, ut gregem tibi commissum tecum Dominus sustinere dignetur, nec te uspiam deserere, sed adesse adiutor in opportunitatibus, faciens cum Ecclesia sua misericordiam per sacerdotium tuum, qualem spirituales viri ut faciat, lacrymis cum gemitibusque interpellant."

42. Ibid., 22.2. "Scias itaque, domine beatissime et plenissima caritate venerabilis, non desperare nos, imo sperare vehementer, quod Dominus et Deus noster per auctoritatem personae quam geris, quam non carni, sed spiritui tuo impositam esse confidimus, multas carnales foeditates et

Augustine then moves to a discussion of Paul's Romans 13:13–14, the passage that was the key to the final door separating Augustine from the Catholic Church, according to the *Confessions*. He says that the African Church does well on distancing itself from the wantonness and chambering, but not so well on the next two pairs—drunkenness and rioting and envies and strife.[43] In 22.4, Augustine says that the transmarine church, particularly in Italy, provides the lead. Augustine says these are the infirmities of the African Church Rioting and drunkenness are particularly problematic according to Augustine. They are "considered so permissible and tolerable that they are practiced not only on holy days, when blessed martyrs are honored—a lamentable sight to anyone who looks on such festivities with more than a carnal eye—but even on any and every day." He goes on in 22.3:

> Were this depravity only immoral and not sacrilegious as well, we might think of putting up with it with what power of endurance we could. Are we to put up with it in the disgraceful debauchery of private life and of those festivities that are confined to private houses, and receive the Body of Christ in the company of those with whom we are forbidden to eat bread? At least let such disgraceful practice be removed from the cemeteries where the bodies of the saints are laid, and from the place where the sacraments are celebrated, and from the house of prayer. For we who dare forbid the use in private of that which, when practiced in holy places, is called a tribute to martyrs?[44]

He then presses his argument, saying that:

> If Africa were the first to attempt the removal of these abuses, she would be worthy of imitation by all other countries. But since they have been repressed and done away with through the greater part of Italy and in all, or nearly all, the other churches across the sea, partly because they were never in use, partly because, when they did arise or were of long standing, the scrupulousness and censure of saintly bishops, truly contemplating the life to come. . . . [H]ow can we hesitate to correct this grave moral corruption, especially after the precedent set by so many others?[45]

---

aegritudines quas Africana Ecclesia in multis patitur, in paucis gemit, conciliorum gravi ense et tua possit sanare."

43. Ibid., 22.3.

44. Ibid. "Quae foeditas si tantum flagitiosa et non etiam sacrilega esset, quibuscumque tolerantiae viribus sustentandam putaremus. Quanquam ubi est illud, quod cum multa vitia enumerasset idem Apostolus, inter quae posuit ebriosos,ita conclusit, ut diceret cum talibus nec panem edere? Sed feramus haec in luxu et labe domestica, et eorum conviviorum quae privatis parietibus continentur, accipiamusque cum eis corpus Christi, cum quibus panem edere prohibemur; saltem de sanctorum corporum sepulcris, saltem de locis sacramentorum, de domibus orationum tantum dedecus arceatur. Quis enim audet vetare privatim, quod cum frequentatur in sanctis locis, honor martyrum nominatur?"

45. Ibid., 22.4. "Haec si prima Africa tentaret auferre, a caeteris terris imitatione digna esse deberet: cum vero et per Italiae maximam partem, et in aliis omnibus aut prope omnibus transmarinis

Lamenting that the "disease (*tanta pestilentia*)" might have taken too great a toll on the African Church already, Augustine, taking early steps towards the campaigner for the Catholic cause, implores Aurelius to take action.

> But the disease wrought by this evil habit has become so chronic that complete recovery seems to me to be impossible, unless by the authority of a council; or if any one church has to begin the treatment, it appears foolish to try to change anything the Church of Carthage retains, and very presumptuous to desire to keep anything the Church of Carthage has rectified. And to carry through that reform here, what bishop could be more desirable than the one who, as a deacon, denounced such abuses?[46]

Reform is to be done "not harshly . . . but by education rather than by formal commands, by persuasion rather than by intimidation."[47] He distinguishes between treatment of the "multitude (*multitudine*)" and the "few (*paucorum*)," where one has greater latitude for "severity (*severitas*)." Even there:

> If there be any intimidation let it be done with sorrow by the threats of future punishment from the Scriptures, then the fear we inspire will not be of ourselves or our authority, but of God speaking in us. In this way an impression will first be made on the spiritually minded or on those most nearly so, and by their influence and gentle, but urgent, expostulation the rest of the crowd will be subdued.[48]

Thus, in 393, we have the first of many councils under Aurelius. The strategy of persuasion is used against the opponents of the Catholic party, as well as to maintain party discipline. Over time, however, persuasion would give way to *severitas* against those within and without. The shift can clearly be seen in the works of Augustine and in the positions taken by the African Catholic Bishops'

Ecclesiis, partim quia nunquam facta sunt, partim quia vel *orta vel* inveterata, sanctorum et vere de vita futura cogitantium episcoporum diligentia et animadversione exstincta atque deleta sunt, . . . dubitare quomodo possumus tantam morum labem, vel proposito tam lato exemplo emendare?"

46. Ibid. "Sed tanta pestilentia est huius mali, ut sanari prorsus, quantum mihi videtur, nisi concilii auctoritate nonpossit. Aut si ab una ecclesia inchoanda est medicina; sicut videtur audaciae, mutare conari quod Carthaginensis Ecclesia tenet, sic magnae impudentiae est, velle servare quae Carthaginensis Ecclesia correxit. Ad hanc autem rem quis alius episcopus esset optandus, nisi qui ea diaconus exsecratabatur?"

47. Ibid. "Non ergo aspere, quantum existimo, non duriter, non modo imperioso ista tolluntur; magis docendo quam iubendo, magis monendo quam minando. Sic enim agendum est cum multitudine: severitas autem exercenda est in peccata paucorum."

48. Ibid., 22.5. "Et si quid minamur, cum dolore fiat, de Scripturis comminando vindictam futuram ne nos ipsi in nostra potestate, sed Deus in nostro sermone timeatur. Ita prius movebuntur spiritales vel spiritalibus proximi, quorum auctoritate, et lenissimis quidem sed instantissimis admonitionibus caetera multitudo frangatur."

Councils. Before going on to talk about the councils, I will give brief sketches of the group that would compose what I call the elite core of the African Catholic clergy.

The Elite Core

Augustine, viewed from the modern period, casts a long and imposing shadow. In his own day, he was also somewhat of an impressive figure. Because of temporal distance, however, it is not often the case that we give a fair representation of Augustine in light of his contemporaries. Augustine was the chief spokesman for, and theorist of, Catholicization, but he did not act alone. Augustine worked collegially with a group of North African clergymen. Below, I will discuss a few key individuals: Valerius, Aurelius, Alypius, Severus, Evodius, and Possidius. I call these the elite core because, aside from Valerius and Aurelius, these figures were shaped in Augustinian communities before becoming bishops, and were, thus, possibly inclined to share the vision for Catholicization that Augustine promoted. Possidius records the following about this phenomenon.

> While the divine teachings were achieving success, some of the men who were serving God in the monastery with and under the direction of holy Augustine began to be ordained clerics for the Church of Hippo. Thus the truth of the preaching of the Catholic Church became daily better known and more evident, and so did the way of life of these holy servants of God with their continence and austere poverty. Other Churches therefore began eagerly to ask and obtain bishops and clerics from the monastery that owed its origin and growth to this memorable man, with the result that the Church was established and consolidated in peace and unity. I myself know of about ten holy and venerable men of continence and learning, some of them quite outstanding, whom blessed Augustine gave upon request to the various churches. These men, inspired by the ideals of that holy community and being now scattered among the Churches of the Lord, founded monasteries in their turn; as zeal for the spread of God's word increased, they prepared brothers for the priesthood and then advanced them to other Churches. The Church's teaching on saving faith, hope, and love thus became known through many and among many, not only in all parts of Africa but also in regions overseas. By means of published books, which were translated into Greek, all this teaching was able, with God's help, to make its way from this one man and through him to many. Consequently, as it is written, sinners saw and were angered; they gnashed their teeth and wasted away (see Psalm 112:10). But your servants, as it is said, kept peace with those who hated peace, and when they spoke they were attacked without cause (Psalm 120:7).[49]

---

49. Possidius, *Life of Saint Augustine*, introduction by Michele Pellegrino (Villanova, PA: Augustinian Press, 1988), 11.

As the conciliar records that we will examine shortly show, the Catholic Church in Africa was suffering a shortage of clergy.[50] In response to this problem, Augustine provided a partial solution by becoming responsible for developing and reproducing leadership that had a rippled impact on Africa. This, of course, included the characters I designate as the elite core, but extends far beyond them as well. Building this core was crucial for re-establishing vital episcopal collegiality among African Catholic bishops and with bishops overseas.[51]

Valerius of Hippo[52]

About the shrewd Valerius little is known. According to Possidius, he was the Catholic bishop of Hippo but "Greek by birth." Because he was "insufficiently master of the Latin language and literature," he drafts Augustine into priesthood, and encourages him to write and preach.[53] These were somewhat irregular moves, and he received criticism for them. But over time, they proved effective for the growth of the Catholic party in Africa.

> Contrary to the usual practice of the African Churches, he gave his priest permission to preach the gospel in church even when he himself was present and to hold frequent public discussions. For this reason some bishops were critical of him. This venerable and far-sighted man knew for sure, however, that this was the usual practice in the Eastern Churches. And because he had regard for the good of the Church, he was unconcerned about his detractors, provided only that he saw a priest accomplishing what he knew that he himself, though bishop, could not do. As a result, a lamp lit and burning and raised on a candlestick was now giving light to all who were in the house

---

50. This shortage, "inopia clericorum," gets mentioned in the *Breviarum Hipponense* 37 as the reason why Catholics are entertaining taking converts from Donatism into the clergy. For further discussion of this problem and Augustine's key role in establishing a monastic seminary model of recruitment as a partial solution, see Remi Crespin, *Ministère et sainteté: Pastorale du clergé et solution de la crise donatiste dans la vie et la doctrine de saint Augustin* (Paris: Études Augustiniennes, 1965), 53ff.

51. Paul Zmire, "Collegialité Episcopal," in *Recherche Augustiniennes* (Paris: Institut d'Études Augustiniennes, August 1971), 7:3–71. Zmire describes the phenomenon of episcopal collegiality from c. 300, the rise of Donatism, to 430, the Vandal invasion, although there is plenty of reference to Cyprian and his age. What clearly emerges is that under the primacy of Aurelius, a self-assured Catholic episcopacy developed in Africa. Although Zmire's focus is on the fitness of the organization to fight Donatism and paganism, the same structures, as we shall see, worked well to combat a myriad of religious competitors.

52. Marie Aquinas McNamara, *Friends and Friendship for Saint Augustine* (Staten Island, NY: Alba House, 1964), 126–129.

53. Possidius, 5.2.

(see John 5:35; Matthew 5:15). News of this spread abroad, and, following the good example given, some other priests began with episcopal permission to preach to the people in the presence of their bishops.[54]

Because Valerius saw the value of Augustine's potential contributions to the African Catholic Church, he was willing to go against established tradition. He pushed Augustine, but was also accommodating.[55] In allowing Augustine his requested time to study, Valerius already had in mind, or was persuaded by, the ultimate goal that Augustine presented: a well-prepared servant of the church. That servant Valerius named as his co-bishop in 395. This assured Valerius that at his death Augustine would be his successor.

Aurelius of Carthage[56]

If Augustine was the architect of Catholicization, then Aurelius was its structural engineer. From *Epistle* 22, we have seen Augustine recognizing that his project of shaping social order was one that hinged on Aurelius and the power and authority he wielded as Bishop of Carthage, Primate of Proconsular Africa. The longevity of their ecclesial careers is almost parallel, with Aurelius having a slightly longer record of service. He was a deacon by 382. His episcopate began around 391 and continued for over thirty years. During the years from 393 until 408, and the fall of Stilicho, Aurelius presided over plenary African councils that met to address the general issues that Augustine raised in his *Epistle* 22 with methodical detail. Below, only the councils that led up to the Edict of Unity in 405 will be discussed. The council first met at Hippo in 393; then in Carthage in 397 and 399, twice in 401, and once in 402, 403, and 404.

Although Augustine and Aurelius worked very closely together and agreed about much of the actions that the Catholics took, there was an important difference of opinion between them. Anne-Marie La Bonnardière points out that Augustine tended to favor persuasion in controversy with non-Catholics, while Aurelius was willing to employ coercion much more quickly.[57] Augustine's

---

54. Ibid., 5.2–5.

55. Valerius even allowed Augustine to write a letter to a Donatist challenging his position on rebaptism in Valerius's name. See *Epistle* 29.

56. The best treatment of Aurelius that I have found is that of Anne-Marie La Bonnardière. See her article "Aurelius episcopos," in *Augustinus-Lexicon*, edited by C. Mayer (Basel: Schwabe & Co., 1986). For a good discussion of Aurelius in English, see McNamara, 144–147.

57. La Bonnardière, "Aurelius episcopos." "Augustine désireux d'user de la persuasion, temporise le plus longtemps possible, tandis qu'Aurelius—soutenu d'ailleurs par Alypius—opte pour des solutions plus sévères et immédiates. Selon l'heureuse mule de Pietri: 'Augustin compose alors qu'Aurelius résiste.'"

preference for persuasion is expressed in *Epistle 22*,[58] and is, as we shall see, evident in his actions up until a shift emerges around the fall of 403 and into the winter of 404.

Alypius of Thagaste[59]

Of the elite core, as a friend of Augustine's from youth, Alypius had the longest continuing relationship with Augustine. The friendship was an intimate one, such that Augustine features Alypius prominently in the *Confessions*,[60] and even refers to him as "the brother of his heart."[61] From *Epistle 22* we see that, aside from being converted and baptized with Augustine, Alypius was also a brother with him in the monastic communities of Thagaste and Hippo. In 394, he is made Bishop of Thagaste, being the first among many who flow from Augustine's community into the Catholic clerical leadership of Africa.[62]

Severus of Milevus[63]

Severus was, like Alypius, part of the Thagaste and Hippo communities. He, too, was referred to as a friend on the most intimate terms. And he, too, was made a bishop. When Severus was dragged into the episcopate in 396, he was made the shepherd of Milevus, a great distance from Hippo and Thagaste. In spite of the distance of over 200 miles that separated them, Severus was, nevertheless, a key member of the elite core and an active promoter of the plan of Catholicization.

Evodius of Uzalis[64]

Another hometown acquaintance of Augustine's who became a member of his monastic communities before being drafted into the episcopacy was Evodius.

58. *Epistle* 22.5, in *Augustine: Select Letters.*

59. McNamara, 129–132.

60. In fact, Augustine provides a brief sketch of Alypius that serves as a sort of mini-*Confessions* for Alypius in Book 6.

61. Augustine, *Confessions* 9.4.7.

62. In *Epistle* 24, in the Augustinian corpus, Alypius is addressed as a bishop. The letter is from Paulinus of Nola and his wife, Therasia, to Alypius thanking him for the gift of works of Augustine.

63. McNamara, 137–141. See also *Encyclopedia of the Early Church*, 1992 ed., s.v. "Severus of Milevus," by F. Scorza Barcellona.

64. McNamara, 132–137. See also Evodius of Uzalis in *Augustine Through the Ages.*

Judging from some of Augustine's correspondence, Evodius had a potentially volatile personality. Augustine spins this quality favorably as zeal for the Church. It is, thus, interesting that Evodius is then chosen for the mission to Honorius in 404. This mission was part of what secured the Edict of Unity.

Possidius of Calama[65]

Although Possidius, the disciple and biographer of Augustine, was a part of Augustine's community in Hippo,[66] he had not been a lifelong friend of Augustine's. He became Bishop of Calama around 397. After 403, Possidius became involved in a clash with the Donatists. This was a key event, precipitating Augustine's shift from persuasion to coercion. Thus, it also precipitates the actions taken at the Council of Carthage in 404, which led to Evodius's mission to Ravenna.[67]

On Faith and the Creed, the Councils, and the Early Implementation of Catholicization

When Augustine proposed using councils to reform the African Catholic Church in 392, he was calling for the reinvigoration of a tradition of Church governance that could be tied back at least to Cyprian, who convened seven councils during 248–250. After Cyprian, we have no documentation for an African Council until 348, when there was the celebration of a brief reunion between the Catholics and the Donatists. Again, we have no documentation until a council at Carthage in 390. After Augustine's letter of 392, Aurelius presided over a series of councils that were the "key"[68] or "linchpin" of "an ambitious program to revitalize the Catholic Church in Africa."[69]

---

65. Possidius. See also *Augustine Through the Ages*, 1999 ed., s.v. "Possidius," by Mark Vessey; and McNamara, 141–144.

66. Possidius, 15.1.

67. In 408–409, Possidius was sent on a mission to Emperor Honorius.

68. Charles Munier, "L'influence de saint Augustin sur la legislation de son temps," in *Augustinus Afer: Augustin Afer: Saint Augustin: africanité et universalité: Actes du colloque international Alber-Annaba*, 1–7 avril 2001 Paradosis, volume 45/1 et 45/2, edited by Pierre-Yves Fux, Jean-Michel Rössli, Otto Wermelinger (Fribourg: 2003), 109–123.

69. *Augustine Through the Ages*, 1999 ed., s.v. "Councils of North African Bishops," by Jane Merdinger; *Encyclopedia of the Early Church*, 1992 ed., s.v. "Carthage, V. Councils," by Charles Munier.

Hippo, October 393[70]

The first of these councils was held at Hippo in 393. The location of the council is significant for at least two reasons. First, the location seems to show the degree to which Augustine, even as a priest, was so important for the conciliar reform movement that he was suggested to his friend Aurelius. Second, perhaps Aurelius and the Catholics saw an opportunity to make gains in Numidia, where the Donatists had been traditionally strong until the recent schism in their ranks.[71] The record from the council has been lost, but the council at Carthage in 397 represents the actions of the Hippo council. These canons come down to us as the Hippo Breviary.[72] Before getting to this collection, I will discuss Augustine's unique contribution to the council, his sermon *On Faith and the Creed*.

In addition to the Hippo Breviary, the other record of note is Augustine's treatise *On Faith and the Creed*. At the Council of Hippo, Augustine was asked to preach to the assembled clergy. The topic was the creed, and the sermon, as found in *On Faith and the Creed*, has lost much of its homiletic style through Augustine's reworking of the material. In spite of the problems getting at the original sermon, I think that it is important to take note of Augustine's concern to establish the essential parameters of the Catholic faith in Africa. But what was the content of that faith? What creed did he expound? These are difficult questions to answer, and here I rely on the work of E. P. Meijering. He rules out the possibility of the creed that Augustine uses as being either Nicean or African.

> Nothing can be said in this matter with absolute certainty. What seems certain is that Augustine does not follow the North African Creed in the *De fide et symbols*, and that it seems more likely that he follows the *Vetus Romanum* than the Confession of Milan. Augustine obviously inserted the words from the Creed into his argument in the way which suited him best. Given that the two Creeds from which the words

70. See *Concilia Africae A. 345–A. 525*, vol. 149 of *Corpus Christianorum: Series Latina*, edited by Charles Munier (Turnhout, Belgium: Brepols, 1974), 20–53. For an English translation, see Charles J. Hefele, *A History of the Councils of the Church*, volume 2: AD 326–AD 429 (Edinburgh, 1896), 395–402. See also *The Canons of the CCXVII Blessed Fathers Who Assembled at Carthage. Commonly Called the Code of Canons of the African Church* (*NPNF* Series 2, vol. 14).

71. La Bonnardière suggests that the location showed prudent judgment on Aurelius's part in the wake of the Donatist council of the Maximinianist schism within Donatism that had just condemned Primianus, the Donatist bishop of Carthage, in June 393. See her article "Aurelius episcopos," 555.

72. Merdinger, "Councils of North African Bishops." See F. L. Cross "History and Fiction in the African Canons," *Journal of Theological Studies* 12 (1961): 227–247, particularly for his assertions about the nature of the problems associated with the way in which canons of the various councils have come down to us.

could have been taken are so similar, it is impossible to determine with certainty from which of the two Creeds Augustine is drawing. We can provide no more than probable explanations.[73]

Accepting Meijering's judgments, it is interesting to note that, whether Roman or Milanese, it is an overseas creed that is the standard by which Augustine has come to know and understand the Catholic faith. Further, it is this creed that he represents as the foundation for his reformation of the African Catholic Church, and thus, is the foundation for the Catholicization of Roman Africa as a whole.

On Faith and the Creed

Although Augustine does not state the creed in its entirety, a hypothetical reconstruction can be made. Meijering provides one such reconstruction in his commentary. It runs as follows:

> I believe in God the Father Almighty, and in Jesus Christ,
> Son of God, only begotten of the Father, Our Lord,
> Who was born through the Holy Spirit from the Virgin Mary,
> Who was crucified under Pontius Pilate and buried,
> On the third day he was raised from the dead,
> Ascended into heaven
> Sat at the right hand of the Father
> From where he will come and judge the living and the dead
> And in the Holy Spirit, the Holy Church
> Remission of sins, and the resurrection of the flesh.[74]

In the reworked form, published shortly after the conference, Augustine provides an exposition of the creed that consistently upholds Catholic doctrine against rival interpretations of the nature of the Trinity and the Church. Meijering argues that in doing this, Augustine adheres closely to the tradition of acknowledged Catholic teaching of writers like Tertullian, Hilary, and Ambrose, but without explicitly naming them. Augustine is, however, often explicitly clear about denouncing

73. E. P. Meijering, *Augustine: De Fide et Symbolo* (Amsterdam: J. C. Gieben Publisher, 1987), 8–12.

74. Ibid., 11. "Credo in Deum Patrem omnipotentem, et in Jesum Christum, Filium Dei, Patris unigenitum, Dominum nostrum, qui natus est per Spiritum sanctum ex Maria virgine, qui sub Pontio Pilato crucifixus est et sepultus. Tertio die resurrexit a mortuis, ascendit in caelum, sedet ad dexteram Patris, inde venturus et iudicaturus vivos et mortuos, et in Spiritum sanctum, sanctam ecclesiam, remissionem peccatorum, camis resurrectionem."

schools of doctrine by name that diverge from the Catholic faith.

In his defense of the Catholic faith, it is interesting to note that, in the clause on the church, the church is not designated as Catholic. Thus, Augustine needs to say: "[W]e believe in the holy church, doubtlessly the Catholic one."[75] He gives further explanation in the apparent openness in the creed by adding that:

> For the heretics and the schismatics call their congregations churches but the heretics in supposing falsely about God, they violate the faith. The schismatics also, departing improperly from fraternal love, break away. Although they believe what we believe. On which account neither the heretics belong to the Catholic Church because it loves, nor do the schismatics because it loves its neighbor.[76]

By evoking Jesus's teaching on the two great commandments, Augustine defines the "holy Church" as the Catholic Church, in that it is only the Catholic Church that both rightly professes about God and rightly holds communion with its fellow Christians.

Hippo Breviary

The Hippo Breviary, compiled in 397, contains a representation of the most significant actions of the Council of Hippo in 393. As it has come down to us, it contains a Latin version of the Nicene Creed, five canons (A–E), and then another thirty-seven canons (1–37).[77] As F. L. Cross says: "The Hippo council evidently has high ambitions. It appears to have aimed at drawing up, at least in outline, a complete body of canon law." He further contrasts the Hippo project with "the clearly ad hoc twenty canons of Nicaea."[78] The canons cover a variety of issues, from establishing that all churches will follow the date of Easter established by Carthage (Canon A) to mandating that "[t]he sons of bishops and clergy may not join in secular plays, or witness them" (Canon 11). These two examples reveal two categories of laws found in the Hippo Breviary and in other canons of subsequent councils. Canon A is an example of laws on church order, while Canon 11 reflects the moral reform initiative. A third category of laws has to do with relations to non-Catholics. An example of this kind of law is seen in Canon 37:

---

75. Ibid., 137. "[C]redimus et sanctam ecclesiam, utique catholicam."

76. Ibid., 138. "[N]am et haeretici et schismatici congregationes suas ecclesias vocant. sed haeretici de Deo falsa sentiendo ipsam fidem violant; schismatici autem discissionibus iniquis a fraterna caritate dissiliunt, quamvis ea credant quae credimus. quapropter nec haeretici pertinent ad ecclesiam catholicam, quoniam diligit Deum; nec schismatici, quoniam diligit proximum."

77. *Concilia Africae A. 345–A. 525*, vol. 149 of *Corpus Christianorum*, 20–53. For an English translation, see Hefele, 395–402.

78. Cross, 227–247.

The old rule of the Councils, that no Donatist ecclesiastic shall be received into the Church otherwise than among the laity, remains in force, except as regards those who have never rebaptized, or those who desire to join the Church with their congregations (that is, such shall retain their clerical office). But the transmarine Church shall be consulted on this point, as also on the question whether the children of Donatists, who have received Donatist baptism, not of their own free will but at the desire of their parents, are to be excluded from being accepted for the service of the altar, on account of the error of their parents.[79]

In this canon we have Catholicity being promoted in two ways. On the one hand, they want to establish discipline that makes clear distinctions between Catholics and Donatists. On the other hand, effort is made to affirm Catholicity by virtue of the geographic universality that the African Catholics share with churches overseas. What really anchors the importance of this council for Catholicization is the way the council establishes its own authority on a perpetual basis,[80] and the way in which the bishop of Carthage is acknowledged as the leader of Catholic action.[81]

Carthage, June 397

In 394 a council met in Carthage, but it is unclear as to whether it was a plenary or only a regional council. At any rate, the acts are lost. In 395 and 396, the African Catholic bishops did not meet due to political instability. Gildo, the *Comes Africae,* revolted against Honorius and allied himself with Optatus, the Donatist bishop of Thamugadi. Together they made a grab for political and religious power that would have, if successful, embraced Proconsular Africa and Numidia.[82] During a relative lull, the Catholic bishops of Africa were able to meet at Carthage in 397.

One of the most important of this council's actions was the compilation and reaffirmation of the canons of Hippo. This council did more than just that, however. Carthage 397 put forth canons that sought to craft a distinctly Catholic church discipline. It seems that the disputed election of Caecilian in 311, and the ensuing schism that made for two main parallel Christian communities, framed some of this legislation. For example, Canon 48 forbade rebaptisms, re-ordinations, and

79. See Hefele, 400–401; *Concilia Africae,* 43–44.

80. Canon 5 makes provision for the annual council encompassing "all provinces (omnes prouinciae)." *The Canons of the CCXVII Blessed Fathers Who Assembled at Carthage (NPNF* Series 2, vol. 14).

81. Aside form having the authority to set Easter given in Canon A, in Canon 5 for the other provinces the bishop of Carthage also was given power to settle disputes over ecclesiastical appointments.

82. On Gildo, see *Encyclopedia of the Early Church,* 1992 ed., s.v. "Gildo," by W. H. C. Frend. For an account of the revolt, see Frend, *The Donatist Church,* chap. 9, 208–226.

translations of bishops. One would expect these responses to Donatism. However, what one would not expect is that the Africans would take these positions using a non-African council, the Council of Capua, as a precedent.[83] Again with reference to overseas churches, the Africans decide that at least three bishops need to be present to consecrate a new bishop,[84] and that if the consecration is disputed, then one or two more are to be added to the number of those ordaining and the objections are to be discussed where the candidate is to serve. Only after the candidate has been cleared in public may he be ordained.[85]

Another interesting aspect of this collection of canons is the way in which Aurelius, as Primate of Africa, has the importance of his office enhanced. Carthage, as had been the custom, now, formally, is recognized as the church that sets the date for Easter.[86] A note from the earlier, probably regional, council of June 397 says that no bishop should go across the sea without a formal letter from the primate of Africa. Also, a number of the canons have the opinions of Aurelius included along with the language of the law itself.

Carthage, June 401[87]

Once again, the revolt of Gildo intensified and prevented the Catholics from assembling a plenary council in 398. In 399, they met at Carthage, but the canons do not survive. There is a note that survives, however, indicating that the Africans sent a request to the emperors that the churches might have the right of refuge for anyone who might flee to them.[88] There was also no plenary in 400, and Charles

---

83. Canon 48 (*NPNF* Series 2, vol. 14). "Illud autem suggerimus mandatum nobis, quod etiam in Capuensi plenaria synodo videtur statutum, ut non liceat fieri rebaptizationes, reordinationes, vel translations episcoprum."

84. Canon 49, Ibid.

85. Canon 50, Ibid. "Sed illud est statuendum, ut quando ad eligendum conuenerimus, si qua contradictio fuerit oborta, quia talia tractata sunt apud nos, non praesumant ad purgandum eum qui ordinandus est tres iam, sed postuletur ad numerum supradictorum unus uel duo, et in eadem plebe cui ordinandus est discutiantur primo personae contradicentium, postremo etiam illa quae obiciuntur pertractentur; et cum purgatus fuerit sub conspectu publico, ita demum ordinetur."

86. Canon 51, Ibid.

87. *NPNF* Series 2, vol. 14, 472–483; Helefle, 421–427; *Concilia Africae*, 194–205.

88. *NPNF* Series 2, vol. 14, 470; *Concilia Africae, Reg. Eccl. Carthag. Excerpta V. Notitia concilii Carthaginensis 27 aprilis 399*, 193 lines 387–396. According to Munier in *Encyclopedia of the Early Church*, the Catholics asked Honorius to allow the churches the right of asylum conceded to the temples by the law of January 29 (*CT* 16.10.15). This does not make sense. I am suspicious that Walford mistranslated Munier because that law says that some temples are to be preserved as "public works." Other temples in the countryside, according to 16.10.16, are to be destroyed. The law says nothing about asylum. As a matter of fact, 16.10.14 actually revokes any

Munier thinks that conflict with polytheists over the laws of 399 was the reason.[89] Thus, the next plenary council rich with records is to be found in 401. In fact, 401 had two plenary councils.

The first of these plenaries was held at Carthage on June 15, 401, and the second was on September 15. At the first, Aurelius, lamenting a shortage of clergy, says that they should send envoys to Anastasius of Rome and Venerius of Milan to inform them that:

> [T]he need of clergy is so great that many churches are in such destitution as that not so much as a single deacon or even an unlettered clerk is to be found. I say nothing of the superior orders and offices, because if, as I have said, the ministry of a deacon is not easily to be had, it is certainly much more difficult to find one of the superior orders. [And let them also tell these bishops] that we can no longer bear to hear the daily lamentations of the different peoples almost ready to die, and unless we do our best to help them, the grievous and inexcusable cause of the destruction of innumerable souls will be laid at our door before God.[90]

Given this state of affairs, the African Catholics then propose that children of Donatists may be ordained after becoming Catholics. They even consider accepting Donatist clergy who would join the Catholic Church and bring their congregations

---

previously standing "privileges to civil priests." This was probably in response to the fact that a law of 399, *CT* 16.10.15, had granted the right of asylum to temples. See Munier, *Encylopedia of the Early Church*.

89. Munier, *Encylopedia of the Early Church*.

90. *NPNF* Series 2, vol. 14, 470; *Concilia Africae, Reg. Eccl. Carthag. Excerpta V. Notitia de gestis concilii Carthaginensis 16 iunii 401,* 194–295 lines 398–430. "Aurelius episcopus dixit: Ecclesiarum Dei per Africain constitutarum necessitates mecum optime nouit caritas uestra, sanctissimi fratres, et quoniam praestitit Dominus ut ex aliqua parte sancti coetus uestri esset congregata praesentia, uidetur mihi ut has easdem necessitates, quas pro sollicitudine nostra indagare potuimus, in medium proferamus; quas cum adprobauerit uestra sinceritas, sit consequens aligendum esse unum de nostro numero consacerdotem qui, auxiliante Domino orationibus uestris, et has ipsas suscipere possit et nauiter peragendas implere, perrecturus ad transmarinas Italiae partes, ut tam sanctis fratribus et consacerdotibus nostris, uenerabili sancto fratri Anastasio sedis apostolicae episcopo, quam etiam sancto fratri Venerio sacerdoti Mediolanensis ecclesiae, necessitatem ipsam ac dolorem atque inopiam nostram ualeat intimare. Ex his enim sedibus hoc fuerat prohibitum, quo nouerint communi periculo prouidendum, maxime quia tanta indigentia clericorum est, multaeque ecclesiae ita desertae sunt, ut ne unum quidem diaconum, uel inliteratum, habere reperiantur. Nam de ceteris superioribus gradibus et officiis tacendum arbitror, quia, ut dixi si ministerium diaconii facile non inuenitur, multo magis superiorum honorum inueniri non posse certissimum est. Et quotidianos planctus diuersarum paene emortuarum plebium iam non sustinemus, quibus nisi fuerit aliquando subuentum, grauis nobis et inexcusabilis innumerabilium animarum pereuntium causa apud Deum mansura est."

with them as another partial solution to their manpower shortage. At this council, however, they do not act unilaterally. Instead, they ask the opinions of the "aforesaid brothers." That is, they ask Rome and Milan for their opinions.[91]

Canon 64 provides another example of the importance that the churches of Italy hold for the Africans. Apparently, manumission of slaves done publicly in churches had been practiced in Italy, and the Africans proclaim, "Concerning the publishing of manumissions in church, if our fellow bishops throughout Italy shall be found to do this, it will be a mark of our confidence to follow their order."[92]

The Africans also decide at this council to request of the emperors that the remaining polytheist temples be destroyed,[93] that the associated "pagan feasts" be restrained,[94] and that on Sundays and feast days no plays may be performed.[95] They also request that the emperors grant clergy exemption from forced public testimony in cases that were already tried in an ecclesial court where the losing party then seeks remedy in civil court. Relating also to clergy, it is ruled that if any are condemned by a trial of bishops, "he may not be defended either by the churches over which he presided, nor by anyone whatever, under pain of loss both of money and office, and let them order that neither age nor sex be received as an excuse."[96]

Carthage, September 401

Shortly thereafter, the efforts to be on good terms with their Italian colleagues pay dividends. At the second plenary council of 401, the African Catholics are able to read a letter of encouragement from Anastasius, Bishop of Rome, in their struggle against the Donatists. Referring to that letter, Aurelius's comments introduce the canons from that council as follows:

> When the letters of our most blessed brother and fellow priest, Anastasius, bishop of the Church of Rome, had been read, in which he exhorted us out of the solicitude and sincerity of his paternal and brotherly love, that we should in no way dissimulate with regard to the wiles and wickednesses of the Donatist heretics and schismatics, by which they gravely vex the Catholic Church of Africa, we thank our Lord that he hath vouchsafed to inspire that best and holy archbishop with such a pious care for the members of Christ, although in diverse lands, yet builded together into the one body of Christ.[97]

91. Canon 57 (*NPNF* Series 2, vol. 14).
92. Canon 64, Ibid.
93. Canon 58, Ibid.
94. Canon 60, Ibid.
95. Canon 61, Ibid.
96. Canon 62, Ibid.
97. *NPNF* Series 2, vol. 14, 475; *Concilia Africae, Reg. Eccl. Carthag. Excerpta V. Notitia de gestis concilii Carthaginensis 13 septembris 401*, 199 lines 565–577.

Emboldened by this support, the Africans decide to act "leniently and pacifically (*leniter et pacifice*)"[98] towards the Donatists. They decide to go ahead and receive Donatist clergy into the Catholic Church even though they now understand that a council, which met in foreign parts, ruled against it. Pragmatically, and strategically, it seemed to be a good move. What had seemed to be solid resistance for decades now seems to be vulnerable. The crack in the structure of Donatism came about in the Maximianist schism. The Catholics seem to be trying to exploit this schism at many turns. In Canon 67, they state their intent to prod secular officials to take note of the disruption caused by the schism and to

> aid the common mother, the Catholic Church, that the episcopal authority may be fortified in the cities; that is to say that by their judicial power and with diligence out of their Christian faith, they enquire and record in the public acts, that all may have a firm notion of it, what has taken place in all those places in which the Maximianists, who made a schism from them, have obtained basilicas.

At the same time, they send legates to Donatists, "both those they held as bishops and (lay) people,"[99] inviting them to return to Catholic unity. Those legates will be careful to point out what is recorded in the municipal acts as to how the main Donatist hierarchy should treat the schismatic Maximianists.

> For in this case it is shown them by divine grace, if they will but heed it, that their separation from the unity of the Church is as iniquitous as they now proclaim the schism of the Maximianists from themselves to be. Nevertheless from the number, those whom they condemned by the authority of their plenary council, they received back with their honours, and accepted the baptism which they had given while condemned and cut off.

They conclude the act regarding the peaceful delegation to the Donatists thusly:

> And thus let them see how with stupid heart they resist the peace of the Church scattered throughout the whole world, when they do these things on the part of Donatus, neither do they say that they are contaminated by communion with those whom they so receive for the making of peace, and yet they despise us, that is the Catholic Church, which is established even in the extreme parts of the earth, as being defiled by the communion of those whom the accusers have not been able to win over to themselves.

The air of condescension permeates Canon 69 and the Catholic Church's official position in Africa regarding the Donatists. In spite of the claims that they desire

---

98. Canon 66 (*NPNF* Series 2, vol. 14).

99. Canon 67, Ibid.; Canon 69, Ibid. "[E] numero nostro ad ipsorum Donatistarum sive quos habent episcopos sive ad plebs mittantur."

peace, the Catholics did not view the proposed peace as being between equals. The Catholics were not thinking, "let's work things out between us"; they were thinking, "come to your senses." The main body of Donatists did, in fact, see the Maximianists as so iniquitous as to warrant forced return brought about by the invited intervention of the secular power.

Over the next decade, as the Donatists charged Catholics with using the coercive power of the state against them, Augustine would remind them of their earlier practices against the Maximianists. No doubt also being mindful of the Donatists, the Catholics take care to guard against rebaptisms. Allowance is made, however, to baptize someone who may have been baptized as an infant when they have no memory of baptism and when a good faith effort is made to establish that no one can attest to a prior baptism.

Canon 83 provides a ruling that does not explicitly mention the Donatists, but was surely mindful of them. The African Catholics mandate a crackdown on martyr cults.

Of False Memories of Martyrs.

> Item, it seemed good that the altars which have been set up here and there, in fields and by the wayside as Memories of Martyrs, in which no body nor reliques of martyrs can be proved to have been laid up, should be overturned by the bishops who rule over such places, if such a thing can be done. But should this be impossible on account of the popular tumult it would arouse, the people should none the less be admonished not to frequent such places, and that those who believe rightly should be held bound by no superstition of the place. And no memory of martyrs should at all be accepted, unless where there is found the body or some reliques, on which is declared traditionally and by good authority to have been originally his habitation, or possession, or the scene of his passion. For altars which have been erected anywhere on account of dreams or inane quasi-revelations of certain people, should be in every way disapproved of.[100]

The Donatists had a tradition of reverence for martyrs that perhaps even played a part in the start of the schism. According to Optatus, Lucilla, a wealthy woman who had been criticized by Caecilian before he was elected bishop, was offended, opposed his election, and supported one of her servants, Majorinus, as a rival bishop.[101] From then on, reverence for martyrdom was distinctive of the Donatist

---

100. Canon 83, Ibid.

101. See Optatus 1.16–19 Optatus, *Optatus: Against the Donatists*, translation and introduction by Mark Edwards (Liverpool: Liverpool University Press, 1997). For discussion of the incident see Frend, *The Donatist Church*, 17ff. See also Victor Saxer, *Morts, Martyrs, Reliques en Afrique chrétienne*. Théologie historique 55 (Paris: Beauchesne, 1980), 233–235; and Bernhard Kriegbaum, *Kirche der Traditoren oder Kirche der Martyrer: Die Vorgeschichte des Donatismus*. Series: Innsbrucker theologische Studien, Bd. 16 (Innsbruck: Tyrolia, 1986), 101ff.

religion. This legislation is a natural follow through on the agenda set out by Augustine in *Epistle* 22. Reflecting on Romans 13:13, Augustine had questioned the "rioting and drunkenness" practiced "on holy days, when blessed martyrs are honored" as well as on "any and every day." Augustine asked Aurelius:

> At least let such disgraceful practice be removed from cemeteries where the bodies of the saints are laid, and from the place where the sacraments are celebrated, and from the house of prayer. For who dare for bid the use in private of that which, when practiced in holy places, is called a tribute to the martyrs.[102]

An important step in controlling and Catholicizing the cult of the martyrs is to firmly establish who is and who is not a martyr, and bring the verifiable cultic sites under Catholic episcopal control. Though this was their intent, they are keenly aware of the possibility that they would encounter popular backlash. On those occasions, the bishops then are to maintain that "the people should none the less be admonished not to frequent such places, and that those who believe rightly should be held bound by no superstition of the place."[103]

Several issues of church discipline are also addressed. Bishops, priests, and deacons can be married, but they must be celibate in marriage.[104] Clergy must not defect their churches to take another church, and no bishop may ordain a monk from another diocese, nor may he take a monk from another diocese and make him head of their monastery.[105] It is reiterated that bishops must attend the councils. Bishops who are serving as intercessors (*intercessori*)[106] must find a bishop for that congregation within a year, even if there is popular support for them remaining. If a member of the clergy has been excommunicated, then they have up to a year to appeal the decision. These general rules clearly can have particular application on two cases addressed in the canons. In Canon 77, we learn of a Cresonius of Villa Regis who is to be summoned by his primate to the next plenary council or else the council will rule against him.[107] We do not know what charge was leveled against him. Following this, in Canon 78, we learn some sketchy facts of Equitius, who caused some scandal in the church of Hippo-Diarrhytus. A delegation of twenty bishops, including Augustine, Alypius, and

---

102. *Epistle* 22.3, in *Augustine: Select Letters*.

103. Canon 83 (*NPNF*, Series 2, vol. 14).

104. Canon 71, Ibid.

105. Canon 80, Ibid.

106. Apparently interim pastors.

107. Canon 77 (*NPNF*, Series 2, vol. 14). "Quod si uenire contempserit, in se cognoscat sententiam promulgandam."

Evodius, is sent to sort out the matter in a way that will ultimately lead to the ordination of a new bishop.[108]

Again the emperors are petitioned to allow manumission in the churches.[109] They are also asked to "all together destroy" the last vestiges of idolatry[110] and to appoint defenders under the authority of the church.[111]

Lastly, it is agreed that when a letter needs to be written on behalf of the entire council, Aurelius will have the authority to compose such a letter. We can justly assume that this would be done with the consultation of Augustine and Alypius especially.

Milevis, August 402

In an unusual move, the plenary council met at Milevis. The chief causes for not meeting in Carthage were issues of church discipline. To resolve them, the plenary council descends on the hospitality of Augustine's disciple Severus, reiterates previous canons going all the way back to Hippo 393, and passes new legislation as well. Precedence of honor among bishops is established by seniority. Thus, except for Carthage, which has precedence in Proconsular Africa as well as precedence over the other North African providences, primacy in the other provinces is determined by who was ordained first.[112] It is also declared that persons who are ordained to the episcopacy in all of the African provinces (*per prouincias Africanas*) must, in letters from their ordainers, certify the act bearing the name of the consul and the date, so that seniority can be clearly established.

A case against Quodvultus of Centuria is suspended because a key accuser of the unstated crime has withdrawn his testimony. A case against a Maximian of Bagai was carried through, however, and he was expelled from his See. Again, we are not given the details of the case.

In what seems to be a follow-up on Canon 80, from Carthage in September 401, in light of controversy in Milevis, it is decreed that even if someone has only read in one diocese, he may not be taken to be clergy by another bishop in their province.[113]

---

108. Canon 78, Ibid.

109. Canon 82, Ibid.

110. Canon 84, Ibid. "Item placuit ab imperatoribus gloriosissimis peti, ut reliquae idolatriae non solum in simulacris sed in quibuscumque locis vel lucis vel arboribus omnimodo deleantur."

111. Canon 75, Ibid. These could be *defensor ecclesiae*, but given that the expressed concern is for the poor, these *defensors* might be *defensor plebs*.

112. Canon 86, Ibid.

113. Canon 90, Ibid.

Carthage, August 403

Returning to Carthage, a pivotal council is held in 403. The African Catholics decide to take the offensive against the Donatists in a confrontational way. Under the banner of peace, they launch a two-pronged attack. First, as Aurelius states, it is the decision of the council to met the Donatists head-on.

> Canon XCI (Greek xciv.) Of holding meetings with the Donatists.

> Aurelius, the bishop, said: What has come out in the handling of your charity, I think this should be confirmed by ecclesiastical acts. For the profession of all of you shews that each one of us should call together in his city the chiefs of the Donatists either alone and with one of his neighbour bishops, so that in like manner in the different cities and places there should be meetings of them assembled by the magistrates or seniors of the places. And let this be made an edict if it seems good to all. And all the bishops said: It seems good to all, and we all have confirmed this with our subscription. Also we desire that your holiness sign the letters to be sent from the council to the judges. Aurelius, the bishop, said: If it seems good to your charity, let the form of summoning them be read, in order that we all may hold the same tenour of proceeding. All the bishops said: Let it be read. Laetus the Notary read.[114]

Second, as can be teased out from what is written above, these meetings are to be arranged by the local lay authorities, either magistrates or seniors.[115] As described in Canon 92, these meetings were to allow each side to state their case through representatives that each side chooses. Following is the form of invitation that the Catholics used:

> We, sent by the authority of our Catholic Council, have called you together, desiring to rejoice in your correction, bearing in mind the charity of the Lord who said: Blessed are the peacemakers, for they shall be called the children of God; and moreover he admonished through the prophet those who say they are not our brothers, that we ought to say: Ye are our brethren. Therefore you ought not to despise this pacific commonitory coming of love, so that if ye think we have any part of the truth, ye do not hesitate to say: that is, when your council is gathered together, ye delegate of your number certain to whom you in trust the statement of your case; so that we may be able to do this also, that there shall be delegated from our Council who with them delegated by you may discuss peacefully, at a determined place and time, whatever question there is which separates your communion from us; and that at length the old error may receive an end through the assistance of our Lord God, lest through the animosity of men, weak souls, and ignorant people should perish by sacrilegious dissension. But

---

114. Canon 91, Ibid.
115. Canon 92, Ibid. "[P]er magistratus uel seniors locorum conueniant."

if ye shall accept this proposition in a fraternal spirit, the truth will easily shine forth, but if ye are not willing to do this, your distrust will be easily known.[116]

Unfortunately, but not unpredictably, the Donatists did not accept the olive branch, dripping and slick with such sentiments.

Carthage, June 404

Aside from refusing to meet in city after city, town after town, the militant Circumcellions executed some dramatic attacks. One of these fell on Possidius, who was beaten but survived. Another attack was planned to ambush Augustine, but he escaped through an accidental, or providential, wrong turn on his journey. As a result, the Catholics decided to ask for greater support from the emperor. The following is the request from the African Synod that Evodius carried to Honorius at Ravenna.

[As the Donatists had failed to respond to efforts made to bring them to a discussion, but had replied by acts of violence, the delegates of the council to the Emperors were instructed to ask as follows:]

As we have fulfilled our episcopal and peace-seeking duty towards them, and they, who could make no reply to the truth, were turned to horrible acts of violence such as laying ambushes for numerous bishops and clergy (not to speak of laity) and the seizure or attempted seizure of various churches, it is for the Imperial Clemency to counsel as to how the Catholic Church, which has borne them in Christ from her sacred womb, and nourished them with firmness of faith, should be fortified by their foresight, lest audacious persons get the upper hand in a religious era, by terrorizing a defenceless population since they cannot lead them astray and so corrupt them. For the hateful band of the Circumcellions, in which they rage, has often been mentioned and proclaimed in laws, and it has been condemned by frequent sanctions of our above-mentioned most religious Emperors; against their fury we can gain a security that is not extraordinary or alien to holy Scripture, since the Apostle Paul, as is related in the faithful Acts. If the Apostles even averted a conspiracy of powerful opponents by Military aid. But the subject of our request is that protection be provided openly for the various orders in the Catholic Churches in individual cities and various areas on certain neighbouring estates. At the same time one must ask that they confirm the law originating from their father of pious memory, Theodosius, by which a penalty of ten pounds of gold is laid upon those heretics who ordain or are ordained, or upon landowners on whose property heretical congregations assemble. The object of its confirmation is to bring it to bear on whose against whom on account of their ambushes, exasperated Catholics have entered a suit, so that by fear at least of legal action they may refrain themselves from heretical or schismatical

116. Ibid.

wickedness, who fail to be amended or corrected by the thoughts of everlasting punishment. [Similarly we request the law about inheritances be reconfirmed with safeguards against those who become Catholics merely to secure an inheritance.][117]

Ironically, by the time Evodius and Theasius reached Ravenna, Honorius, having already been influenced by an episcopal petitioner from Africa, had made up his mind. The plea of Maximian of Bagai persuaded Honorius to issue stronger measures against the Donatists.[118]

Carthage, June 405

It seems that the African Council of Catholic bishops did not care how Honorius made his decision; they only cared about what he would legislate and what he would enforce. So, gladly taking the legislation, and, no doubt, encouraging its enforcement at the first plenary council since the promulgation of the Edict of Unity, the bishops took care to thank the emperor.

Augustine's Catholicism: Africa

From the preceding accounts of the councils, the influence of overseas churches on the African project of Catholicization is apparent. The project was collaborative. But, as we see from *Epistle* 22, Augustine played the catalytic role. As Paul Zmire[119] has shown, the collegiality that the Africans sought to strengthen was not just with transmarine bishops, but amongst themselves as well. Bonds made with letters of communion were cemented in common theology and views on church discipline. I am in agreement with Robert Evans's evaluation with the development of Augustine's thought on the Church. It is clear that the overseas churches, particularly the Milanese church, contributed to his views of Catholicity; however, not all that he advocated and all that was done can be accounted for by appealing to the overseas churches alone.[120] Also, as Zmire, Munier, and Jane Merdinger have shown, despite the concerns for collegiality, particularly with Rome, the Africans, even the African Catholics, had a keen sense of their own tradition and independence.[121] Augustine returned to Africa from Italy with a Christian frame of mind shaped by his experience

---

117. Canon 93, Ibid.

118. Augustine mentions the event in *Epistle* 88.7, *Augustine: Select Letters*. See the discussion of the incident and background of Maximian in Frend, 266–267.

119. Zmire, 1–74.

120. Evans, 78ff.

121. Brisson, Kriegbaum.

of the churches there. To judge from his recollections in the *Confessions*, little of his experience of Christian Africa, pre-Italy, had a positive impact on him. His self-understanding upon return was a highly Platonized mentality, developed in Milan, that led him to withdraw from the world. When drawn into the ministry, Augustine felt compelled to take a "crash course" in reading the Bible. Perhaps he also took a crash course in reading the culture. In his early years, his theological influences seem to be those from outside Africa, particularly Ambrose. By at least 394, however, Augustine starts to take up African sources as well, particularly Cyprian. The African influence on Augustine's Catholicism comes mainly from three sources: Cyprian, Optatus, and Tyconius. It is to these three figures that we now turn.

Optatus

In the generation before Augustine, Optatus of Milevis was the great champion of Catholic Christianity. Around 367, Optatus wrote a work in six books known as *Against the Donatists*.[122] In this work, written against Parmenian, Optatus provides arguments for the truth of the Catholic Church being founded in its name, which shows that it is universal, whereas the Donatists in their name show their falsity and particularity.[123] A seventh book, which addresses some Donatist criticisms and appendices that have supporting documentary evidence, dates from around 384. Although there is some dispute, Mark Edwards, Mark Vessey, and F. Scorza Barcellona agree that the material for the seventh book is, at its base, from Optatus. It may have been the case that either he himself left it in an unpolished state or a follower took the work that Optatus had completed until that point and attempted to add a seventh book. Whatever transpired, this work was of great help to Augustine in a number of ways. Speaking of Optatus's relationship to Augustine, Geoffrey Grimshaw Willis says:

> It is therefore apparent how important the work of Saint Optatus is as preparing the ground for Saint Augustine. To some degree this is true theologically, especially in respect of the appeal to the State, the origin of the sacraments, the evil of the schism

---

122. Optatus, *Optatus: Against the Donatists*, translation and introduction by Mark Edwards (Liverpool: Liverpool University Press, 1997). Optatus, Catholic Bishop of Milevis (fl. 365–385), is not to be confused with the Donatist bishop Optatus of Thamgadi (d. c. 398). In addition to Edwards's introduction, see *Augustine Through the Ages: An Encyclopedia*, 1999 ed., s.v. "Optatus," by Mark Vessey; and *Encyclopedia of the Early Church*, 1992 ed., s.v. "Optatus, of Milevis," by F. Scorza Barcellona. See Willis, *Saint Augustine and the Donatist Controversy*, 23–25, and chap. 4, "Saint Augustine's Doctrine of the Church," for a discussion of Optatus's treatise against the Donatists.

123. Optatus, 2.1.2; and 3.9.

and the unity of the Church. . . . But the dependence of Saint Augustine on the work of Optatus is even more obvious in matters of historical fact. Optatus co-ordinated for Augustine the documents relevant to the history of the schism, and provided a first-hand and trustworthy picture of the Church conditions in Africa in the middle of the fourth century. Frequently Augustine praises him, and in one passage goes so far as to rank him with his beloved Saint Cyprian.[124]

With reference to Catholicization, it is on the doctrine of the Church where Optatus has his impact. Against a contemporary, the Donatist bishop Parmenianus, Optatus argues that the Church must be geographically extended throughout the whole world.

> You, brother Parmenianus, have said that it exists only among you; unless, perhaps, you aspire to a special claim of sanctity for yourselves on the grounds of pride, so that the church exists where you wish or does not exist where you do not wish. So in order that it may be among you in a tiny portion of Africa, in the corner of a little region, is it therefore not to be with us in another part of Africa? Is it not to be in the Spanish provinces, Gaul, Italy, where you are not? If you want it only to be among yourselves, is it not to be in the three provinces of Pannonia, in Dacia, Moesia, Thrace, Achaia, Macedonia and in the whole of Greece, where you are not? So that it can be among you, is it not to be in Pontus, Galatia, Cappadocia, Pamphilia, Phrygia, Cilicia, or in the three provinces of Syria and in the two Armenias and in the whole of Egypt and Mesopotamia, where you are not? And through so many innumerable isles and other provinces, which can scarcely be numbered, where you do not exist, shall it exist? Where then will the name "catholic" have its proper application, when the reason for calling it catholic is its international and universal diffusion?[125]

The universal extension of the Church is a key argument to which Augustine frequently turns in his polemics against the Donatists. Optatus's influence here is clear, but when Augustine writes *Against Parmenius* and *Against the Letter of Petilianus*, the argument is buttressed with an interpretation of a biblical passage that, in fact, comes from a Donatist.

Tyconius[126]

Surprisingly, it is Tyconius, a Donatist lay-theologian and biblical scholar, who has perhaps the greatest influence on Augustine's understanding and articula-

124. For those passages of praise, Willis points the reader to *C. Parm.* 1.3.5, *De Unit Eccl.* 19.50; *DDC* 2.40.61. *De Unit Eccl.* 19.50 (Willis, 25).

125. Optatus, 2.1. This is argued throughout Book 2.

126. Tyconius is known mainly through Augustine's references to him, a brief but significant entry by Gennadius in his *De Viribus Illustribus (Lives of Illustrious Men)*, 18, in *NPNF* Series 2,

tion of what it means to be Catholic. In the Donatist controversy, Augustine repeatedly and consistently interprets Genesis 22:18 as a prophecy speaking of the present extension of the Church. Further, he gives it an imperative force. The Church *must* be spread throughout the world. This command from God is what the Donatists blatantly oppose by their separation. The argument from "the blessed seed of Abraham"[127] appears early in Augustine's writings against the Donatists, and is present in the arguments presented at the Council of Carthage in 411.[128] It is even found in his last extant anti-Donatist writing, *Against Gaudentius (Contra Gaudentium)*.[129] This text is first used in anti-Donatist fashion in *Contra litteras Petiliani*.[130] Augustine seems to be indebted to Paul, as filtered through Tyconius,

---

vol. 3, and his own surviving works. Gennadiustells of four of Tyconius's works, *De Bello intestino, Expositiones diversarum causarum, Liber Regularum,* and a commentary on the Revelation. Unfortunately *De Bello intestino* and *Expositiones diversarum causarum* are lost, and the Revelation Commentary is preserved only in fragments. Only the *Liber Regularum survives* intact. The survival of the *Liber Regularum is* possibly due to Augustine's endorsement of it, most notably in his *De doctrina Christiana* 3.30.42. See *Augustine Through the Ages: An Encyclopedia*, 1999 ed., "Tyconius," by Paula Fredriksen. See also Manlio Simonetti, "Tyconius" in *Patrology*, vol. 4, 119–122; and *The Book of Rules of Tyconius*, edited by F. C. Burkitt (Cambridge University Press, 1894).

127. Augustine does not always quote Genesis 22:18 directly. But the idea is present that there is a promise given by God to Abraham that through his seed all peoples would be blessed. For Augustine, as said above, the meaning is that Christianity is in his day spread all over the world, and not just confined to the Donatists. From the biblical text, it is also important to note that this blessing gets repeated in Gen. 26:4 and 28:14. Also, as we shall see later, it gets linked to passages like Ps. 2.

128. *Gesta Collationis Carthaginiensis anno 411*, 1.55; 3.55. I conducted a search in the texts contained in the CETEDOC database using the parameter "semine tuo." Other parameters of course could be used; however, I selected this one as a starting point. Further work on this topic will allow me to explore subtleties of references to the "blessed seed of Abraham." The above parameter "your seed" marks references that could be referring to God's or the angel's direct speech to Abraham in the biblical text.

The CETEDOC database references texts from the following collections:
Corpus Christianorum, Series Latin (c) Brepols
Patrialogiae Latinae Supplementum (c) Brepols
Corpus Scriptorum Ecclesiaticorum Latinorum (c) Hoelder, Pichler, Tempsky
Sources Chrétiennes
S. Bernadi Opera Omnia (c) Edizioni Cistercensi
Bibla Sacra juxta vulgatam versionem (c) W. Württembergische Bibelenstalt.

129. Augustine, *Contra Gaudentium* 1.15.16; 1.33.42 (*NPNF* vol. 1).

130. Around the year 400, Augustine came into possession of a fragment of a letter of Petilianus, the Donatist bishop of Cirta, written to his presbyters against the Catholic Church. Petilianus was the most prominent Donatist bishop of his time, even exceeding the prestige of

for his interpretation of "the blessed seed" in support of his understanding of Catholicism. Further, although Tyconius uses Genesis 22:18 in support of the assertion of the geographic extension of the Church, Augustine is original in his polemical application of the text.[131]

A key part of Augustine's argument against Petilianus is the claim that the names of the two groups show their true natures: one was particular, the other universal. This theme was an argument that goes back at least to Optatus. Augustine first gives it in his *Psalm Against the Party of the Donatists*, 1, line 278 (393–394):

> [E]go catholica dicor et uos de donati parte.

I am called "Catholic" and you (are called) the party of Donatus.[132]

What distinguishes *Against the Letter of Petilianus* from *Psalm Against the Party of the Donatists* and Optatus's *Against the Donatists"* is Augustine's argument from "the blessed seed of Abraham."

> In conclusion, the Testament is said to have been given to the flames by certain men in the time of persecution. Now let its lessons be read, from whatever source it has been brought to light. Certainly in the beginning of the promises of the Testator this is found to have been said to Abraham: "In thy seed shall all the nations of the earth be blessed" (Gen. 22:18) and this saying is truthfully interpreted by the apostle: "To thy seed," he says, "which is Christ" (Galatians 3:16). No betrayal on the part of any man

the Donatist bishop of Carthage, Primianus. Augustine's reply to these letters elicited further response from Petilianus. The work that comes down to us as *Contra litteras Petiliani* captures this back and forth correspondence that probably ranged over two or three years. Hombert dates Books 1 and 2 between 400 and 402; Book 3 he dates between 403 and 405 (Hombert, 189–193). See Augustine's comments and Sister Mary Inez Bogan's notes in Saint Augustine, *Retractations* 2.51, translated by Sister Mary Inez Bogan, *Retractations* Fathers of the Church Series, vol. 60 (Washington: Catholic University of America Press, 1968. See also Chester D. Hartranft, "Introductory Essay: Writings in Connection with the Donatist Controversy," in *The Nicene and Post-Nicene Fathers*, First Series, Vol. IV: *St. Augustine Writings Against the Manichees and Against the Donatists*, translated by J. R. King (Grand Rapids: Eerdmanns, 1983).

131. An important spur to my approach is W. H. C. Frend, who, drawing on A. Pincherle, states in his book *The Donatist Church* that: "It seems clear that much of his thought in his formative years between 386 and 396, as illustrated by the commenting on the Pauline Epistles, which date from that period, was influenced by Tyconius's teaching. Time and again, in unexpected places, such as in the midst of a speculation on the significance of the numbers 40 and 50 in the Bible (*De Diversis Quaestionibus*, lxiii), Augustine lets drop some aside which hints at the source of his exegesis. With Ambrose, Tyconius may perhaps have shared the honor of finally winning Augustine from Mani to Christ" (Frend, *The Donatist Church*, 205).

132. My translation.

has made the promises of God of none effect. Hold communion with all the nations of the earth, and then you may boast that you have preserved the Testament from the destruction of the flames.[133]

Augustine argues that the Donatists are persisting to be particular in the face of the prophetic blessing given to Abraham that his seed would be a blessing to all people. This is the promise fulfilled only in the *Catholic,* that is, *Universal,* Church. The Donatists claim that they kept the Scriptures, or Testament, inviolate in the Great Persecution, but Augustine, taking the idea of "keeping" in a different sense, claims that they have not truly kept the Testament because they have failed to heed the Testator, God. Here Augustine is persuasively interpreting "Testament" in legal terms to portray the Donatists as guilty. If God, as Testator, said to Abraham that all the nations of the earth would be blessed through his seed, how then can the Donatists claim to be faithful if they have broken communion with all the other churches?

Augustine refers to the "blessed seed" directly or indirectly several times throughout the tangled correspondence. It comes up once in Book 1, at least five times in Book 2,[134] and once at the end of Book 3.[135] Augustine is not simply reading Genesis 22:18 and concluding that it really is a prophecy about the universal extent of the Church of Christ. How does he arrive there if not by a literal reading? Where does Augustine derive this interpretation?

We find our answer in *Contra epistulam Parmeniani* (403–404), where we see the blessed seed used against the Donatists. Interestingly, however, the usage does not originate there with Augustine; it comes from Tyconius. The *Contra epistulam Parmeniani* is another strange piece of correspondence. At the beginning of the work, Augustine says that a letter of Parmenianus, the famed but deceased Donatist bishop, has fallen into his hands. This letter is written against Tyconius, "a man gifted with a penetrating spirit and grand eloquence, but a Donatist."[136] Augustine proceeds to explain that Parmenianus wrote to censure Tyconius because he began to advance some teachings from his study of scripture that ran counter to the Donatist party line.

> Tyconius indeed being surrounded by all the words of the Sacred Pages awoke and saw the church of God spread throughout the whole world, as it had been foreseen and foretold so much beforehand, by the hearts and by the mouths of the saints. Which principles he undertook to demonstrate and affirm against those from his party, that

133. Augustine, *Contra litteras Petiliani* 1.23.25 (*NPNF* vol. 4).
134. Ibid., 2.8.20; 2.14.33; 2.36.84; 2.39.93; 2.65.146.
135. Ibid., 3.50.62.
136. Ibid. "Hominem quidem et acri ingenio praeditum, et uberio sed tamen Dontistam."

there is not a sin of humans so great and so criminal that it might be able to stand against the promises of God, neither could it be, by what is done within the church, however impious, that the promise of God to the Church, be made empty, even that it must be everywhere to the ends of the earth which was being held in trust to the Fathers and is now shown.[137]

Augustine continues, saying that despite the power and eloquence with which Tyconius argued from many texts of scripture, Parmenianus and other Donatists refused to be persuaded. To Augustine, it is plain that Tyconius should have re-united with the Catholics, given his views. Tyconius never took this option, even after he was excommunicated sometime after receiving Parmenianus's letter of censure. In Augustine's telling of the tale, Parmenianus had no substantial arguments to martial against Tyconius's proofs from scripture; here is where we come to the significance of the blessed seed.

Tyconius brings forth the thunder of the Divine Testament which is made in the promise to Abraham, and in the promise to Isaac and Jacob of which God himself the testator says, I am the God of Abraham, the God of Isaac, and God of Jacob (Ex 3:6). This is my name forever. But that one (Parm.) opposes our sacred stories. What is said to Abraham? In your seed all the people will be blessed (22:18). What is said to Isaac? And blessed in your seed will be all the peoples of the earth, just as because Abraham your father heard my voice (26:4). What was said to Jacob? (28:13). I am the God of Abraham your father, and God of Isaac, do not fear. The earth indeed on which you sleep, I give to you and your seed: and thus will be your seed in dry earth and will be filled in the sea and in Africa and in Aquilon and in the Orient and blessed in you are all the tribes of the earth and in your seed. Lest it be though this spoken of the Jews. The Apostle says "What may be the seed of Abraham, in whom it is said all the peoples must be blessed" explaining, "It says that the promises have been given to Abraham and his seed: It does not say seeds as in many but seed as in one. And your seed which is Christ (Gal 3:16). In Christ therefore all people have been blessed as much in authority/power, as in truth and those who want to say they are Christian oppose (this). What then can they argue against this?[138]

Parmenianus seems to accept the texts as fulfilled prophecies, and argues instead that the churches beyond Africa, once true and healthy, are now false and contaminated by their communion with *traditores* (1.2.2, 1.4.6).

---

137. Ibid. "Tichonius enim omnibus sanctarum paginarum vocibus circumfusus evigilavit, et vidit Ecclesiam Dei tota orbe diffusam, sicut de illa tanto ante per corde et ora sanctorum praevisum atque praedictum est. Quo percepto suscepit adversu ipsos suos demonstrare et asser-ere, nullius hominis quamvis sceleratum et immane peccatum praescribere promissis Dei, nec id agere quorumlibet intra Ecclesiam constitutorum quamlibet impietatem, ut fides Dei de Ecclesia futura et diffundenda usque ad terminos orbis terrae quae promissis Patrum retena est evacuetur."

138. Ibid., 1.2.2.

In *Contra epistolam Parmeniani,* the blessed seed is used by Augustine as an anti-Donatist polemic for the first time. But ironically, the fact that the blessed seed can be interpreted to show that the Church is universal against the standard Donatist position is presented by Tyconius, a Donatist.

To clarify the picture of Augustine's dependence on Tyconius, we can see that first Augustine had used the universality of the Church as an anti-Donatist polemic without appealing to the blessed seed, as we have argued above. Second, if we compare what Augustine says with what Tyconius said in the *Liber Regularum (Book of Rules)* and the Revelation Commentary, there is striking agreement. Considering just the *Book of Rules,* for example, there is an important reference to the universal extension of the Church in the third rule. Here the main focus is to reconcile the claims that "no one can ever be justified by the works of the law" with the fact that, in the Old Testament, "there have always been some who do the law and are justified."[139] At this point, Tyconius, taking up Paul's arguments from Romans and Galatians, argues: "Thus, the seed of Abraham comes not from the law but from the promise and has remained uninterrupted from Isaac on."[140] He asserts that those who participate in the benefits of the promise are those who live by faith.[141] He says that the promise became an obligation when God said: "All the nations of the earth will be blessed in you because you obeyed and, for my sake, did not spare your beloved son" (Gen. 22:18, 16).[142]

These ideas seem to be consistent with Augustine's description of Tyconius's opinions given in *Parm.* Does this mean that the *Liber Regularum* was the work that got Tyconius into trouble with Parmenianus? Not necessarily. Paul Monceaux accepts the order of writings given by Gennadius as the order of publication. He goes on to argue that the two lost works caused the initial problem. In his reconstruction of events, Tyconius writes on the internal conflicts of the Donatists. *De bello intestine* receives criticism from Parmenianus and others, so he writes a follow-up on different questions that were raised against him, which he entitles *Expositiones diversarum causarum.* Parmenianus then calls a Donatist council, where Tyconius is tried and excommunicated. Tyconius, still persistent in his views, writes his book of rules, *Liber Regularum,* followed by a sustained example of the application of those rules in the Apocalypse Commentary.[143]

---

139. Tyconius, *Liber Regularum* 3.1 (*NPNF,* vol. 1).

140. Ibid., 3.3.

141. Ibid., 3.10.

142. Ibid., 3.16.

143. See Paul Monceaux, *Histoire Littéraire de L'Afrique Chretienne,* vols. 1–6 (Paris: Ernest Leroux, 1901), 5:167ff.

Yet we may nevertheless assume a consistency in Tyconius's thought. What, then, did Augustine learn from Tyconius's works that he went on to incorporate into his own approach in order to develop the polemical use of the blessed seed? Setting aside Tyconius's intent, it should be clear that if the contents of his earlier work reflected similar views, it is easy to see how and why Parmenianus and Augustine interpreted Tyconius as supporting the Catholic position. Tyconius seems to say that the Church is universal in fulfillment of prophecy, that its unity contains both wicked and righteous, and that, furthermore, the two "must 'grow together until harvest'" (Matt. 13:30).[144]

Tyconius's method of interpretation is plainly laid out for us in his rules, and it is undeniable that Augustine greatly respected Tyconius's methods. This is not to say that Augustine slavishly followed Tyconius. As we have noted already, Augustine went beyond Tyconius at certain points. This is true even with respect to the use of the blessed seed. Tyconius is clearly not employing it to exalt the Catholic position, whatever his intent; yet his method or methods are used by Augustine. Some scholars argue that Tyconius's interpretations are Donatist in that they speak against persecutors. Rather than interpreting these persecutors as Catholics, given the turmoil with the Donatist movement and given the fact that he had open disputes with the main leadership represented by Parmenianus, the persecutors can also be interpreted as Parmenianus and the Donatist leadership who were trying to enforce a Donatist orthodoxy. Tyconius alternatively may have had both the Donatists and the Catholics in mind as he criticized persecutors and those who live according to a kind of "law." He sees himself giving prophetic utterances for what he believed to be the last days.

The Church was indeed universal for Tyconius, including even sinners, and the separation of the wheat from the chaff that must wait until the harvest. For Tyconius, however, the harvest was imminent; for Augustine it was not. Augustine accepted the prophetic imperative of the blessed seed necessarily being fulfilled in the present extension of the Church, and he accepted the claim that separation would come at the harvest. However, he interpreted this allegorically rather than typologically; that is, he did not see the imminent coming of the harvest.

Cyprian[145]

Though the end of Cyprian's episcopacy was more than a century before the beginning of Augustine's, it had a profound and inescapable influence on Augustine and the development of his program of Catholicization. He was probably pushed and

---

144. Tyconius, *Liber Regularum* 3.26.
145. On Cyprian and his writings, see Quasten's introduction to *Patrology*, 2:340–383.

pulled this way because of the significance that Cyprian had for African Catholics, especially Donatists. Noting that both African Catholics and Donatists kept a feast on the anniversary of Cyprian's martyrdom and revered him greatly, W. H. C. Frend says:

> The Catholics esteemed him as an example of ecclesiastical discipline and charity, to whom the unity of the Church had in practice meant more than the illusion of purity in its visible membership. . . . On the other hand, the Donatists saw in Cyprian not merely the bishop and martyr but the supreme authority whose teaching provided a complete justification for their breach with Caecilian.[146]

Cyprian's shadow cast itself over the program of Catholicization on several significant issues. In holding councils, both Catholics and Donatists stand in the important organizational tradition of Cyprian, who was born to a non-Christian Carthaginian family of status. He became a rhetor, achieving wealth and fame in his own right before his conversion in the 240s. Within a few years of his conversion, he became a priest, and then Bishop of Carthage by 249. By 251, Christians of the empire were suffering under the persecution of Decius. Under Cyprian, seven councils were held in Carthage that dealt with questions of the lapsed and baptism of heretics raised by the persecution.[147] Cyprian led the African Church through schism by taking a middle ground between a party supporting confessors, who claimed authority to reinstate the lapsed, and extreme rigorists, who saw no way for their restoration. Cyprian's claim was that the lapsed could be restored under episcopal discipline.[148] He also led the African Church to rebaptism of those baptized in heretical or schismatic traditions.[149]

The organizational coherence and collegiality of the African Church receded, only to reappear and be torn in the wake of another persecution, that of Diocletian. With spotty appearances in the mid-fourth century and in the 390s, councils emerge into prominence for Catholics and Donatists. On the Donatist side, particularly with the development of the schism led by Maximian against Primian, councils played an important role.[150] For the Catholics, we have seen how councils

---

146. Frend, *The Donatist Church*, 130–131.

147. See *Encyclopedia of the Early Church*, 1992 ed., s.v. "Carthage: Councils," by Charles Munier.

148. See particularly Cyprian, *On Unity* (*De Unitate*) and *Letter* 33, "The Problem of the Lapsed" in Greenslade, S. L. *Early Latin Theology Selections from Tertullian, Cyprian, Ambrose, and Jerome.* The Library of Christian classics, v. 5. London: SCM Press, 1956.

149. See particularly *Epistles* 69 and 73, in *Augustine: Select Letters*.

150. See Frend, *The Donatist Church*, 214–220; see also Clemens Weidmann, *Augustinus und das Maximinianistenkonzil von Cebarsussi, Zur historischen und textgeschichtlichen Bedeutung*

were crucial for the implementation of Catholicization. Responding to the opportune moment brought about by the Maximianist schism, the Catholics begin their own series of councils in 393 at Hippo. From Augustine's *Epistle* 22, it cannot be clearly established that the "sword" of councils was taken up because Aurelius and Augustine knew that Cyprian had wielded it with great effect. It is reasonable to assume that the connection was obvious. It can be argued that Augustine did not have detailed knowledge of Cyprian until 400, when he writes *On Baptism*. Yet it is most likely the case that even if he did not know the material relating to the councils of Cyprian, he knew of them by reputation. Clearly, in the writing of *On Baptism*, Augustine developed a way of understanding Cyprian and his conciliar action that allowed him to partially reclaim him from the Donatists.

Cyprian was a figure whose legacy was contested by Catholics and Donatists, who both claimed to be the true inheritors of Cyprian. On a number of issues, Catholics and Donatists argued over who was the correct interpreter of Cyprian. For example, as we saw in *Epistle* 22, Augustine was concerned about the riotous nature of the celebration of the martyrs. Cyprian was the ideal martyr in Donatist tradition.[151] Augustine sought to show how Cyprian transcended the provincialism of the Donatists. This case was made in terms of interpreting his theology and in terms of appropriately venerating him and other martyrs.

Another important example is found in *On Baptism*. There we have Augustine taking up the issue of Cyprian's theology of baptism that seems to be more in agreement with the Donatist position than the Catholic.[152] In this work of seven books, Augustine, with much belaboring of his points, discusses some of Cyprian's letters and records of the Carthaginian council in 256. Augustine concedes that clearly Cyprian approved of, and even practiced, rebaptism.

> "Cyprian," say they (the Donatists), "whose great merits and vast learning we all know, decreed in a Council, with many of his fellow-bishops contributing their several opinions, that all heretics and schismatics, that is, all who are severed from the communion of the one Church, are without baptism; and therefore, whosoever has joined the communion of the Church after being baptized by them must be baptized in the Church."[153]

---

von Enarratio in Psalmum 36, 2, 18–23 (Wien: Verlag der Österreichischen Akademie der Wissenschaften, 1998).

151. Evans, 68. See also "The Donatist Passion of Cyprian," in *Donatist Martyr Stories*, by Maureen Tilley (Liverpool: Liverpool University Press, 1996). Tilley provides an informative general introduction to the volume as well as introductions and notes to each story.

152. Augustine is fulfilling a promise he made in *Contra epistulam Parmeniani* 2.14.32 to take up the Donatists' claims that Cyprian supported their doctrine of baptism.

153. Augustine, *De* bautismo 2.1.2, in *Oeuvres de saint Augustin*, introduction by A. C. De Veer.

Augustine goes on to argue that, even though Cyprian held this position, one that Augustine considers an error, Cyprian's "humility," along with his love of peace and unity, support the Catholic claims against the Donatists because, Augustine argues, he did not break communion with those with whom he disagreed. One passage, illustrating this concession and affirmation, Augustine quoted from the Council of Carthage of 256:

> When, on the calends of September, very many bishops from the provinces of Africa, Numidia, and Mauritania, with their presbyters and deacons, had met together at Carthage, a great part of the laity also being present; and when the letter addressed by Jubaianus to Cyprian, as also the answer of Cyprian to Jubaianus, on the subject of baptizing heretics, had been read, Cyprian said: "Ye have heard, most beloved colleagues, what Jubaianus, our fellow-bishop, has written to me, consulting my moderate ability concerning the unlawful and profane baptism of heretics, and what answer I gave him, giving a judgment which we have once and again and often given, that heretics coming to the Church ought to be baptized, and sanctified with the baptism of the Church. Another letter of Jubaianus has likewise been read to you, in which, agreeably to his sincere and religious devotion, in answer to our epistle, he not only expressed his assent, but returned thanks also, acknowledging that he had received instruction. It remains that we severally declare our opinion on this subject, judging no one, nor depriving any one of the right of communion if he differ from us. For no one of us sets himself up as a bishop of bishops, or, by tyrannical terror, forces his colleagues to a necessity of obeying, inasmuch as every bishop, in the free use of his liberty and power, has the right of forming his own judgment, and can no more be judged by another than he can himself judge another. But we must all await the judgment of our Lord Jesus Christ, who alone has the power both of setting us in the government of His Church, and of judging of our acts therein."[154]

Augustine repeatedly highlights the fact that, though Cyprian wrote to Jubaianus endorsing rebaptism and that this council endorses it, Cyprian says, "It remains that we severally declare our opinion on this subject, judging no one, nor depriving any one of the right of communion if he differ from us." For Augustine, then, Cyprian prizes unity over purity. And so, for Augustine, Cyprian's Catholicity must be understood in terms of the Church's encompassing communion, not in terms of wholeness or purity as the Donatists argue.[155]

Though a number of scholars see the Donatists as being closer to Cyprian, at times it seems that Augustine's arguments are under-appreciated. Evans, for example, criticizes Augustine for "failure to take seriously the Cyprianic basis,

---

154. Ibid., 2.2.3. See also, for example, *De baptismo* 3.1; and 5.25.

155. For discussion of these differing views of Catholicity, see Evans, 214; and Brisson, 138ff.

the Cyprianic logic, of the Donatists." For Evans, this is demonstrated by Augustine citing concessions made by Donatists in 336 to accept Catholics into their communion without rebaptism, and again in 394–395 to accept back their own schismatic Maximianist bishops without forcing rebaptism on those they had baptized.[156] Referring to this latter incident, Evans says: "The Donatists in effect decided that in the context of the 390s, the Cyprianic call to separation and permanent deposition of schismatic bishops was less compelling than the same call in respect to lapsed bishops. Apostasy is more serious than schism."[157] A more convincing explanation could be that purity can, at times, be relativized by concerns regarding power and social order. This line of reasoning can also be used to explain the puzzling concession from Cyprian in the statement from the Council of Carthage 256. On the one hand, Cyprian worked to gain an African consensus in support of purity. On the other hand, once it became clear that Stephen of Rome was intractable in his opposition, Cyprian opted for a position that emphasized episcopal autonomy and freedom.[158] Similarly, Primianus and his supporters against the Maximianists could have been doing what they felt necessary to avoid a two-front war. On the one hand was the carrot: easy, honorable readmittance to the main body of Donatists. On the other hand was the stick: the employment of the secular power of Count Gildo, who, in alliance with Optatus, used imperial laws against heresy to repress dissenters from the main Donatist fold. Particularly if one is making claims about purity and persecution, those cases seem fair examples to cite for an opponent to raise the charge of inconsistency.

Conclusion

By the early years of the fifth century, Augustine had taken Milanese Neoplatonism, tinged with Catholic Christian doctrine and ascetic worship, and applied it to the African context. Augustine also used this overseas Catholicism to reinterpret the traditional view of Cyprian held by the Donatists, and to combine it with both the Catholic tradition of universalism found in Optatus and the exegetical approach to "the blessed seed" gained from Tyconius to drive his plan of Catholicization. The development of Augustine's thought reveals a genius for innovation and incorporation. He worked to craft a social order with

---

156. Evans, 71.

157. Ibid., 74.

158. On this point and its relationship to the version of Cyprian's *De unitate* that gives a lesser view of the chair of Peter and a clearer affirmation of the collegiality of bishops, see Brisson, 110ff.

a strong sense of group identity, and one with sturdy, but elastic, ties that bind and regulate the group.[159] Thus, as a kind of "centrist discourse,"[160] Augustine's Catholicism stands between the rigorism of the Donatists and the all embracing synthetic polytheism of the pagan Roman Empire. As Patout Burns has shown, however, Augustine's interpretation of Cyprian differed from the Donatists in that, according to the rhetoric addressed towards each other, they were living in two different empires. The Donatists claimed, to Catholics like Augustine, that they were living in the same persecuting empire that Cyprian did. Augustine claimed that that persecuting empire was dying, if not already dead, as the prophecy of the "blessed seed" was being fulfilled. For Augustine, the Church was broad and expanding, and the danger was not persecution but feigned adherence. I am in agreement with Burns, who says:

> [T]he boundary dividing the church from the world, the line which separated those on their way to salvation from those who would never be drawn free from the *massa damnata*, could not be defined behaviorally. Indeed, Augustine's theory of sin and grace, which his African colleagues approved, drew a crooked, almost indistinct border between love and lust within the human heart.[161]

However, I have one slight disagreement when he goes on to say:

> Yet on one very significant point, Augustine held quite firmly to Cyprian's behaviorally defined perspective: no one could be saved outside the unity of the church. This principle had been the foundation for Cyprian's rejection of the Novatianist program of life-long penance and appeal to the mercy of Christ. In Augustine's theology it became a premise in the argument for the transmission of Adamic sin and the gratuity of divine election to grace and glory. He might have justified the principle by appeal

159. Thus this would be a high grid/high group society in Mary Douglas's system. My thinking is influenced by Mary Douglas immediately from *Natural Symbols* and mediated through J. Patout Burns, *Cyprian the Bishop* (London: Routledge, 2002), and a brief essay available on Burns's Web site relating to Douglas's model to the North African context, "The Analytical Model: Adapted from Mary Douglas 'Cultural Bias,'" in *The Active Voice* (Boston: Routledge & Kegan Paul, 1982), 183–254; and Lim.

160. I am indebted to Michael Gaddis's insights found in his paper "Finding the Middle Way: Centrist Discourse in Late Antique Ecclesiastical Politics," for which I had the opportunity to act as commentator at the American Society of Church History Annual Meeting in 2004, Washington D.C., in the session "Heresy, Authority, and Interpretations in Early Christianity."

161. Patout Burns "Appropriating Augustine Appropriating Cyprian," *Augustinian Studies* 36:1 (2005) 113–130, 129.

to human intention because most of those—traditionalists or Donatists—with whom he dealt were deliberately outside Christian or Catholic unity.[162]

In general, I think Augustine did set the limits of salvation at the doors of the Catholic Church. Yet there is at least one example of setting that door ajar. In his Sermon on the Kalends, of January 1, 404, he states in very strong terms his position on salvation that seemingly confirms Burns' claim that Augustine rejected the possibility of salvation outside of Catholic unity:

> And so, brothers and sisters, let us spurn the malign mediator, the self-deceiving and deceitful mediator, the mediator who does not reconcile but separates more and more. Let no one promise you any kind of purification outside the Church, whether in temples or anywhere else, by means of sacreligious sacred rites. Let nobody do so outside the unity even by means of Christian sacraments, because even if the sacrament is to be found outside the unity—which we cannot deny and dare not violate—still the power and saving effect of the sacrament, making one *a fellow heir with Christ* (Rom 8:17), is only to be found in the unity and *in the bond of peace* (Eph. 4:3) of the Church.
>
> Let no one turn you away from God, no one from the Church; no one from God your Father, no one from the Church your mother. We had two parents who gave birth to us for mortality, we have two who give birth to us for immortality, God and the Church. Those gave birth to heirs to succeed them, these give birth to heirs to abide with them. Why else, after all, are we born of human parents, except in order to succeed them when they are dead? But we are brought forth by our Father, God, and our mother, the Church, in such a way as to live with our parents forever. Any who go off to sacrilegious rites or magical arts, or go consulting astrologers, augurs, diviners about their life or anything to do with this life, have cut themselves off from their Father, even if they do not leave the Church. If any, though, have cut themselves off from the Church by the division of schism, even though they may seem to themselves to be holding on to the Father, they are most perniciously forsaking their mother, while those who relinquish both Christian faith and mother Church are deserting both parents. Hold on to your Father, hold on to your mother. You are a little child; stick to your mother. You are a little child; suck your mother's milk, and she will bring you, nourished on milk, to the table of the Father.[163]

In this same sermon, however, Augustine puts forward an important, but underdeveloped, caveat.

> But one must not say anything rashly about those who have not worshiped any idols, nor bound themselves over to Chaldean or magical rituals, in case perhaps it has

---

162. Ibid., 129–130.
163. Augustine, *Sermon* 198:42, in *Newly Discovered Sermons.*

escaped our notice how the savior, without whom nobody can be saved, has revealed himself to them in some manner or other.[164]

Though it contradicts Burns' claim about Augustine's Catholic exclusivity, this puzzling off-handed comment actually supports and extends Burns's assertions about the interior nature of the line separating the saved from the damned. Not only is the "crooked, almost indistinct" line drawn in the heart, it must, in the face of divine freedom and mystery, be extended into the world. So, though he understands himself as a bishop, a shepherd, and a guardian, Augstine must, even as he works to construct a Catholic social order, yield place to his God's will and not his, nor anyone else's, including that of his council of episcopal colleagues. Or is this the case? I must concede that the concession on the part of Augustine is, to my knowledge, unparalleled in his writings.

Whatever the case, Augustine's Catholicizing plan is achieved in interesting ways through sermons like the one on the Kalends quoted above. We will look at that sermon and a series of other sermons more closely in Chapter 5. First, however, we will examine the various styles of communication that are part of his totalizing discourse, as, in the next chapter, we focus on Augustine's rhetoric.

164. Ibid., 198:37. "Sed de illis qui nulla coluerunt neque aliquibus chaldaicis aut magicis sacris sese obstrinxerunt, temere aliquid dicendum non est, ne forte nos lateat quod eis aliquo modo saluator ille reuelatus sit, sine quo saluari nemo potest."

CHAPTER FOUR

Rhetoric

Rhetoric and Social Order

Richard Lim, in his book *Public Disputation, Power, and Social Order in Late Antiquity*, published in 1995, gives a "social history of public disputation in Late Antiquity." He does this by "showing how within various late antique groups the reception and practice of public disputation, as one of many forms of open competition, consistently depended on the principles underlying notions of authority, group solidarity, and social order."[1] Lim does not attempt to give a comprehensive history of public disputation; rather, he uses selected examples to shed light on the connection between rhetoric and social order, and its meaning for the development of Christianity. He begins by showing how the link is well established in Greco-Roman traditions of philosophical dispute. By Chapter 3 he shows how the Manichees adopted public disputation as a tool of recruitment that proved very successful in Africa—until Augustine renounced Manicheism, embraced Catholic Christianity, and took on the Manichees in public debate. Augustine was successful against the Manichees beginning in the 390s for two reasons. First, Augustine turned the Manichee tactic against them. He went on the offensive in proposing perplexing questions that highlighted the inconsistency of their positions. Second,

---

1. Lim, ix.

he had the public debates recorded and published. Getting the debates on the record exposed the Manichees to wider ridicule, on the one hand, and potential repression from the government, on the other hand, for Manichaeism had been technically outlawed.

When Augustine tried to use the same strategy with the Donatists, not just personally but as a concerted strategy put forth by the Council of Carthage 403, he and his colleagues were rebuffed. Chief among the reasons given by the Donatists was an unwillingness to meet on equal terms with the sons of *traditores*; however, one might suppose that there was a reticence to be treated as the Manichees had been. The Catholics were calling for peaceful meetings with an air of superiority and with explicit appeals to secular officials to enforce anti-heretical legislation against the Donatists. Being unable to use exactly the same strategy that was successful against the Manichees, Augustine innovates. Since public disputation was not possible, Augustine creates the sense of it in his published works and in his sermons. His major anti-Donatist works in the first decade of the fifth century evoke the sense of a public disputation that has been recorded and circulated. In all cases, Augustine displays his skill as a rhetorician trained for excellence in public debate. Aside from having real talent in those situations, Augustine's genius can be seen moving every controversy he could to a setting that was most comfortable to him. Given that the Donatists were avoiding the deployment of this strategy through his colleagues, they adjusted. The African Catholics fell back to Augustine as their "spin doctor." He took on the Donatists through his correspondence, preserved either in his letters or in treatises, and he also responded to requests to preach in various locations. Most notable, and most often among these venues outside of Hippo, was Carthage. When Augustine traveled to preach, he would, in effect, give a virtuoso solo public disputation. He would rhetorically construct his opponents' position and demolish it. These sermons also would be recorded and circulated.

Rhetoric Then and Now

As we have seen, Augustine's vision of social order that I call Catholicization, with respect to the Catholic Church in Africa, entailed internal and external components. Internally, the church must reform; externally, the church must engage in offensive and defensive strategies so that it can promote its truth claims over and against its competitors in the religious marketplace.[2] We have also seen that in the beginning, as he expressed his Catholicization plan to Aurelius, Augustine desired to accomplish it "by education rather than by formal commands, by persua-

---

2. Augustine, *Epistle* 22:2–4, in *Augustine: Select Letters*.

sion rather than by intimidation."[3] Even conceding some limited role for stronger measures, he wants to use words and avoid physical violence. Given his stated preference for using words to execute his plan it, is apparent that we must attend to Augustine's rhetoric.

Two basic ranges of meaning of rhetoric, traditional and modern, are relevant for this study. In the traditional range, rhetoric as a classical discipline is our starting point. It involves technical definition and analysis of oratory in a tradition developed initially in the Greek-speaking world, but which became adopted and adapted to Latin usage.[4] I will also use the term "rhetoric" as it came to be used in the latter part of the twentieth century to describe persuasive discourse in a broad sense.[5] With respect to the study of Christianity in late antiquity, two published series of lectures, one by Peter Brown and the other by Averil Cameron, are important examples of this broad sense of the term "rhetoric."

In her Sather Lectures, published in 1991 as *Christianity and the Rhetoric of Empire: The Development of Christian Discourse,* Averil Cameron drew attention to the neglected examination of the rhetorical strategies that Christians developed within the Roman Empire in late antiquity. Instead of concerning herself overly much with the content of Christian expression, she investigates the modes and forms of expression themselves. Her aims are twofold: first, to show "that a large part of Christianity's effectiveness in the Roman Empire lay in its own capacity to create its own intellectual and imaginative universe," and second, "to show how its own literary devices and techniques in turn related to changing contemporary circumstances."[6] Avoiding the technical, or as I say the traditional, sense of the term "rhetoric," Cameron uses it as "characteristic means or ways of expression."[7] This broader definition, derived in large part from trends developed in literary and social criticism of the twentieth century, helps her to investigate relationships of social power. "Rhetoric" and "discourse"[8] are terms that can seem to be hopelessly vague, but, when used with care, they help manage the fluidity and ambiguity that is inherent in communication.

---

3. Ibid., 22:5.

4. For good historical overviews of the rhetorical tradition up to Augustine's time, see M. L. Clarke, *Rhetoric at Rome*, 3rd ed. (New York: Routledge, 1996); and Stanley Porter, "Historical Survey of Rhetoric," in *Handbook of Classical Rhetoric in the Hellenistic Period 330 B.C.–A.D. 400* (Boston: Brill, 2001).

5. "Discourse" is another term similarly derived and is virtually synonymous with the term "rhetoric" except for the fact that persuasion seems to be implied. See *Encyclopedia of Contemporary Literary Theory*, 1993 ed., s.v. "discourse" and "rhetoric."

6. Cameron, *Christianity and the Rhetoric of Empire*, 6.

7. Ibid., 13.

8. *Encyclopedia of Contemporary Literary Theory*, 1993 ed., s.v. "discourse" and "rhetoric."

Brown is also concerned with rhetoric and social power, as is evident in the title of his Curti Lectures, *Power and Persuasion in Late Antiquity*, published in 1992. Both he and Cameron, in focusing on power, are embracing approaches in academic research that have been influenced particularly by Michel Foucault's[9] investigations into social relations as constructed and maintained by language.[10] Both Cameron and Brown acknowledge the influence of Foucault's *The Care of the Self*.[11] Cameron notes in particular Foucault's investigation of Christianity's "totalizing discourse,"[12] while Brown focuses on the way in which concern for the self developed from the early empire into late antiquity that could be was seen in numerous instances as a concern for deportment, self-mastery, and asceticism in the face of power exercised in the violence of social control.[13] Language and rhetoric, or discourse, define and govern roles of dominance and submission in such a way that all persons in society participate in a "network of relations" that can be called a matrix of power. As such, "power is exercised rather than possessed: it is not the 'privilege,' acquired or preserved, of the dominant class, but the overall effect of its strategic positions—an effect that is manifested and sometimes extended by the position of those who are dominated."[14] In *Power and Persuasion,* Brown shows how the dominant classes' "strategic positions" were founded upon *paideia,* the Greek term for the educational system that maintained the social order.[15]

In their discussion of rhetoric, both Cameron and Brown focus on the eastern Roman Empire, although they do treat figures such as Ambrose and Augustine at points. In contrast, my focus is on Augustine and the west, particularly Roman Africa, with only occasional references to the east. Although Augustine's relationship to the classical canons of rhetoric will be considered, the chief aim is to describe Augustine's methods of persuasion in the broad sense, not specifically articulated in terms of Augustine's adherence to, or departures from, the rules of classical rhetoric. Both of these meanings, although basic in one sense, become complex upon further investigation. The tradition of rhetoric, of which Augustine found himself a teacher, was ancient and rich. Though essentially Greek in origin, it was appropriated and developed for particular needs in the Latin context. Our

9. Ibid., s.v. "Michel Foucault," by Michael Clark.

10. Cameron, *Christianity and the Rhetoric of Empire,* 2; Brown, *Power and Persuasion,* 50–51.

11. Michel Foucault, *The Care of the Self,* translated by Robert Hurley (New York: Random House, 1986).

12. Cameron, *Christianity and the Rhetoric of Empire,* 2.

13. Brown, *Power and Persuasion,* chap. 2, "Paideia and Power," and chap. 3, "Poverty and Power."

14. Michel Foucault, *Discipline and Punish* (New York: Random House, 1995), 26–27.

15. Brown, *Power and Persuasion,* chap. 2.

first steps in this chapter will involve examining Augustine's relationship to this tradition, not from the perspective of self-understanding, as with Chapter 2, but from the perspective of the relationship between theory and practice.

The second sense of rhetoric that I use is broad, but also rich, because it captures a major shift in the academic study of rhetoric largely begun in the latter half of the twentieth century.[16] After discussing Augustine and his relationship to classical rhetorical theory and practice, the chapter will shift to a discussion of some of the newer methods of rhetorical analysis and how they can be beneficial for understanding Augustine and Catholicization. Of particular interest are insights derived from the analysis of political rhetoric.

Augustine and Ancient Rhetoric

Augustine's Education

Rhetoric stood at the pinnacle of the Greco-Roman educational system. The nature, structure, and goals of education relevant to understanding Augustine have been described by a number of scholars, but perhaps the most influential has been the work of Henri Irénée Marrou. In *A History of Education in Antiquity,* Marrou gives a comprehensive description of education in the Mediterranean world from ancient Greece to the dawn of the Middle Ages.[17] In his earliest major work, *Saint Augustin et la fin de la culture antique,* Marrou's aim was to understand Augustine in the context of the late Roman Empire, and thus, the view of education was focused on illuminating the context of Augustine.[18] The educational system of Augustine's time was a product of Roman adoption of "Hellenistic prototypes" in "principles, syllabus and methods."[19] The system was three tiered, with select young males starting with a first master, or schoolmaster, at around age seven; moving to a grammarian at around age eleven; and then, finally, reaching the school of the

16. *Encyclopedia of Contemporary Literary Theory,* 1993 ed., s.v. "Rhetorical Criticism," by David Goodwin.

17. Marrou's *A History of Education in Antiquity* was first published in 1956 and again in 1982.

18. Originally published in 1938, Marrou added a *Retractatio* in 1949. Marrou's reevaluation of his work does not lead him to completely overturn his earlier arguments. However, there is one key point that Marrou sought to correct. In the original work, he portrayed the culture of late antiquity as decadent and in decline. In the *Retractatio,* he describes the culture as being in transition and not decline. He also expresses changes of mind brought about by more than a decade of further study.

19. Marrou, *A History of Education in Antiquity,* 265.

rhetor at around age fifteen.[20] Under the instruction of the schoolmaster, Augustine learned the basics of reading and writing.[21] Moving on to the grammarian, Marrou says that the teaching Augustine received "consisted of essentially two aspects, the theoretical study of the language and its laws and the explication of great writings of grammar and literature."[22] Augustine pursued his grammatical study at Maduara, and once finished, he began his rhetorical training.[23] It was under that instruction that Augustine, as did many other young men, sharpened the skills developed at a basic level under the grammarian. Marrou states that:

> It is in effect with the rhetor that one received the essential formation of letters; the grammarian only laid the foundation, prepared the material; only the rhetor could complete the edifice of culture; it is thanks to his lessons that one could become what each was ambitious to be: an orator, a *vir eloquentissimus.*[24]

By the standards of the late empire, Augustine indeed became a most eloquent man. From teaching grammar and rhetoric, with his appointment in Milan as the city teacher of Rhetoric (*civitati rhetoricae magister*),[25] Augustine was poised to fulfill his and his parents' ambitions to rise above their modest station in life; however, as we have seen in Chapter 2, turns in the path led him to other things.

Augustine the Grammarian

Taking the schoolmaster's training as basic and rudimentary, we can focus on what was gained from the grammarian and the rhetor. Both dealt with eloquence as it was understood in terms of a rich literary tradition. In simple terms, as Marrou

20. Ibid.
21. Augustine, *Confessions* 1.19.14.
22. Henri Irénée Marrou, *Saint Augustin et la fin de la culture antique* (Paris: Boccard, 1938), 10. "Considérons d'abord l'enseignement du grammaticus: il comprend essentiellement deux aspects, l'etude théorique de langue et de ses lois, l'explication des grands écrivains grammaire et littérature."
23. As discussed in Chapter 2, Augustine's schooling was interrupted by lack of money. He returned home for a period of time, but then with the financial patronage of Romanianus, a wealthy benefactor, he was able to continue his studies in rhetoric at Carthage.
24. Marrou, *Saint Augustin et la fin de la culture antique*, 47. "C'était en effect chez le rhéteur qu'on recevait l'essentiel de le formation du lettré; le grammairien ne faisait que poser des fondements, préparer des matériaux; seul le rhéteur pouvait achever l'édifice de la culture; c'est grâce à ses leçons qu'on pouvait devenir ce que chacun ambitionnait d'être: un orateur, *vir eloquentissimus.*"
25. Augustine, *Confessions* 5.13.23.

shows, the instruction of the two can be distinguished in the following way: the grammarian focused on analysis and the rhetor on expression. The grammarian took up the canon of great authors and developed the tools in the student for understanding the structure of the language in the text.[26] The rhetor dealt with those issues as well, but put greater emphasis on imitation. The student was taught how to take the understanding of the possibilities of expression as determined by the tradition and present apt words for whatever occasion might be presented to the orator.[27]

The grammarians have often been obscured in the shadow of the rhetors, but Robert Kaster's *Guardians of Language: The Grammarian and Society in Late Antiquity* does much to bring their contributions to light.[28] Kaster focuses on grammarians of the fourth and fifth centuries to explore "the interplay of social status, individual skill and social relations." Kaster derives the title *Guardians of Language* from the sources that describe the role and work of the grammarian. Of particular interest to us is Augustine's designation of the grammarian as "guardian of articulate speech" found in the *Soliloquies*.[29] Kaster says about the grammarian:

> He was to protect the language against corruption, to preserve its coherence, and to act as an agent of control: thus, early in his history we find the grammarian claiming the right to limit the grant of citizenship (*civitas*) to new usages. But by virtue of his command of the poetic texts, the grammarian's guardianship extended to another, more general area, as guardian of tradition (*historiae custos*). The grammarian was the conservator of all the discrete pieces of tradition embedded in his texts, from matters of prosody (to which Augustine refers in his characterization), to the persons, events, and beliefs that marked the limits of vice and virtue.[30]

Such were the things that pertained to the grand sweep of what Kaster calls the "burden" of the grammarian. It also involved, according to Kaster, the arbitration of

> three competing forces: the habit of contemporary usage (*consuetudo; usus*), the authority (*auctoritas*) of classical literary models, and nature (*natura*), that is, the natural

---

26. For a good overview of the Romanized role of the grammarian see Marrou, *A History of Education in Antiquity*, 274–283.

27. Again Marrou provides a good overview. He notes that the rhetor was also distinguished by higher pay and higher social status (Marrou, *A History of Education in Antiquity*, 284–291).

28. Robert Kaster, *Guardians of Language: The Grammarian and Society in Late Antiquity* (Berkeley: University of California Press, 1988), xi.

29. Kaster translates "vocis articulatae custos" as "guardian of articulate utterance," but "vox" can also be translated "speech" or "language" (Kaster, 17). Quoting *Soliloquies*, 2:19, Kaster also quotes Seneca *Epistle* 95.65, "guardian of the Latin language *(custos Latini sermonis)*."

30. Kaster, 17–18.

properties of the language, determined by the grammarians handbook (*ars*). In practice, the grammarian spent much of his time protecting the nature of the language (and so his own *ars*) against the influence of habit and authority.[31]

Augustine was keenly attuned to the currents of these forces. No doubt he performed these duties as a professional teacher of grammar; he even wrote a work on grammar, as part of a projected series on the liberal arts:

> At the time that I was about to receive baptism in Milan, I also attempted to write books on the liberal arts, questioning those who were with me and who were not adverse to studies of this nature, and desiring by definite steps, so to speak, to reach things incorporeal through things corporeal and to lead others to them. But I was only able to complete the book on grammar—which I lost later from our library.[32]

He goes on to say that he also completed six books *On Music* (*De musica*), as well as the beginnings of works on dialectic, rhetoric, geometry, arithmetic, and philosophy. Regrettably, all that survives of this project are the incomplete *On Music* (387-391) and *On Dialectic* (*De dialectica*, 387). Although *On Grammar* (*De grammatica*) and *On Rhetoric* (*De rhetorica*) are lost, the skills of the grammarian and the rhetorician, as well as glimpses of theory, are evident in his life and work. With respect to the grammarian, Augustine's understanding of the significance of the grammarian in learning a body of literature is evident in *On the Usefulness of Belief* (*De utilitate credendi*, 391–392), for example. There, to Honoratus, Augustine argues for the importance of proper instruction for understanding the Christian texts.

> You need Asper, Cornutus, Donatus and innumerable others if you are to understand any poet whose poems and plays apparently win applause. Will you boldly venture without a teacher to study books, which whatever they may be otherwise, are at least holy and full of divine teachings, and are widely famed with assent of almost the whole human race?[33]

And Augustine definitely sought to establish his view of the nature of the language, even after his conversion, in works like *On the Teacher* (389) and especially in *On Teaching Christianity*, which we will examine in greater detail below. As Augustine's self-understanding moves towards that of a bishop, we can see his grammatical concerns shift and become more Catholic. The grammarian's concern for distinctions is important for understanding Augustine's vision of Catholicization. In the service of the Catholic Church, first as a monk, then as

---

31. Ibid., 19.
32. Augustine, *Retractations* 1:5.
33. Augustine, *On the Usefulness of Belief* 7.17, in *Augustine: Earlier Writings*.

a priest, and then supremely as a bishop, Augustine takes up the task of being a "guardian of sacred language." The technical work of the grammarian can be found most obviously in his commentaries and sermons as he wrestles with the sacred texts and tradition of Catholic Christians. In the following passage from *Expositions on the Psalms* 127 (126), Augustine links the role of guardian, that key role of the grammarian, with the task of the bishop.

> 2. But that which is the house of God is also a city. For the house of God is the people of God; for the house of God is the temple of God. . . . This is Jerusalem: she hath guards: as she hath builders, labouring at her building up, so also hath she guards. To this guardianship these words of the Apostle relate: "I fear, lest by any means your minds should be corrupted from the simplicity which is in Christ." He was guarding the Church. He kept watch, to the utmost of his power, over those over whom he was set. The Bishops also do this. For a higher place was for this reason given the Bishops, that they might be themselves the superintendents and as it were the guardians of the people (*custodiant populum*). For the Greek word *Episcopus*, and the vernacular Superintendent, are the same; for the Bishop superintends, in that he looks over. As a higher place is assigned to the vinedresser in the charge of the vineyard, so also to the Bishops a more exalted station is alloted. And a perilous account is rendered of this high station, except we stand here with a heart that causeth us to stand beneath your feet in humility, and pray for you, that He who knoweth your minds may be Himself your keeper. Since we can see you both coming in and going out; but we are so unable to see what are the thoughts of your hearts, that we cannot even see what ye do in your houses. How then can we guard you? As men: as far as we are able, as far as we have received power. And because we guard you like men, and cannot guard you perfectly, shall ye therefore remain without a keeper? Far be it! For where is He of whom it is said, "Except the Lord keep the city, the watchman waketh but in vain?" (ver. 1). We are watchful on our guard, but vain in our watchfulness, except He who seeth your thoughts guard you. He keepeth guard while ye are awake, He keepeth guard also whilst ye are asleep. For He hath once slept on the Cross, and hath risen again; He no longer sleepeth. Be ye Israel: for "the Keeper of Israel neither sleepeth nor slumbereth." Yea, brethren, if we wish to be kept beneath the shadow of God's wings, let us be Israel. For we guard you in our office of stewards; but we wish to be guarded together with you. We are as it were shepherds unto you; but beneath that Shepherd we are fellow-sheep with you. We are as it were your teachers from this station; but beneath Him, the One Master, we are schoolfellows with you in this school.[34]

Cameron argues that a key part of the emergence of Christian discourse was the construction of symbolic meaning in language. The richness and power of this are displayed in Augustine's rhetoric in this passage. Augustine seeks to persuade his hearers to take up a role appropriate for their individual spiritual formation and

---

34. *Expositions on the Psalms* 127 (126), *NPNF* vol. 8: *Augustin: Exposition on the Psalms,* translated by H. M. Wilkins, 1995; *Ennarationes in Psalmos* 126.

for the collective social order of the Christian community. He employs the images of known relationships that reinforce his position and theirs. The watchman and the city, the bishop and the congregation, the vinedresser and the vineyard, the shepherd and the sheep, and the schoolmaster/grammarian all pile up, creating a rhetorical density in his message. Yet, within Augustine's discourse, there is an inversion that at the same time deconstructs and compounds the message. Augustine acknowledges the bishops' limited capacity to oversee, but invokes, based on the text of Psalm 127, "the Lord" as the ultimate keeper of Israel:

> For we guard you in our office of stewards; but we wish to be guarded together with you. We are, as it were, shepherds unto you; but beneath that Shepherd we are fellow-sheep with you. We are as it were your teachers from this station; but beneath Him, the One Master, we are schoolfellows with you in this school.

Thus, although acknowledging weakness, Augustine re-inscribes the role of the bishop, the grammarian/guardian of sacred language, in a far more significant hierarchy. This hierarchy is not provincial; it is Catholic and totalizing in scope. As a bishop, he guards and distinguishes from heresy and schism the purity of Catholic hierarchy and tradition. Like those grammarians who sought to deny citizenship, Augustine seeks to define who can appropriately take up the name Catholic. This is seen in *On the Creed,* discussed in Chapter 3, and in *On the Usefulness of Belief,* where he tries to convince Honoratus, a man whom he had led into Manicheism, that he should follow him once again into the Catholic Church and reject the arguments of the Manichees against Catholics' reliance on the teaching authority of the Church. At one point Augustine frames the question sharply, saying:

> The name of religion is most honourable and in highest repute. What then hinders thorough discussion and pious and careful investigation of the question whether the Catholic Faith be not the religion which a few may know intimately and guard, while it rejoices in the goodwill and favor of all nations.

He goes on to argue that:

> Among Christians there are several heresies, but all want to be regarded as Catholics and call others beyond their own group heretics. But there is one Church, all will admit, numerically larger taking the whole world into consideration, and sounder in truth than all other, as those affirm who know it.[35]

Augustine thus presents for Honoratus a new way of understanding the Catholic teaching that is reasoned. This reasoned approach involves at its foundation

---

35. Augustine, *On the Usefulness of Belief* 7.19–8.20, in *Augustine: Earlier Writings.*

allegorical interpretation of scripture to handle difficulties that the Manichees raised.[36] Arguing fine points of interpretation blurs the distinction between the roles and skills of the grammarian and the rhetor. This seems to be a goal of the educational system as it related to the formation of men. Ideally, one ought to have command of the skills learned under the grammarian so as to be an effective man of eloquence. Such was the case with Augustine, but, as we have tried to understand what of the grammarian can be found in Augustine's eloquence, let us now consider Augustine as rhetorician.[37]

Augustine the Rhetorician

The academic tradition of rhetoric, as it developed in the Latin world, was primarily shaped by Cicero and Quintillian.[38] In Augustine's training in Carthage, it was Cicero who was the master and model. From the time the Romans adopted rhetoric to the time of Augustine, emphases shifted, but the basic structure of the academic tradition remained essentially that which Cicero and Quintillian had promulgated. There are three types of speeches or oratory, five aspects of speech preparation, six parts of the speech, and three styles of speech delivery. The following chart lays out this basic theoretical structure.[39]

36. Ibid., 3; 4. Augustine also expressed the importance of this for himself as he listened to Ambrose in the *Confessions* 5.3.4ff.

37. O'Meara interestingly sets the roles of grammarian and rhetor in opposition and raises the question: "which of the two aspects appealed more to Augustine? The answer is the second." His reasoning is that even though Augustine employed the technical aids learned in grammar and also rhetoric, "his genius was too great, too independent, too tumultuous to find easy expression in a neatly articulated plan." Thus, O'Meara equates plan and order with the grammarian and inventiveness and innovation with the rhetorician. I think that this is a fair characterization of Augustine. But the correspondence with the roles of grammarian and rhetor of these impulses might be slightly overdrawn. On the one hand, we can recognize that the educational structure was geared towards moving men from the tutelage of the grammarian to that of the rhetorician, so in theory the grammarians' room was preparatory and necessary for the proper formation of men. That formation was only complete, as Marrou argued, when men had been trained by the rhetor. Yet on the other hand, the respective instructors served two distinct social roles, and Augustine did not settle for being a mere grammarian but moved onwards and upward in the social strata to become a rhetorician (O'Meara, 39–40).

38. See, for example, M. L. Clarke, *Rhetoric at Rome*, 3rd ed. (New York: Routledge, 1996). His survey goes from the Greek background of Roman rhetoric in the Republican period through the late empire. Cicero and Quintillian receive more treatment than any other rhetoricians.

39. I rely principally on M. L. Clarke, 23–27.

3 Types Speeches	5 Aspects Preparation	6 Parts of the speech	3 Styles
• Delibrative	• Invention	• Opening	• Grand
• Forensic	• Arrangement	• Statement of Fact	• Middle
• Epidectic	• Style	• Partition	• Plain
	• Memory	• Proof	
	• Delivery	• Refutation	
		• Conclusion	

In addition to this framework, there are many figures of speech that are technical devices involved in the composition and delivery.[40] Thus, the structure that was in place by the time of Augustine was quite complex. But to what degree did Augustine exemplify this complexity?

Several scholars have done meticulous investigation and exposition of Augustine's relationship to classical rhetoric.[41] It is clear from the body of research that Augustine was well acquainted with the canons of oratorical theory, particularly that of Cicero. Trends in Augustine's relationship to classical rhetoric can generally be characterized according to the type of work: letters, treatises, and sermons. Wilfrid Parsons has conducted a careful, quantitative rhetorical analysis of Augustine's letters. Looking at vocabulary and style, she tabulates things such as the use of foreign loan words, tropes, figures of rhetoric, and figures of speech. Parsons concludes that there was not a strong trend in the development of Augustine's style over the course of his career. She does notice variation in Augustine's style, however; but she finds this is to be attributed to subject and addressee.

> Letters of a polemical nature are usually highly rhetorical, elaborately figured, intricately symmetrical. So also are those in which a difficult doctrine is set forth, as if the profundity of the subject called for a complexity of treatment. Some of the letters sound remarkably like sermons (e.g., *Ep.* 130, 151). Purely explanatory letters on the other hand, are usually simple and straightforward in style as are those addressed to superiors (e.g., *Ep.* 102, 147).[42]

Parsons finds Augustine to be noticeably influenced by three elements that "comprehend" all others: "he was African, he was a rhetorician and he was an

---

40. For a definition and discussion of these terms with examples, see *Handbook of Classical Rhetoric in the Hellenistic Period*, "Style," by Galen Rowe.

41. Of particular interest is a series of dissertations done at Catholic University of America. For example, Mary Inez Bogan, *The Vocabulary and Style of the Soliloquies and Dialogues of Saint Augustine* (Ph.D. diss., Catholic University of America, 1935); and Wilfrid Parsons, *A Study of the Vocabulary and Rhetoric of the Letters of Saint Augustine* (Ph.D. diss., Catholic University of America, 1923).

42. Parsons, 276–277.

ecclesiastic."[43] Noting archaism, colloquialism, and neologism as markers of African Latinity, she finds archaisms "insignificant" in the letters compared with the large amount of late Latin vocabulary, and with the neologisms of Augustine.[44] Thus, it can be concluded, at least from his letters, that Augustine was not content to be a mere imitator, conserver, or guardian of tradition. Rather, Augustine varied his style and innovated his vocabulary usage with a view towards communication with an expanding circle. He could effectively communicate with elites who had the benefit of similar education, but he also cultivated skills of communication with the people not privileged to have such an education.

To my knowledge, there has not been the same sort of thorough rhetorical analysis of all of the treatises of Augustine; however, there have been studies on specific treatises and groups of treatises. Mary Inez Bogan, for example, wrote on the style and vocabulary of the *Soliloquies* and the Cassiaciacum dialogues. She finds there Augustine very much the rhetorician in Ciceronian mode. But what of the rest of his career? It is difficult to speak definitively, but what can be said is that there is enough evidence to show that Augustine often envisioned a sophisticated reader or hearer for his treatises and so targeted his rhetoric accordingly.

Along with the letters, there is variation of audience, and thus rhetoric, to be found in Augustine's sermons as well. Once he became a priest, he was immediately pressed into service as a preacher. According to Steven Oberhelman, many of Augustine's early sermons reflect a high level of rhetorical polish that would have been above most of his audience.[45] Over time, however, Augustine developed a simpler extemporaneous style that had greater popular appeal. Oberhelman claims that Augustine did draw on classical or Christian models of oratory for the development of his new style;[46] he modeled himself on the writings of scripture, particularly Paul's letters.[47] In general, Augustine's early sermons were highly rhetorical in style, but as Augustine's career developed in the mid-390s, he became more relaxed and responsive to the audience he found himself preaching to in Hippo. This audience tended to be less educated than he was. As he began to have greater appreciation for the sacred Christian writings, he also came to realize that

43. Ibid., 269.

44. Ibid., 269ff.

45. Steven M. Oberhelman, *Rhetoric and Homiletics in Fourth-Century Christian Literature* (Atlanta: Scholars Press, 1991), 108–109.

46. Ibid., 109–111.

47. This does not mean that we can set into clear opposition biblical and classical language, especially since there has been a great deal of work that demonstrates that classical rhetorical echoes in the scripture as well. What has not been the subject of much investigation, to my knowledge, are the Jewish or Hebraic rhetorical traditions in the Old and New Testaments.

the Scriptures could serve as Virgil and the other writings of the grammarians' canon did, as the basis for a Christian cultural model and its mode of expression. Thus, the humble Latin of the sacred writings became a guide for his new mode of persuasion. Augustine's simpler style is evident in his sermons, but the theory is clearly laid out in *On Teaching Christianity*, to which we will turn now.

Augustine's *De Doctrina Christiana*

Begun as early as 397, *On Teaching Christianity* was not finished until around 427, while he was working on the *Retractations*. Books 1 and 2 were circulating by 398, according to a number of scholars' examination of a fourth-century manuscript, the Leningrad Codex.[48] Once completed in four books, Augustine describes the structure as follows:

> I added a new book and completed the work in four books, of which the first three help us so that the scriptures might be understood, but the fourth how that which we understand might be declared publicly.[49]

Augustine presents a guide to exegesis and preaching that draws on the work of the grammarian, primarily in Books 1 through 3, and the rhetor, primarily in Book 4.[50] Book 4, after reminding readers of the structure, gives an interesting disclaimer:

> In the first place, then, I wish by this preamble to put a stop to the expectations of readers who may think that I am about to lay down rules of rhetoric such as I have

---

48. I rely on Kenneth B. Steinhauser, who in conversation with William M. Green, "A Fourth Century Manuscript of Saint Augustine," *Revue Bénédictine* 69 (1959): 191–197; and Almut Mutzenbecher, "Codex Leningrad Q.v.I.3 (Corbie). Ein Beitrag zu seiner Beschreibung": *Sacris erudiri* 18 (1967/1968): 406–450, examines this manuscript and makes some interesting proposals. First, he agrees with Green and Mutzenberger [AU.] that this is an authentic fourth-century manuscript that has Augustine's *Epistle 37 introducing De diversis questionibus ad Simplicianum, Contra epistulam Manichaei quamvocant fundamenti, De agane christiano*, and the first two books of *De doctrina Christiana*. Second, he argues for seeing the collection as a *Festschrift* for Simplicianus. Kenneth Steinhauser "Codex Leningradensis Q.v.I.3.: Some Unresolved Problems," in *De doctrina Christiana: A Classic of Western Culture*, edited by Duane W. H. Arnold and Pamela Bright (Notre Dame, IN: University of Notre Dame Press, 1995).

49. Augustine, *Retractations* 2.4. "Addidi etiam novissimum librum et quattuor libris opus illud implevi; quorum primi tres adiuvant ut scripturae intelligantur, quatrus auten quomodo quae intelligimus proferenda sint."

50. In fact, Book 4, which contains the rhetorical theory such as it is, was at times circulated independently of the other three books, and was even one of the earliest of Augustine's works to be printed and have a wide circulation.

learnt and taught too, in the secular schools, and to warn them that they need not look for any such from me. Not that I think such rules of no use, but that whatever use they have is to be learnt elsewhere; and if any good man should happen to have leisure for learning them, he is not to ask me to teach them either in this work or any other.[51]

We may ask, what is Augustine trying to do in Book 4, and how does he distinguish it from the rules of rhetoric that he learned? Before tackling these questions, however, it is important to take up another; that is, how are the last two books, particularly with their usages of Tyconius and Cicero, relevant to the late fourth and early fifth centuries when Augustine broke off writing? First, as we shall see, Augustine's consideration of the importance of Tyconius and Cicero might have been a significant reason why he stopped writing. Second, works from around 400 show a familiarity with those two authors consistent with what Augustine writes thirty years or so later.

Augustine attempts to present some basic instruction on eloquence without becoming overly immersed in the technical mechanics of rhetoric. With Cicero as his guide, even though he does not mention him by name, he provides a simple guide for preachers focused on the appropriate value of three styles: the grand, the middle, and the plain, which correspond to three aims: teaching, delighting, and persuading.

> He then who, in speaking, aims at enforcing what is good, should not despise any of those three objects, either to teach, or to give pleasure, or to move, and should pray and strive, as we have said above, to be heard with intelligence, with pleasure, and with ready compliance. And when he does this with elegance and propriety, he may justly be called eloquent, even though he does not carry with him the assent of his hearer. For it is these three ends, viz., teaching, giving pleasure, and moving, that the great master of Roman eloquence himself seems to have intended that the following three directions should subserve: "He, then, shall be eloquent, who can say little things in a subdued style, moderate things in a temperate style, and great things in a majestic style": as if he had taken in also the three ends mentioned above, and had embraced the whole in one sentence thus: "He, then, shall be eloquent, who can say little things in a subdued style, in order to give instruction, moderate things in a temperate style, in order to give pleasure, and great things in a majestic style, in order to sway the mind."[52]

51. *De Doctrina Christiana (DDC)* 4.2, Oxford Early Christian Texts, translated by R. P. H. Green (New York: Oxford University Press, 1996).

52. *DDC* 4.17.34. "Qui ergo nititur dicendo persuadere quod bonum est, nihil illorum trium spernens—ut scilicet doceat, ut delectet, ut flectat—, oret atque agat ut, quemadmodum supra diximus, intellegenter, libenter, oboedienterque audiatur. Quod cum apte et convenienter facit, non immerito eloquens dici potest, etsi non eum sequatur auditoris assensus. Ad haec enim tria, id est ut doceat, ut delectet, ut flectat, etiam illa tria videtur pertinere voluisse idem ipse Romani

Instead of presenting the canon of secular authors as models, Augustine presents, first, biblical examples like Paul,[53] and, second, extra-biblical examples like Ambrose and Cyprian[54] as models for the three styles.

The key element that Augustine sees as distinguishing his enterprise is truth or wisdom. Presentation of truth or wisdom is primary, and eloquence should serve them. "Now, the art of rhetoric being available for the enforcing either of truth or falsehood, who will dare to say that truth in the person of its defenders is to take its stand unarmed against falsehood?"[55]

Comparing Augustine to Cicero, Quintillian, and even the *minor ars* of the late empire, we find that Augustine's treatment of rhetoric, although conversant with those other guides, is far simpler in covering the basic aspects of rhetoric and not nearly as comprehensive. Sister Thérèse Sullivan, in her commentary on Book 4 of *On Teaching Christianity*, charts Augustine's indebtedness to Cicero and other classical sources of rhetorical theory in *On Teaching Christianity* and other works as well. Cicero's *De Oratore* and *Orator* provide the richest sources that Augustine mines in Book 4. Sullivan finds traces of Aristotle, the anonymous *Rhetorica Ad Herennium*, and Quintillian.[56] Though a great number of topics are mentioned with reference to these classical authorities, Augustine explicitly says, in the above quotation from 4.2, that he is not producing a Christian *Ars rhetorica*, and this is, in fact, debatably the case. On the one hand, Augustine's Book 4 lacks the comprehensiveness of the *ars* tradition; on the other hand, it might be fair to say that Augustine gave what he thought was essential for a Christian *ars*.

What we have in *On Teaching Christianity* is evidence that Augustine turned the tools of his education away from the maintenance of elite Roman culture to the establishment of a broader Christian culture.[57] This Christian culture is also literary and not free from the establishment of accompanying elites; however, with Augustine we see clear and conscious efforts to expand the range of address and

---

auctor eloquii, cum itidem dixit: Is erit igitur eloquens, qui poterit parva summisse, modica temperate, magna gran diter dicere, tamquam si adderet illa etiam tria, et sic explicaret unam eamdemque sententiam, dicens: Is erit igitur eloquens, qui ut doceat poterit parva summisse, ut delectet modica temperate, ut flectat magna granditer dicere." See also Cicero, *The Orator* 29, 101.

53. *DDC* 4.7.20–21; 39–44.

54. Ibid., 4.2.45–50.

55. Ibid., 4.2.3.

56. *S. Aureli Augustini Hipponiensis Episcopi De Doctrina Christiana Liber Quartus: A Commentary, with a Revised Text, Introduction, and Translation* by Thérèse Sullivan (Washington, D.C., 1930), 8–13.

57. Marrou, Cameron, and Frances M. Young, *Biblical Exegesis and the Formation of Christian Culture*. Peabody, Mass: Hendrickson, 2002.

inclusion. For Augustine, the Christian culture embraces the elites and common people, the literate and nonliterate alike. In fact, for Augustine, an essential aspect of Christian culture is this inclusive thrust that can be found in the central narrative of the Christian story that embraces creation, the fall, redemption, and judgment in the figure of Jesus Christ. God, in Jesus the Word, creates, man falls, Christ humbles himself in the incarnation to redeem man through his death and resurrection, and he will come again in judgment. Time and again, Augustine focuses on the opposition between pride and humility and the way that Jesus's humility is the remedy for the human pride of which Augustine says he was so guilty. Augustine sees himself putting his rhetorical skill to work for humble aims, which contrast with those aims he had as a professional rhetor. Rather than focusing on garnering praise and fame or promoting ambition, he focuses on convincing people to take up this humble way of life.

In a way, Augustine, as he portrays himself in the *Confessions,* is coming full circle in his use of rhetoric. The opposition between the rhetorician's search for fame and the philosopher's search for truth is proverbial. But with Augustine, we find a marriage of the skill set of the rhetor with the skill set of the philosopher, and, more important, his aims. Ironically, it is Cicero who is the key guide for this journey. For Augustine, the reading of Cicero's *Hortensius* symbolized a call to pursue truth. As he says in the *Confessions,* he was diverted from the strict pursuit of this aim by ambition. The readers and hearers, of course, know the end of the story, that Augustine finds truth in the teaching of the Catholic Church. He says that it is the estimation of the texts of this Church, in comparison to the writings of Cicero, that first drove him from the truth, however. The irony comes to full light when we consider that Augustine began writing *On Teaching Christianity* before writing the *Confessions.* It is true that the work was not finished until around 427, but, accepting the arguments of Kenneth Steinhauser, the first two books were finished by 398. While it is true that the most prominent use of Cicero is found in Book 4, he is far from absent in the rest of the work. In fact, the underlying theme of the superiority of wisdom or truth over eloquence is Ciceronian. Consider, for example, the following:

> But as some men employ these coarsely, inelegantly, and frigidly while others use them with acuteness, elegance, and spirit, the work that I am speaking of ought to be undertaken by one who can argue and speak with wisdom, if not with eloquence, and with profit to his hearers, even though he profit them less than he would if he could speak with eloquence too. But we must beware of the man who abounds in eloquent nonsense, and so much the more if the hearer is pleased with what is not worth listening to, and thinks that because the speaker is eloquent what he says must be true. And this opinion is held even by those who think that the art of rhetoric should be taught: for they confess that "though wisdom without eloquence is of little service to states,

yet eloquence without wisdom is frequently a positive injury, and is of service never." If, then, the men who teach the principles of eloquence have been forced by truth to confess this in the very books which treat of eloquence, though they were ignorant of the true, that is, the heavenly wisdom which comes down from the Father of Lights, how much more ought we to feel it who are the sons and the ministers of this higher wisdom? Now a man speaks with more or less wisdom just as he has made more or less progress in the knowledge of Scripture; I do not mean by reading them much and committing them to memory, but by understanding them aright and carefully searching into their meaning.[58]

Thus, Augustine, from Cicero, claims whatever may be the case for service to the state, so much the more in service of God ought truth or wisdom be of supreme value. So we see that while recounting his initial acquaintance with Cicero and his life of ambition as a rhetorician, Augustine in the *Confessions* is hinting at what is apparent in *On Teaching Christianity*, namely, that pursuit of wisdom or truth is superior to eloquence. Thus, his return to Cicero. I do not mean to say that it is an uncritical embrace of Cicero; on the contrary, the connection seems to be one about which Augustine has some degree of ambivalence. This fact may be one of the potential reasons for the interruption of the work.

Charles Kannengiesser has argued persuasively for a number of other factors, but the role of Cicero is not addressed.[59] He sees *On Teaching Christianity* as a work designed to be a handbook for the reformation in the Catholic ranks of Africa. I find great support in his arguments for my view that Augustine was involved in a project of Catholicization. Why then the interruption, if such a guide was in desperate need? It seems as if Tyconius is the shadow that haunted the project.

58. *DDC* 4.5.7 "Sed cum alii faciant obtunse, deformiter, frigide, alii acute, ornate, vehementer, illum ad hoc opus unde agimus iam oportet accedere, qui potest disputare vel dicere sapienter, etiamsi non potest eloquenter, ut prosit audientibus, etiamsi minus, quam prodesset si et eloquenter posset dicere. Qui vero affluit insipienti eloquentia, tanto magis cavendus est quanto magis ab eo in his quae audire inutile est, delectatur auditor et eum quoniam diserte dicere audit, etiam vere dicere existimat. Haec autem sententia nec illos fugit qui artem rhetoricam docendam putarunt. Fassi sunt enim sapientiam sine eloquentia parum prodesse civitatibus, eloquentiam vero sine sapientia nimium obesse plerumque, prodesse numquam. Si hoc ergo illi, qui praecepta eloquentiae tradiderunt, in eisdem libris in quibus id egerunt, veritate instigante coacti sunt confiteri, veram, hoc est supernam quae a Patre luminum descendit sapientiam nescientes, quanto magis nos non aliud sentire debemus, qui huius sapientiae filii et ministri sumus? Sapienter autem dicit homo tanto magis vel minus, quanto in Scripturis sanctis magis minusve profecit, non dico in eis multum legendis memoriaeque mandandis, sed bene intellegendis et diligenter earum sensibus indagandis."

59. Charles Kannengiesser, "The Interrupted *De doctrina christiana*," in *De Doctrina Christiana: A Classic of Western Culture*, edited by Duane W. H. Arnold and Pamela Bright (Notre Dame, IN: University of Notre Dame Press, 1995), 3–13.

In *Epistle* 41, Augustine opens by praising Aurelius effusively for allowing priests to preach and closes by saying that he has not forgotten a request of Aurelius's. Augustine acknowledges this debt but asks, almost desperately, for Aurelius's opinion of the Donatist exegete. He writes:

"Our mouth is filled with laughter, and our tongue with singing," by your letter informing us that, by the help of that God whose inspiration guided you, you have carried into effect your pious purpose concerning all our brethren in orders, and especially concerning the regular delivering of a sermon to the people in your presence by the presbyters, through whose tongues thus engaged your love sounds louder in the hearts than their voice does in the ears of men. Thanks be unto God! Is there anything better for us to have in our heart, or utter with our lips, or record with our pen, than this? Thanks be unto God! No other phrase is more easily spoken, and nothing more pleasant in sound, profound in significance, and profitable in practice, than this. Thanks be unto God, who has endowed you with a heart so true to the interests of your sons, and who has brought to light what you had latent in the inner soul, beyond the reach of human eye, giving you not only the will to do good, but the means of realizing your desires. So be it, certainly so be it! Let these works shine before men, that they may see them, and rejoice and glorify your Father in heaven. In such things delight yourself in the Lord; and may your prayers for these presbyters be graciously heard on their behalf by Him whose voice you do not consider it beneath you to hear when He speaks by them! May they go on, and walk, yea, run in the way of the Lord! May the small and the great be blessed together, being made glad by those who say unto them, "Let us go into the house of the Lord!" Let the stronger lead; let the weaker imitate their example, being followers of them, as they are of Christ. May we all be as ants pursuing eagerly the path of holy industry, as bees labouring amidst the fragrance of holy duty; and may fruit be brought forth in patience by the saving grace of stedfastness unto the end! May the Lord "not suffer us to be tempted above that we are able, but with the temptation may He make a way to escape, that we may be able to bear it"!

Pray for us: we value your prayers as worthy to be heard, since you go to God with so great an offering of unfeigned love, and of praise brought to Him by your works. Pray that in us also these works may shine, for He to whom you pray knows with what fullness of joy we behold them shining in you. Such are our desires; such are the abounding comforts which in the multitude of our thoughts within us delight our souls. It is so now because such is the promise of God; and as He hath promised, so shall it be in the time to come. We beseech you, by Him who hath blessed you, and has by you bestowed this blessing on the people whom you serve, to order any of the presbyters' sermons which you please to be transcribed, and after revisal sent to us. For I on my part am not neglecting what you required of me; and as I have written often before, I am still longing to know what you think of Tychonius' seven Rules or Keys.[60]

---

60. Augustine, *Epistle* 41.2, in *Augustine: Select Letters*. "Nam et ego quod iussisti non negligo, et de Tychonii septem regulis vel clavibus, sicut saepe iam scripsi, cognoscere quid tibi videatur exspecto."

Against the backdrop of this letter, the story that Kannengiesser reconstructs is as follows. After Augustine is allowed to preach as a priest, and with the support of Aurelius, it becomes a promoted practice in the African Catholic Church. With this new structure, the need becomes even greater to train and improve the overall ability of the clergy to teach and preach the Catholic faith. Thus the need for a *De Doctrina Christiana*, which is the request that Augustine has not forgotten. Though it is not explicitly stated in the title, it is implicit that the work is really *De Doctrina Catholica Christiana*. A problem arises for Augustine's execution of this work, however. I agree with Kannengiesser that other writings were not a sufficient distraction, and that there must be some other factor or factors involved. The main thing for Kannengiesser is Tyconius.[61] Tyconius was a Donatist, a dissenting one, but it is clear that such dissent did not lead him to join the Catholic Church. Kannengiesser speculates that Aurelius might have told Augustine that the timing was not right for presenting a Donatist so favorably.[62] Augustine complies and publishes the work without the Tyconius material. As Kannengiesser further argues, it is probable that at least Books 1 and 2 circulated by 400. Thus, Augustine still was able to provide some guides for the clergy. It is possible that the material of the earlier part of the work was most significant because it presented how to find truth through what Augustine argues are the proper interpretive guidelines. When Augustine finally does finish the work thirty years later, he indeed gives a cautious but favorable review that adds to the basic interpretive guides he has already given.

> One Tychonius, who, although a Donatist himself, has written most triumphantly against the Donatists (and herein showed himself of a most inconsistent disposition, that he was unwilling to give them up altogether), wrote a book which he called the Book of Rules, because in it he laid down seven rules, which are, as it were, keys to open the secrets of Scripture. And of these rules, the first relates to the Lord and His body, the second to the twofold division of the Lord's body, the third to the promises and the law, the fourth to *species* and *genus*, the fifth to times, the sixth to recapitulation, the seventh to the devil and his body. Now these rules, as expounded by their author, do indeed, when carefully considered, afford considerable assistance in penetrating the secrets of the sacred writings; but still they do not explain all the difficult passages, for there are several other methods required, which are so far from being embraced in this number of seven, that the author himself explains many obscure passages without using any of his rules; finding, indeed, that there was no need for them, as there was no difficulty in the passage of the kind

61. For more on the influence of Tyconius on Augustine's *De doctrina Christiana*, see Karla Pollmann, *Doctrina Christiana: Untersuchungen zu den Anfängen der christlichen Hermeneutik unter besonderer Berücksichtigung von Augustinus, De doctrina Christiana* (Freiburg, Schweiz: Universitätsverlag, 1996).

62. I will add that it might have been just as awkward to present Cicero in 397 rather than when he did, in 427.

to which his rules apply. As, for example, he inquires what we are to understand in the Apocalypse by the seven angels of the churches to whom John is commanded to write; and after much and various reasoning, arrives at the conclusion that the angels are the churches themselves. And throughout this long and full discussion, although the matter inquired into is certainly very obscure, no use whatever is made of the rules.[63]

Augustine goes on to give examples of each of the rules; scholarship, beginning in the last quarter of the twentieth century, has shown evidence that his use of Tyconius was at best misunderstanding him and at worst intentional misrepresentation.

A key criticism is understood by considering Pamela Bright's *The Book of Rules of Tyconius: Its Purpose and Inner Logic.*[64] In this work, she shows the importance of understanding Tyconius's strategy of prophetic exegesis that reads the Old and New Testament through "mystical rules." She also makes clear the error of Augustine and the epitomizers who follow him. They all fail to understand the "precise ecclesiological focus of Tyconius." For example, about Rule 2: Of the Bipartite Body of the Lord (*De Domini corpere bipertito*), Augustine says:

> [B]ut this indeed is not a suitable name, for that is really no part of the body of Christ which will not be with Him in eternity. We ought, therefore, to say that the rule is about the true and the mixed body of the Lord, or the true and the counterfeit, or some such name; because, not to speak of eternity, hypocrites cannot even now be said to be in Him, although they seem to be in His Church. And hence this rule might be desig-nated thus: Concerning the mixed Church. Now this rule requires the reader to be on his guard when Scripture, although it has now come to address or speak of a different set of persons, seems to be addressing or speaking of the same persons as before, just as if both sets constituted one body in consequence of their being for the time united in a common participation of the sacraments. An example of this is that passage in the Song of Solomon, "I am black, but comely, as the tents of Cedar, as the curtains of Solomon." For it is not said, I was black as the tents of Cedar, but am now comely as the curtains of Solomon. The Church declares itself to be at present both; and this because the good fish and the bad are for the time mixed up in the one net. For the tents of Cedar pertain to Ishmael, who "shall not be heir with the son of the free woman."[65]

But consider what Tyconius himself says about the same passage on the same rule:

> Again, the bipartite character of Christ's body is indicated in brief: "I am black and beautiful" (Song of Solomon 1:5). By no means is the church—"which has no spot or wrinkle" (Eph. 5:27), which the Lord cleansed by his own blood—black in any part,

63. *DDC* 3.30.42.

64. Pamela Bright, *The Book of Rules of Tyconius: Its Purpose and Inner Logic* (Notre Dame: University of Notre Dame Press, 1988).

65. Augustine, *DDC* 3.32.45.

except in the left-hand part through which "the name of God is blasphemed among the gentiles" (Rom. 2:24). Otherwise it is wholly beautiful, as he says: "you are wholly beautiful, my love, and there is no fault in you" (Song 4:7). And indeed she says why it is that she is both black and beautiful: "like the tent of Kedar, like the tent-curtain of Solomon" (Song 1:5). She shows that there are two tents, one royal and one servile. Yet both spring from Abraham, for Kedar is Ishmael's son. And furthermore, in another passage, the church groans that it has dwelt so long with this Kedar, i.e., with the servant descended from Abraham: "Woe is me that my sojourn has been so lengthy, that I have lived among the tents of Kedar. Too long has my soul been on sojourn. With those who hate peace, I was peaceful; when I spoke to them, they made war against me" (Ps. 120:5–7). Yet we cannot claim that the tent of Kedar is outside the church. She herself mentions the "tent of Kedar" and "of Solomon"; and that is why she says, "I am black and beautiful." Those who are outside the church do not make it black.[66]

In her discussion of the comparison of this rule, Bright says:

> For Tyconius, it is not a question of the "true church" and the "counterfeit church." It is rather a question of the bipartite Church in which the "right" and the "left" will be visibly and irrevocably separated at the Judgment when the time for repentance is over, but until the Judgment there is to be no visible separation (Matt. 13:29) of the membership of the Church.[67]

---

66. Tyconius, *The Book of Rules*. "Iterum breviter bipertitum ostenditur Christi corpus: Fusca sum et decora. Absit enim ut Ecclesia quae non habet maculam aut rugam, quam Dominus suo sanguine sibi mundavit, aliqua ex parte fusca sit nisi in parte sinistra per quam nomert Dei blasphematur in gentibus. Alias tota speciosa est, sicut dicit: Tota speciosa es proxima mea et reprehensio non est in te. Etenim dicit qua de causa sit fusca et speciosa: Ut tabernaculum Cedar ut pellis Salomonis. Duo tabernacula ostendit, regium et setuile: utrumque tamen semen Abrahae; Cedar enim filius est Ismahel. Alio denique loco cum isto Cedar, id est cum seruo ex Abraham, diuturnam mansionem, sic ingemescit Ecclesia dicens: Heu me quoniam peregrinatio mea longinqua iacta est, habitaui cum tabernaculis Cedar, multum peregrinata est anima mea. Cum odientibus pacem eram pacificus, cum loquebar illis debellabont me. Non possumus autem dicere tabernaculum Cedar praeter Ecclesiam esse. Ipse autem dicit tabernaculum Cedar et Salomonis unde fusca sum inquit et decora; non enim Ecclesia in his qui foris sunt fusca est. Hoc mysterio Dominus in Apocalypsi septem angelos dicit, id est Ecclesiam septiformem, nunc sanctos et praeceptorum custodes, nunc eosdem multorum criminum reos et paenitentia dignos ostendit. Et in Evangelio urium praepositorum corpus diversi meriti manifestat dicens: Beatus ille seruus quem adueniens dominus illius inuenerit ita facierttem, et de eodem: Si autem nequam ille seruus, quem Dominus dividit in duas partes. Dico numquid omnem dividet aut findet?"

67. Pamela Bright, "Tyconius and His Interpreters: A Study of the Epitomes of the Book of Rules," Kannengiesser, Charles, Pamela Bright, and Wilhelm H. Wuellner. *A Conflict of Christian Hermeneutics in Roman Africa: Tyconius and Augustine*. Berkeley, CA, USA: Center for Hermeneutical Studies in Hellenistic and Modern Culture, 1989. 23–39.

There is thus a subtle but important difference between Tyconius and Augustine in their ecclesiology and method of interpretation. Tyconius influenced Augustine in both areas. It does not seem that Augustine's distortion of Tyconius was intentional, for, at least by the time he finished *On Teaching Christianity*, he was comfortable enough to acknowledge his debt to Tyconius. Yet he was also comfortable enough to raise criticisms and say that his endorsement was qualified. I think it then unlikely that Augustine would knowingly distort Tyconius; he had nothing to hide and nothing to gain. If that is the case, then I think that his failure to grasp the subtlety of Tyconius's hermeneutic led to him missing the subtlety of his eschatological bipartite ecclesiology. Augustine saw the use of the keys as an activity, whereas it may be more accurate to describe their use as a "passivity," for, according to Bright, Tyconius places the emphasis of interpretation on attending to the "logic" of scripture. She writes: "From Augustine onwards, the interpreters of *The Book of Rules* did not recognize the 'keys' or 'windows' that Tyconius provided as access to the understanding of the mysteries of the Church sealed within the 'recesses' of scripture by the Spirit."[68]

To sum up, Augustine condensed his training into manageable guides for the common priest or bishop, and, at the same time, pressed on towards his goal of moving people to embrace truth. The interpretive rules of Tyconius and the delivery skills of Cicero are of great help, but their successful use, Augustine claims, depends on love.[69] It is now appropriate to look at rhetoric and persuasion in the broader terms of modern rhetorical analysis.

Augustine and Modern Rhetorical Theory

With modern rhetorical theory, as it developed in the latter half of the twentieth century, we find a combination of lines of continuity with traditional rhetoric as well as important new avenues of inquiry. According to David Goodwin, classical rhetoric experienced a revival of sorts as an area of study, but along with this revival came redirection. Some scholars sought to understand communication more broadly, with varying degrees of attention to classical rules. Some left off consideration of those rules altogether and sought to understand dynamics of persuasive communication that were not limited to speeches and the classical rules for speeches. Another aspect of innovation was the way in which rhetorical criticism interfaced with fields as diverse as sociology, anthropology, psychology, linguistics, and literary theory. Movements of the postmodern mood, such as structuralism and

---

68. Ibid., 38.
69. Augustine, *DDC* 3.37.56.

post-structuralism, became currents where one could find rhetorical analysis in the broad sense.[70] Occasionally, rhetorical analysis in this broad sense was applied to the study of Christianity in late antiquity, as seen with the studies of Cameron and Brown mentioned above. They both treat Augustine at points in their analysis, and so they provide some important foundational work for the investigation here.

Cameron sketches the outlines of the development of Christian discourse that created an intellectual and imaginative world. She also shows some of the ways in which that world was rooted in lines of non-Christian discourse. Related to the development of new imaginative worlds are shifts in power relations. Cameron and Brown investigate the way these power shifts were associated with the emergence of Christian discourse. What follows in the rest of this chapter is consideration of the way in which Augustine was involved in the construction of an imaginative world, the way in which that world was rooted in contemporary lines of discourse, and the way in which the emerging Catholicizing discourse was related to shifts in social power.

New Worlds

The educational system that we have discussed served to create and maintain an imaginative world that in turn created and maintained a social order. The guardians of this prevailing social order and its imaginative world were the grammarians and rhetoricians. They made men of power to rule. Focusing on Africa, works of men like Virgil and Cicero served to establish the accepted language of discourse for the elite. By the standards of common people, this Latin was archaic, but for those who wielded, or wanted to wield, power, this form and style of Latin were a code that insured recognition by others of the elite. The imaginative and intellectual world that was created was populated by figures such as Aeneas, and was concerned with the life and duty of the wise man. It was a world where eloquence and wisdom existed in tension. It was a world that was not readily open to innovation that challenged tradition, as it was imposed from the top down by the government of the empire, on the one hand, or that challenged tradition that emerged out of local contexts, on the other.

What can be described as religion often mediated between countervailing forces of the imperial and the local, of tradition and innovation. In Roman Africa, for example, the local tradition, extending back to Phoenician settlement, of Baal and Tanit merged with the Roman cults Saturn of Juno (Caelestis).[71] Appropriate

---

70. *Encyclopedia of Contemporary Literary Theory*, 1993 ed., s.v. "Rhetorical Criticism," by David Goodwin.

71. For an argument for the endurance of Punic civilization and particularly ritual and mentalities associated with religion, see Frend, *The Donatist Church*, 36ff.

temples, priesthoods, and rituals gave opportunity for the local elites to reconcile tensions and give expression to an imaginative and intellectual world that confirmed their status. Activities ranging from serving on the town council to sponsoring games and giving to the poor were done in accordance with the imaginative and intellectual world constructed from the adjudication of various traditions.[72] The emergence of Christianity participated in this delicate navigation. At certain times and in certain places, it was smooth sailing; at other times and in other places, the going was quite rough.[73] Cameron argues that Christian discourse from Constantine onwards, on the one hand, became more pervasive by way of accommodation and assimilation, and, on the other hand, contained a paradoxical element that resisted imperial takeover.[74]

Going back to the second and third centuries, Cameron traces two aspects of the Christian movement in its diverse complexity that distinguished it as a substantially different worldview. First, it was figural,[75] and second, it was narrative.[76] She argues that Christianity emerged in a space where wider movements, like the second sophistic and romance literature, provided lines of continuity for its discourse. Its innovation came with the development of figures and the narratives creatively held in tension with history and transcendent reality. With Jesus Christ as central, Christians, in varying degrees and in various ways, spoke of the whole sweep of human history from beginning to end, of the alienation of humans from the divine and their reconciliation—all with reference to the preexistence, earthly life, death, resurrection, and return of Jesus of Nazareth.

Key elements in the development of this discourse were the diverse writings composed by Christians, creedal definitions of its teachings, and its network of teachers. By the end of the second century, a Catholic tradition can be said to have emerged, at least in incunabula, marked by its canon, creed, and clergy. From our twenty-first-century vantage point, we can be led astray in thinking solely in terms of a Bible, particular creeds, and an institutional church. There was a diversity

---

72. See Brown, *Power and Persuasion*, 78ff.

73. Ibid., chap. 3, 71–117. This chapter describes the way in which Christian monks and bishops became leaders of a "populist" kind of force that could be very powerful in late antique cities. Thus they provided an alternative system of patronage. For more on the kind of tension that developed between Augustine and civic notables, see Claude Lepelley, "Saint Augustin et la cité romano-africaine," in *Jean Chrysostome et Augustin*, edited by Charles Kannengiesser (Paris, 1975), 13–39. More will be said below about this article and other important work from Lepelley.

74. Cameron, *Christianity and the Rhetoric of Empire*, 155.

75. Ibid., chap. 2.

76. Ibid., chap. 3.

of Christian writings just as there was a diversity of Christian communities and tenets that united them. Looking at what Augustine participated in, we can see the development of a tradition that was styled as "Catholic" by Augustine and his colleagues. New figures, new narratives, and ways of reading already established narratives were crucial to the advancement of a Christianity that was Catholic, and thus, for Augustine, true Christianity, over and against alternatives.

We have seen that during most of his career before his conversion, Augustine had a strong commitment to the elite culture, its texts, and its imaginative and intellectual world drawn principally from its non-Christian past, as well as a strong aversion to Catholic Christianity, its texts, and its imaginative worlds. Augustine says that his standard of eloquence was Cicero, and that by comparison the Bible seemed barbaric. With Ambrose, however, Augustine was exposed to a new way of reading that enabled him to reconstruct his imaginative world. Augustine then in turn takes up the use of the Bible as the cornerstone of his new rhetoric. Increasingly throughout the 390s, the Bible, and in particular Genesis and the writings of Paul, formed the shaping of Augustine's thought. As Augustine became immersed in this Catholic tradition, he became an advocate and innovator of it as well. Against the Donatists, for example, we have seen that Augustine took up the figure of the "blessed seed of Abraham" out of the Genesis narrative to present a Catholicized prophetic reading of the text, patriarchal history, and the relatively recent history of the controversy between the Catholics and the Donatists. This same figure Augustine used, as we shall see, against non-Christian polytheists to hasten the waning of their social power. In both cases, the text was claimed for the Catholic cause and used to buttress truth claims espoused by Augustine and his colleagues.

Though the Bible was the raw material for the development of the new imaginative world, it is clear that there are lines of continuity with the traditional canon of authors. Cicero, as we have seen, is an enduring model for Augustine. Beyond Cicero, there is a host of authors that can be found to have a lasting presence in Augustine. In Plotinus, for example, Augustine found a philosopher that led him in the way of wisdom. The way in which the *Confessions* weaves together the language and imagery of the prodigal son and Plotinus's narrative of the fallen soul is clear testament to this fact.

Another way in which the emerging Christian discourse was rooted in the traditional discourse was the way in which verbal contestation worked in late antiquity. Oratorical training, in fact, initially served to prepare the Greek citizen for democratic participation. By the late empire, the use for training had dropped out and public performance became more important. As the empire came to swirl with various religious and philosophical currents, public disputation became the way these options were introduced and tested. Lim, as we have seen, portrays this trend and how Augustine was part of it.

Conclusion: Augustine the Power-Shifting Spin Doctor[77]

The cultivation and maintenance of power was done through the educational system. Eloquence, developed by men, was the basis of the structure of the social elite that was dominated by men. From the Roman republic to the early and then late empire, the extent of this circle expanded, in terms of numbers of people, but the literary culture was a constant, crucial element. Even when access could be gained to the elite through alternate roots, such as through the military, the sheer weight of tradition tended to block any sure, steady progress by that route over time.

For a few years now, the term "spin doctor" has been used to designate someone whose role it is to take negative public perception of a candidate or a party and spin it or turn it into a positive perception. Since the historic, extremely negative publicity that former president of the United States Bill Clinton received, the meaning of spin doctor has grown to be even more negative in its connotation. That is, the spin doctor is increasingly seen as someone who is tasked with trying to cover up some misdeeds of a candidate or party. A more neutral evaluation can be found in some of the scholarly literature on public relations and political discourse. Spin doctoring has become defined, studied, and even imitated. The neutral and more positive evaluations of spin doctoring come from those who recognize the role as a political function imbedded in modern media culture.

I want to evoke some of the politically charged nature of the designation by calling Augustine a spin doctor. But I want to back off the almost overwhelming negativity associated with the term to play up some positive, or at least neutral, meanings. From the developing literature, we can recognize the spin doctor as someone savvy enough about communications, public relations, and marketing to

---

77. Main Entry: spin doctor. Function: noun. Date: 1984: a person (as a political aide) responsible for ensuring that others interpret an event from a particular point of view, http://www.m-w.com/cgi-bin/dictionary, accessed (March 25, 2011). Despite *Merriam Webster's* designation of the coinage, the functions, if not the concept go further back in history. See also "The Spin Doctor: An Alternative Model of Public Relations," *Public Relations Review* 20, no. 1 (Spring 1994): 19–27; Frank Esser, Carrsten Reinemann, and David Fan, "Spin Doctors in the United States, Great Britain and Germany: Metacommunication about Media Manipulation," *Press/Politics* 6, no. 1 (Winter 2001): 16–45; and Ray Boston, "Spinning for a Living," *History Today* 46, no. 9 (September 1996): 8–9.

get across clearly and persuasively the message of a candidate or party in the public political arena. Augustine, in some sense, was the "cover person" for the Catholic Church in Africa, but he was also the great communicator of the Catholic Church in Africa in its efforts to be dominant, both religiously and socially. Although Augustine does not take on significance in relation to the kinds of media that are present today, he was astute and savvy enough in the uses of the media of his time to advance the aims of his party, the Catholic Church. Thus, Augustine is the Spin Doctor, the Catholic Church is the party, and the message to be communicated is that, in terms of humans' relationship with the Divine, there is only one way that works: that is, the Catholic way. The Catholic way is universal in its extent, both geographically and socially. The Catholic Church is for all lands and for all classes, the elite and nonelite alike.

The Road to Unity
and Its Aftermath

CHAPTER FIVE

Catholicization and the Preaching Tours of Augustine

In a sermon given on January 1, 404, Augustine quips about the growth of the Church and the decline of its opponents.

> But now that it [the Church] has grown up and in the name of Christ is widely and copiously spread abroad, aren't those to be more lamented than ever, whose hearts are still closed right until now, and who *love what is futile and seek what is false* (Ps. 4:3)? Yes of course, those few who have remained cut off from the human race by heaven knows what stiff-necked, unreasonable obstinacy are surely entitled to greater compassion, because they are wasting away with a worse disease, which resists the healing power even of such a great authority.
>
> (9) And if only it were just the pagans we had wring our hands over! We would then be wringing them for practically nobody. Let Christians stop going to the theaters; the pagans will slink away from them, even if not out of shame at what a small audience they constitute.[1]

Explicitly, pagans are named; implicitly, a distinction is being made between true Catholic Christians and false Christians who may believe, or do, a number of things

---

1. *Sermon* 198/ D 26/ M62. *The Works of Saint Augustine: A Translation for the 21st Century: Part III, Sermons*, Vol. 11: *New Sermons*, translated and notes by Edmund Hill, O.P.; and edited by John E. Rotelle, O.S.A. (Hyde Park, NY: New City Press, 1998). All translations of sermons will be taken from this *Works of Saint Augustine* unless otherwise noted.

not in accordance with Catholic teaching. This kind of rhetoric from Augustine presents itself as descriptive, but, in fact, the reality does not quite correspond to what Augustine says. In this chapter, we shall examine the rhetoric, the reality, and the gap between the two during the period of time from the summer of 403 to the issuing of the Edict of Unity in February 405. Augustine, in the rhetoric of sermons like the one quoted above, promotes Catholicization, his ideal for social order that was developed from his personal convictions and in collaboration with others. Catholicization, as a plan for Africa, was first clearly seen in his *Epistle* 22. Beginning with the Council of Hippo in 393, the prime institutional engine for Catholicization was put into motion. In examining these sermons, we focus on the way Augustine promotes Catholicization as a preacher,[2] using his rhetoric to try and move people to his particular vision of social order. He confronts a lived world that is a different reality than the one that he rhetorically constructs in his preaching. Delight is an aspect of what he does, but it is subordinated to instructing people in the truth of the Catholic faith and moving them to live according to that truth.

The key examples that I will be examining are his sermons given at the African Catholic Bishops' Councils between August 403 and June 404. Before commenting on them, however, we will need to say more about the historical context, particularly its political and military contexts. This will help us understand the way in which Augustine and his colleagues moved towards the relationship with the government that brought about the Edict of Unity, a real and symbolically powerful action that put the Catholicization of Roman Africa prominently on the imperial agenda.

Social Political Context

The problem of the empire's stability was an old one. By the early fifth century, there were still internal problems of succession and external problems of rival states over the limes and barbarian tribes looking for better land and lives. First Diocletian, and then Constantine and his successors, brought the empire through the fourth century in ways that helped it to be much more stable than the third century had been. By the late fourth century, the empire had recovered from Julian's death in a disastrous campaign against Persia in 363, the death of Valens in another disaster at Adrianople against the migrating Visigoths, and the rise and fall of a few would-be emperors. Theodosius emerged as successor and eventually brought the empire under his sole control by 394, having crushed Eugenius the

---

2. A central aspect of his episcopal self-understanding. See Chapter 2.

Usurper. Theodosius ruled and waged war well, but he died that following year, in January 395. He left a unified empire to his two sons: Arcadius ruled in the east and Honorius the west. Both were boy emperors and were heavily guided by a series of ministers at court. For our interests, we must consider the role of Stilicho as Theodosius's designated regent for Honorius in the west.[3]

Stilicho rose to power as a commander and confidant of Theodosius.[4] In 384, he had taken an important diplomatic mission to Persia, and shortly thereafter, he married Theodosius's niece Serena. By 392–393, he had received the rank *magister militum* (master of soldiers). Also in 393, Stilicho participated with Theodosius in putting down a bid for power by Eugenius in the west. His position of power was further established when upon Theodosius's death, Stilicho claimed to have received guardianship of both of Arcadius and Honorius from the dying emperor, effectively making him ruler of the eastern and western halves of the empire.[5] Stilicho then placed his supporters in high offices. Strangely, although he had both eastern and western armies under his command, he returned the eastern armies to the control of Arcadius. Stilicho's control in the west was more secure, and in 399, he bound himself to Honorius as a father-in-law by giving the young emperor his daughter in marriage.

Honorius was barely ten years old when his father died, and Arcadius was seventeen or eighteen. A consensus of historians holds that neither distinguished themselves as strong and independent rulers. Honorius was under the influence of Stilicho until 408, when another faction in the western court, headed by Olympius,

3. For histories of the period, see Peter Brown's brief, illustrated *The World of Late Antiquity* (New York: Harcourt Brace Jovanovich, 1971). For an exhaustive study, see A. H. M. Jones, *The Later Roman Empire 284–602: A Social, Economic and Administrative Survey*, 2 vols. (Baltimore: Johns Hopkins University Press, 1992). And for comprehensive state of the field treatments of a number of topics and subperiods, see *Cambridge Ancient History*, vol. XIII: *The Late Empire A.D.*, 3rd ed., edited by Averil Cameron and Peter Garnsey (Cambridge University Press, 1998). Of particular interest is "The Dynasty of Theodosius," by R.C. Blockley, 111–137. Two important studies are John Matthews, *Western Aristocracies and Imperial Court A.D. 364–425* (Oxford: Clarendon Press, 1975); and Stephen Williams and Gerard Friell, *Theodosius the Empire at Bay* (New Haven: Yale University Press, 1994).

4. Peter Heather, "Stilicho," in *Late Antiquity: A Guide to the Postclassical World*, edited by G. W. Bowersock, Peter Brown and Oleg Grabar (Cambridge: Belknap Press of Harvard University Press, 1999). My main secondary sources for extended treatment of Stilicho are John Matthews, *Western Aristocracies and Imperial Court A.D. 364–425;* and Stephen Williams and Gerard Friell. Lastly, primary sources of relevance can be found in the works of the fourth- and fifth-century poet, Claudian, *Claudian*, 2 vols., edited and translated by Maurice Platnauer (Cambridge: Loeb, 1963). See, for example, *On Stilicho's Consulship* in *Claudian*, vol. 2.

5. Matthews, *Western Aristocracies*, 257–59. This claim is attested to by Claudian, *On Stilicho's Consulship*, 2:50ff.

engineered his downfall and execution. Olympius then effectively filled the power vacuum and guided Honorius.[6]

Although Stilicho was not able to assert the same level of influence on Arcadius that he had on Honorius, Arcadius was by no means independent. Ministers such as Rufinus, Eutropius, Anthemius, and others exerted varying degrees of influence over him.[7]

As the effective ruler of the west, Stilicho continued the strongly pro-Catholic policies of Theodosius. With respect to Africa, he even strengthened the imperial support of the Catholics. This was not solely out of religious zeal. There were political and military reasons for that support as well. As regards those issues, the chief catalyst for the African Catholic policy was most likely the revolt of Gildo, Count of Africa.

In 397, Gildo, who had earned favor by helping to put down the rebellion of his brother Firmus, now himself rebelled.[8] He sought greater independence by trying to shift the allegiance of his province from the western emperor to the eastern. Stilicho mobilized forces under the command of Gildo's brother Mascezel. By the summer of 398, Mascezel won victory over Gildo, but lost his life under suspicious circumstances upon his return to Italy to report to Stilicho. This revolt affected the religious policy of Stilicho because the Donatists were implicated as key supporters of Gildo. W. H. C. Frend argues that by as early as 396, Gildo and Optatus, the Donatist bishop of Thamugadi, "were allies in an attempt to impose extreme doctrines of Numidian Donatism on all North Africa." He further claims that "in 398 they were joint leaders of a revolt against Honorius which if successful might have lead to the transfer of allegiance of the African provinces from Ravenna to Constantinople."[9] And thus, the struggle of the Catholics against the Donatists took on added political importance.

Conciliar Catholicization Initiatives

Aside from the alliance of Optatus and Gildo, some Donatists were finding ways to exercise coercive force in Africa. These were the Circumcellions and their supporters.

---

6. Matthews, *Western Aristocracies*, 280ff.

7. John Matthews and Tim Cornell, *Atlas of the Roman World* (Oxford: Phaidon, 1982), 208.

8. For a description of the revolt of Firmus, see Frend, *The Donatist Church*, 197–199, and for discussion of the revolt of Gildo, see Chapter 14, "The Rule of Optatus and Gildo, A.D. 386–98," 208–226.

9. Ibid., 208.

Some Donatist clergy criticized the Circumcellions at times; others found them useful in challenging Catholics. They became particularly troublesome in the 390s, and even after the fall of Gildo into the early years of the fifth century.[10] The violence associated with Gildo's revolt prevented the African Catholic Bishops' Councils from meeting in 395, 396, and 398. In 397, a smaller council met in Hippo in June, and a full council met in Carthage in August. Once the plans of Gildo and Optatus came to nothing, the councils resumed. They actively sought the civil authority's defense and support against the Donatists and other rivals. By 399, measures were sought against pagans. While there was no council in 400, two met in 401; and in the early 400s, there were initiatives taken to challenge Donatist strength. Catholics sent missionaries into areas of Donatist strength in attempts to persuade the leadership and the congregations to switch sides. These efforts were met at times by Circumcellion violence.[11]

On August 25, 403, the council met at Carthage. Led by Aurelius, it decided that the Catholic bishops should engage their Donatist counterparts in debate.[12] This concerted effort at engagement unequivocally presumed the correctness of the Catholic position, which was evidently read as offensive, for the Donatists did not take up the challenge. According to Frend, less than a month later, the Catholics also requested of Proconsul Septmius that "the heretics of the community should be admonished 'in a kindly manner,' so that they could meditate upon their error, and not neglect to recognize it." Additionally, the Donatists were to be brought before the "municipal courts" so that the discussions with the Catholics might be in public.[13]

In response, Primian, the Donatist bishop of Carthage, circulated a letter accusing the Catholics of being persecutors. He wrote: "It would be indignity for the sons of the martyrs to meet with the descendants of the *traditores.*"[14] Augustine and Primian then became engaged in a war of words. We get to eavesdrop on some in *Ennarationes* III on Psalm 36, which we shall examine later. Escalation of rhetoric and escalation of violence between the council of August 25, 403, and the spring of 404 would lead the council of June 404 to send delegates to Ravenna to request from Emperor Honorius even stronger measures against the Donatists.

---

10. Ibid., 210, 211.

11. Ibid., 251. See also the work of Michael Gaddis in his *There Is No Crime for Those Who Have Christ: Religious Violence in the Christian Roman Empire* (Berkeley: University of California Press, 2005).

12. See Chapter 3.

13. Frend, *The Donatist Church*, 258–259, PL. xi, col. 1201.

14. Ibid., 259. Frend is quoting from Monceaux and uses him for discussing the back-and-forth of events between the Donatists represented by Primian and the Catholics represented by Augustine (Monceaux, *Histoire littéraire*, 6:131).

Augustine's controversy with the Donatists looms large during this period, described in many important studies on Donatism and in biographies on Augustine.[15] This is understandable given the prominence of the Donatists in Augustine's writings of the period. According to Pierre-Marie Hombert, Augustine's major anti-Donatist writings all come from this first decade of the fifth century.[16] They are:

> *Contra epistulam Parmeniani* (403–404)
> *Contra litteras Petiliani* (400–405)
> *Contra Cresconium grammaticum et donatistam* (406–407)
> *De baptismo* (404)

Their prominence is, I think, deceptive. Other import rivals of the Catholics get pushed further in the background than is warranted. A closer look at Augustine's treatises, letters, and sermons, and more careful consideration of other sources, such as the African councils' canons, reveal a more complex picture. For example, against the Manichees during this period, Augustine wrote the two following works:

> *Contra Faustum manichaeum* (400–402)
> *Contra Felicem* (404)

Also, *De consensu evangelistarum* (403–404) can be seen to be an anti-pagan work.[17] Augustine himself recognizes the variety of rivals, but reduces the complexity of the religious marketplace to a simple binary. In *Sermon* 62 of 399, he speaks of the

---

15. Bonner, *St. Augustine of Hippo*. Bonner does an introduction and life overview in the first three of his nine chapters, then he devotes two chapters out of the remaining nine to focus on each of Augustine's main controversies. Chapters 4 and 5 address the Manichees, Chapters 6 and 7 the Donatists, and 8 and 9 the Pelagians. This follows a rather convenient chronological path through Augustine's life where these controversies can be seen as sequential. Bonner, of course, knows better than to separate these absolutely, but his structure helps to focus on the nature of each controversy and Augustine's role in it. Having benefited from the work of people like Bonner, I am trying to bring into focus a particular period in Augustine's life where we can witness the simultaneity of his polemics. For studies that focus particularly on Augustine and the Donatists, see Geoffrey Grimshaw Wills, *Saint Augustine and the Donatist Controversy* (London: SPCK, 1950); Frend, *The Donatist Church*; and Maureen Tilley, *The Bible in Christian North Africa: The Donatist World* (Minneapolis: Fortress Press, 1997).

16. Pierre-Marie Hombert, *Nouvelle Recherches de Chronologie Augustinienne*, Collection des Études Augustiniennes, Séries Antiquité 163 (Paris: Institut d'Études Augustiniennes, 2000).

17. For these dates, I follow those of Hombert, which in some cases revise traditional datings. For Hombert's discussion of the rationale for his dating of works of this period as they were found listed in *Retractations* 2.6–2.26, see Hombert, "Premiere Partie," 9–195.

world as being composed of two groups: the Catholics stand on one side and a range of rivals on the other.[18]

> You should know, beloved, that their mutterings against us chime in with those of the heretics, those of the Jews. The heretics, the Jews and the pagans have united against unity. Because it so happens that the Jews, in some places, have been disciplined for their misbehavior, they accuse us, and suspect or pretend that we are always getting them treated like that. Because it has happened in some places that the heretics have paid the legal penalties for their irreligion and their frenzied acts of violence, they are now saying that we on every possible occasion are producing their harassment and eventual destruction. Again because the pagans, should they come to their senses—like the case of silly little boys in the mud and dirtying their hands, until the pedagogue comes up and roughly smacks the mud off their hands and shoves the school book into them; in the same way it is God's will, by means of the rulers who are obedient to him, to scare the heedless, childish minds of pagans into rubbing the dirt off their hands and doing something useful with them.[19]

An important part of the background to this sermon is probably conflict between pagans and Christians in response to a law of 399 ordering the closing of pagan temples.[20] Augustine sees rivals to the unity of the Catholic Church as fitting into three categories: Jews, pagans, and heretics. Looking now to the period between the council of 403 and the council of 404, we will also see Augustine rhetorically reducing a variety of opponents to one of these three categories. But, ultimately, whatever they are, they are a unity against the Catholic unity. This move gives Augustine persuasive leverage for the masses, but also for framing issues for the civil authorities such that all those who are not in the Catholic Church can be addressed by similar legal measures.

Augustine's Preaching Tours

After journeying to Carthage for the council of August 25, 403, Augustine stayed for several weeks, at least until late September. During his stay, he preached on many occasions at churches in the city, and a number of the sermons survive. Othmar Perler and Jean-Louis Maier, drawing on the works of a number of other

18. Frend, *The Donatist Church*, 250; Augustine, *Sermon* 62:18.

19. Augustine, *Sermon* 62:18.

20. Augustine mentions the closing in the *City of God (De Civitate Dei)* 18.54. Hill goes along with the consensus of scholarship in dating this sermon and linking it to the closings. See Hill's note 1 on *Sermon* 62. See also Brown, *Augustine of Hippo*, 227. For the law itself, see *Codex Theodosianus (CT)* 16.10.18.

scholars, date and locate several sermons of that period. Recently, however, Pierre-Marie Hombert has revised the dating of a number of sermons, although the bulk of the chronology that Perler and Maier present remains intact. Thus, the chronology of Augustine's preaching in Carthage after the August council runs as follows:

September 2, 403	*En. Ps.* 44 (Carthage at Basilica Restituta)[21]
September 3, 403	*En. Ps.* 56 (Carthage)
September 13, 403	*En. Ps.* 32.II.1 (Carthage at Mappalia)
September 14, 403	*Sermon* 313 (Carthage at the Tomb of Cyprian)
September 16, 403	*En. Ps.* 32.II.2 (Carthage at Domus Cypriani)
September 17, 403	*S* 32 (Carthage at Basilica Tricliarum)
September ?, 403	*En. Ps.* 36.I, II, and III (Carthage)[22]

Perler and Maier, as well as Hombert, leave open when exactly Augustine arrived in Carthage and when he left. They agree, however, that Augustine returned to Hippo sometime during the fall. It is from there that Perler and Maier have Augustine writing *Epistle* 76, an open letter to Donatist laity.[23]

During the fall, Perler and Maier also place an ambush of the Circumcellions that caught Possidius. In the aftermath, Augustine was drawn into the situation to help prove that Crispinus, the Donatist bishop of Calama, was not Catholic, and, hence, liable to fines against heretics. According to Possidius, Augustine had escaped an ambush by taking a wrong turn on a journey. It is unclear whether Augustine actually went to Calama to bring Crispinus and Possidius together, and to further intervene to have the fine waived even after Crispinus appealed to the emperor. But Augustine was, nevertheless, intimately involved in what happened. The violence of the Circumcellions, and the need for government restraint of that violence, are referred to in a significant way in his later writings, including sermons delivered upon his return to Carthage.

According to Perler and Maier, Augustine did not return to Carthage until early 404.[24] The discovery of sermons by François Dolbeau, however, has forced

---

21. Othmar Perler (with J.-L. Maier), *Les Voyages de saint Augustin* (Paris: Institut d'Études Augustiniennes, 1969), 246–249. Based on the works of Monceaux, Zarb, Kunzelmann, and Rondet, En. Ps. 44; 56; 57; 32.II.1; 32.II.2; *Sermon Guelferb*, 26; and *Sermon* 32 are all given by Perler and Maier as preached in Carthage at the churches listed. Perler and Maier, however, also accept Zarb's placement of *En. Ps.* 57 in September; I will follow Hombert's placement of the sermon in December based on more recent scholarship and in light of the discovery of the Dolbeau collection of sermons. See Hombert, 563–588.

22. Hombert, 12–13.

23. Perler, 247–249.

24. Ibid., 249.

a revision here as well. Dolbeau has placed some of the new sermons in Carthage during December 403. Hombert, following Dolbeau's work,[25] confirms those datings, and takes a series of sermons from the *Ennarationes in Psalmos* that Anne-Marie La Bonnardière placed in December 409 and convincingly argues for shifting the dating to December 404.[26] The revised chronology for Augustine's preaching places the following sermons in December and January, with some, perhaps, spilling over into the spring.

A Sunday in December 403	*Sermon* 114B/ M 12/ D 5 (Carthage)[27]
A Sunday in December 403	*En. in Ps.* 147 (Carthage)
Later in December 403	*S* 361/ M 10/ L 3 (Carthage)
Later in December 403	*S* 362/ M 11/ L 4 (Carthage)
After Christmas 403	*S* 51/ M 58/ L 1 (Carthage)
Also December 403	*En. in Ps.* 103 (Carthage)
	En. in Ps. 80 (Carthage)
	En. in Ps. 146 (Carthage)
	En. in Ps. 2 (Carthage)
	En. in Ps. 57 (Carthage)
	En. in Ps. 66 (Carthage)
January 1, 404	*S* 198/ M 62/ D 26 (Carthage) L 2
January 23, 404–405	*S* 359B/ M 5/ D 2 (Carthage)[28]
End of Winter	*S* 360A/ M 60/ D 24 (Carthage)
	S 360B/ M 61/ D 25 (Boseth)
	S 159B/ M 54/ D 21 (Thignica)
End of Winter	*S De utilitate ieiunii/* M 2 (Carthage)
	S 299A/ M 9/ D 4 (Carthage or Utica)
	S 352/ M 1 (Carthage)

Most of these sermons are in Carthage, but Augustine returns to Hippo by Easter, after preaching in some towns along the way. Augustine goes to Carthage once again in June for the African Catholic Bishops' Council. Having done this brief overview of Augustine's activities between the 403 and 404 councils, we shall

---

25. Hombert, 564, referring to Dolbeau, *Vingt-Six Sermons,* 325.

26. Hombert, 563–588. Hombert refers to the following article by Anne-Marie La Bonnardière "Les *Ennarationes in Psalmos* prêchées par saint Augustin à Carthage en décembre 409," *Recherches Augustiniennes* 11 (1976): 52–90.

27. Hombert, 565–566.

28. *Augustine Through the Ages: An Encyclopedia,* edited by Allan Fitzgerald (Grand Rapids, MI: Wm. B. Eerdmans, 1999); Augustine, *Sermones,* 789, in *Works of Saint Augustine.*

turn back to the two groups of sermons to consider what they can tell us about Augustine and Catholicization in this important period. At the conclusion of the chapter, we will consider the council of 404 as both an event of closure and an inauguration.

The September Group

Carthage had a large Christian community that included a good number of Catholics and Donatists. The collection of sermons that survives shows that Augustine was preaching in at least four different churches at that time, under the authority of his friend Aurelius. The first two sermons, *Enarrationes* 44 and 56, fall on successive days—September 2 and 3, 403. In both of these sermons, Augustine, aside from giving spiritual insight and exhortation for moral improvement, gives criticism of religious rivals. The term "heretics" is frequently used; often, as one might expect, it refers to the Donatists. But sometimes, given the argument where the term is couched, it seems as if Augustine has in mind a non-Nicene heresy of some sort. We also find criticism of pagans and Jews. I will offer commentary on each of the sermons in the September group, but, due to the much larger number of sermons in the second group, I will be more selective there.

Ennarationes 44

Ennarationes 44 opens with Augustine dealing with the title, "'For the sons of Korah, for the things that shall be changed.'" Augustine tells his hearers that the psalm is "sung of the sacred Marriage-feast; of the Bridegroom and the Bride; of the King and His people; of the Saviour and those who are to be saved. . . . His sons are we, in that we are the 'children of the Bridegroom'; and it is to us that this Psalm is addressed." He then focuses on the word "change" to introduce his binary framing of the world.

> 2. Why need I explain what is meant by, "for the things that shall be changed"? Every one who is himself "changed," recognizes the meaning of this. Let him who hears this, "for the things that shall be changed," consider what was before, and what is now. And first let him see the world itself to be changed, lately worshipping idols, now worshipping God; lately serving things that they themselves made, now serving Him by whom they themselves were made. Observe at what time the words, "for the things that shall be changed," were said. Already by this time the Pagans that are left are in dread of the "changed" state of things: and those who will not suffer themselves to be "changed" see the churches full; the temples deserted; see crowds here, and there solitude. They marvel at the things so changed; let them read that they were foretold;

let them lend their ears to Him who promised it; let them believe Him who fulfils that promise. But each one of us, brethren, also undergoes a change from "the old" to "the new man": from an infidel to a believer: from a thief to a giver of alms: from an adulterer to a man of chastity; from an evildoer to a doer of good. To us then be sung the words, "for the things that shall be changed"; and so let the description of Him by whom they were changed, begin.[29]

Augustine and his hearers are those who are "changed" internally according to their commitment to Christ. They are also a part of the "change," in that they participate in what Augustine argues is foretold of the true Church, which is, with respect to the psalm, "the Bride" of Christ (*En. in Ps.* 44:2). In case there was any doubt as to which church he speaks of, in section 5 Augustine says that he desires his interpretations to be understood "consistently with the true Catholic Faith." In explaining this faith in light of the verses of the psalm, he presents readings that portray a Catholic/Nicene Christology. With "[m]ine heart hath uttered a good word," in verse 1, he finds reference to the generation of the son from the father that is from the heart and not from human procreation. He says: "And whence but from His heart, from His very inmost, does God utter the Word?" The "works" then spoken to the King are "in 'the Word,' as in the Word, as in the Only-Begotten, as in the 'Word of God.'"[30] In section 10, picking up "sword" from verse 4, Augustine continues to preach Christologically by interpreting it to mean "Word." However, he also introduces the passage from Matthew 25 where Jesus says he comes not to bring peace but the sword, and where he says that he will be a source of division.

> By what "sword," but that which Christ brought, was this division wrought? And indeed, my brethren, we see this exemplified daily. Some young man is minded to give himself up to God's service; his father is opposed to it; they are "divided against each other": the one promises an earthly inheritance, the other loves an heavenly; the one promises one thing, the other prefers another. The father should not think himself wronged: God alone is preferred to him. And yet he is at strife with the son, who would fain give himself to God's service. But the spiritual sword is mightier to separate them, than the ties of carnal nature to bind them together. This happens also in the case of a mother against her daughter; still more also in that of a daughter-in-law against a mother-in-law. For sometimes in one house mother-in-law and daughter-in-law are found orthodox and heretical respectively. And where that sword is forcibly felt, we do not dread the repetition of Baptism. Could daughter be divided against mother; and could not daughter-in-law be divided against mother-in-law?[31]

29. Augustine, *Ennarationes* 44:1.
30. Ibid., 44:5.
31. Ibid.

This passage is interesting in that the "repetition of baptism" reference clearly implies that Augustine sees Donatism as a heresy. Then, in sections 10 and 11, he invokes a favorite biblical theme used against the Donatists, and learned from Tyconius: "the blessed seed of Abraham."[32] Augustine uses this passage here and elsewhere as a prophecy of the triumph of Christianity. Here it is not directly asserted but mediated through the other passages:

> "Because of truth, meekness, and righteousness." Truth was restored unto us, when "the Truth sprung out of the earth: and Righteousness looked out from heaven." Christ was presented to the expectation of mankind, that in Abraham's Seed "all nations should be blessed." The Gospel has been preached. It is "the Truth." What is meant by "meekness"? The Martyrs have suffered; and the kingdom of God has made much progress from thence, and advanced throughout all nations; because the Martyrs suffered, and neither "fell away," nor yet offered resistance; confessing everything, concealing nothing; prepared for everything, shrinking from nothing.[33]

In this triumphal mind-set, Augustine can even call the Jews to be witnesses to the truth of Catholic Christianity as custodians of the Bible.[34]

> Who then is the God that is "anointed" by God? Let the Jews tell us; these Scriptures are common to us and them. It was God, who was anointed by God: you hear of an "Anointed" one; understand it to mean "Christ." For the name of "Christ" comes from "chrism"; this name by which He is called "Christ" expresses "unction": nor were kings and prophets anointed in any kingdom, in any other place, save in that kingdom where Christ was prophesied of, where He was anointed, and from whence the Name of Christ was to come. It is found nowhere else at all: in no one nation or kingdom. God, then, was anointed by God; with what oil was He anointed, but a spiritual one? For the visible oil is in the sign, the invisible oil is in the mystery; the spiritual oil is within. "God" then was "anointed" for us, and sent unto us; and God Himself was man, in order that He might be "anointed": but He was man in such a way as to be God still. He was God in such a way as not to disdain to be man. "Very man and very God"; in nothing deceitful, in nothing false, as being everywhere true, everywhere "the Truth" itself. God then is man; and it was for this cause that "God" was "anointed," because God was Man, and became "Christ."[35]

Before returning, in section 23, to criticism of the Jews, for crucifying the Christ they failed to see, in section 22 Augustine describes the universality of the

---

32. See above, Chapter 3, where Tyconius is discussed in connection with the African roots of his Catholic worldview.

33. Augustine, *En. in Ps.* 44:12.

34. Ibid., 56:7.

35. Ibid., 44:18.

Catholic Church that is accommodating of different peoples of different languages, even, but nevertheless, held together in unity of belief.

> "On Thy right hand did stand the Queen," in a vesture of gold, clothed about with divers colours." What is the vesture of this Queen? It is one both precious, and also of divers colours: it is the mysteries of doctrine in all the various tongues: one African, one Syrian, one Greek, one Hebrew, one this, and one that; it is these languages that produce the divers colours of this vesture. But just as all the divers colours of the vesture blend together in the one vesture, so do all the languages in one and the same faith. In that vesture, let there be diversity, let there be no rent. See we have "understood" the divers colours of the diversity of tongues; and the vesture to refer to unity: but in that diversity itself, what is meant by the "gold"? Wisdom itself. Let there be any diversity of tongues you please, but there is but one "gold" that is preached of: not a different gold, but a different form of that gold. For it is the same Wisdom, the same doctrine and discipline that every language preaches. In the languages there is diversity; gold in the thoughts.[36]

Moving to conclusion, Augustine returns to the theme of diversity and unity. This time it is to emphasize the unity found in the hierarchy of the Church's "princes" or "fathers," who are the bishops. These bishops serve now, having been established in a reliable succession that goes back to the apostles.

> Think not thyself abandoned then, because thou seest not Peter, nor seest Paul: seest not those through whom thou wert born. Out of thine own offspring has a body of "fathers" been raised up to thee. "Instead of thy fathers, have children been born to thee." Observe how widely diffused is the "Temple of the King," that "the virgins that are not led to the Temple of the King," may know that they have nothing to do with that marriage. "Thou shall make them princes over all the earth." This is the Universal Church: her children have been made "princes over all the earth": her children have been appointed instead of the "fathers." Let those who are cut off own the truth of this, let them come to the One Body: let them be led into the Temple of the King. God hath established His Temple everywhere: hath laid everywhere "the foundations of the Prophets and Apostles."[37]

Ennarationes in Ps. 44 effectively sets the tone for the series that Augustine preaches in Carthage. The polemics against the Donatists, and other heretics, Jews, and pagans, are found throughout. All are not equally present in all sermons; sometimes one or two are foregrounded while the others recede or drop out completely. Overall, however, there is a consistency in his presentation of a Catholic Christianity that stands as the true way to God, whereas all other religious rivals

---

36. Ibid., 44:22.
37. Ibid., 44:29.

are, in one way or another, deficient. I shall move on now to give some examples from other sermons in the first group to illustrate this consistency.

Ennarationes 56

Ennarationes in Ps. 56 focuses on the Jews early on in an interesting way. Noting that the title of this psalm refers to David's flight from Saul, Augustine interprets Christ as David and the Jews as Saul. Thus, according to Augustine, the psalm refers to the incarnation and Jesus's persecution by the Jews.

> For a cavern may be understood as a lower part of the earth. And certainly, as is manifest and certain to all, His Body in a Tomb was laid, which was cut in a Rock. This Tomb therefore was the Cavern; thither He fled from the face of Saul. For so long the Jews did persecute Him, even until He was laid in a cavern. Whence prove we that so long they persecuted Him, until therein He was laid? Even when dead, and, on the Cross hanging, with lance they wounded Him. But when shrouded, the funeral celebrated, He was laid in a cavern, no longer had they anything which to the Flesh they might do. Rose therefore the Lord again out of that cavern unhurt, uncorrupt, from that place whither He had fled from the face of Saul: concealing Himself from ungodly men, whom Saul prefigured, but showing Himself to His members. For the members of Him rising again by His members were handled: for the members of Him, the Apostles, touched Him rising again and believed; and behold nothing profited the persecution of Saul.

In section 7, Augustine gives particularly scathing attacks, again linked to the charge that Jews persecuted Christ.

> The Jews raged against Christ, they were overbearing against Christ. Where? In the city of Jerusalem. For where they reigned, there they were puffed up, there their necks they lifted up. After the Passion of the Lord thence they were rooted out; and they lost the kingdom, wherein Christ for King they would not acknowledge. In what manner they have been given unto reproach, see ye: dispersed they have been throughout all nations, nowhere having a settlement, nowhere a sure abode. But for this reason still Jews they are, in order that our books they may carry to their confusion. For whenever we wish to show Christ prophesied of, we produce to the heathen these writings. And lest perchance men hard of belief should say that we Christians have composed these books, so that together with the Gospel which we have preached we have forged the Prophet, through whom there might seem to be foretold that which we preach: by this we convince them; namely, that all the very writings wherein Christ hath been prophesied are with the Jews, all these very writings the Jews have. We produce documents from enemies, to confound other enemies. In what sort of reproach therefore are the Jews? A document the Jew carrieth, wherefrom a Christian may believe. Our librarians they have become, just as slaves are wont behind their masters to carry documents, in such sort that these faint in carrying, those profit by reading. Unto such a reproach

have been given the Jews: and there hath been fulfilled that which so long before hath been foretold, "He hath given unto reproach those that trampled on me." But how great a reproach it is, brethren, that this verse they should read, and themselves being blind should look upon their mirror! For in the same manner the Jews appear in the holy Scripture which they carry, as appeareth the face of a blind man in a mirror: by other men it is seen, by himself not seen.

More of this kind of polemic continues through to section 11, when he turns to criticizing "the heretics."

But what kind of madness heretics are afflicted with, I pray you observe. They being cut off from the bond of the Church of Christ, and to a part holding, the whole losing, will not communicate with the whole earth, where is spread abroad the glory of Christ. But we Catholics are in all the earth, because with all the world we communicate, wherever the Glory of Christ is spread abroad. For we see that which then was sung, now fulfilled. There hath been exalted above the Heavens our God, and above all the earth the Glory of the Same. O heretical insanity! That which thou seest not thou believest with me, that which thou seest thou deniest: thou believest with me in Christ exalted above the Heavens, a thing which we see not; and deniest His Glory over all the earth, a thing which we see.

Once again, although he does not name them, it is clear that, because they "will not communicate with the whole earth," the heretics to whom he refers are clearly the Donatists. They, of course, are contrasted with the Catholics, who "are in all the earth, because with all the world we communicate." Thus, *En. in Ps.* 56 occupies itself mostly with anti-Jewish polemics, sparsely with anti-Donatist polemics, and no explicit anti-pagan polemics.

Ennarationes 32.II.1[38] (Ex. 2 on Ps. 32), *Sermon* 313C, and *Ennarationes* 32.II.2 (Ex. 3 on Ps. 32)

In mid-September, Augustine preached a series of sermons around the feast of Cyprian. First is *En. in Ps.* 32.II.1 at the Mappalia basilica, then *Sermon* 313C at the tomb of Cyprian, and lastly, *En. in Ps.* 32. II.2. The first, at the Mappalia, is almost absent of the Catholicizing anti-rival rhetoric. The sole exception occurs in

38. That is, *Ennarationes* on Psalm 32, 2nd series, sermon 1. This designation is found in Perler and Maier, 248. There were a total of three sermons on En 32, but only one in the first series. The second series has two given on the Feast of Cyprian. Thus this sermon can also be referred to as *Exposition* 1 on *Ps.* 32, as it is in *Expositions of the Psalms 1–32: The Works of Saint Augustine, A Translation for the 21st Century*, III/15, introduction by Michael Fiedrowicz, and translated and notes by Maria Boulding (Hyde Park, NY: New City Press, 2000).

section 6, where Augustine attacks Jews. Having focused on the "psaltery" of Ps. 32:2, he argues that the ten-stringed instrument signifies the Ten Commandments. Then, in commenting on observation of the Sabbath, he says: "*Observe the day of the Sabbath*, not after a sensual fashion, not as the Jews, whose delight it is to spend their leisure in evil pursuits. It would be better for them to spend the livelong day digging than the livelong day dancing."[39]

The next day provides Augustine with the opportunity to preach about the bishop, who had great significance in the African tradition. Augustine begins with rhetorical flourish:

> Today's anniversary celebration of the passion of this outstanding martyr of Christ, through whom above all others he governed this Church, increased it, adorned it and made it illustrious, does not recall him to our minds as though he had dropped out of them, but rather commends him to us all the more happily and gratefully, fixed permanently as he is in our memories. And so it is my duty with a formal sermon to sermon to praise in the Lord the soul of his servant, so that *the gentle may hear and be delighted.*[40]

This short sermon is full of praise for Cyprian as a model of true Christianity and martyrdom. Not "for this city alone, or for Africa alone,"[41] but

> while this is the duty of all saints, this martyr of ours today gains the reward not only for himself but also for very many others besides. The fact is, he spread the good odor of Christ far and wide by his teaching about Christ, his living in Christ, his dying for Christ.

Augustine is concerned with claiming Cyprian for the Catholic Church and not allowing the Donatists to have any claim on him. Again, without naming them, he states that "he [Cyprian] crushed the effrontery of heretics by his demonstration

---

39. Augustine, *En. in Ps.* 32:6. Here translators Scholastica Hebin and Felicitas Corrigan note that this is an indication of the significance of the presence of a sizable Jewish community in Carthage. This is significant for our understanding of Augustine's polemics. From Augustine's remarks about the Jews to this point in the series, we might conclude that the Jews were only paper rivals. His criticisms were oriented towards the past, towards the text. Here in *En.* Ps. 32:6, Augustine turns from the text to contemporary activities and events, as he does with anti-Donatist and anti-pagan polemics. Thus, Catholicization is not just limited to the internal discourse of texts; rather, it also involves competition with real rivals Augustine, Scholastica Hebgin, and Felicitas Corrigan. *St. Augustine on the Psalms 2, Psalms 30–37. Ancient Christian writers*, 30. Westminster, Md: Newman Press, 1961, 108n22.

40. Psalm 34:2, in Augustine, *Sermon* 313C:1.

41. Ibid.

CATHOLICIZATION AND THE PREACHING TOURS OF AUGUSTINE | 133

and preaching of unity."[42] Clearly, Augustine has in mind the theme of unity in Cyprian as seen in his *On the Unity of the Church*. The Donatists, however, had in mind the Cyprian who was the defender of the purity and holiness of the Church. That Cyprian advocated rebaptism. This fact Augustine had difficulty explaining away, so he focused on Cyprian as the defender of unity. This fact the Donatists had trouble explaining away.[43]

At the Domus Cypriani two days later, Augustine returns to consideration of Psalm 32 in *En. in Ps.* 32.II.2. The early part of the sermon is devoted to expounding upon God's mercy and judgment from verse 5. Augustine argues that from that passage, supported by others, God's mercy was prophesied to spread throughout the world. The apostles are interpreted as sheep among wolves in the spread of that mercy. Augustine then says:

> In fact it is because of the sending of those sheep into the midst of the wolves that we are now keeping sacred the memorials of the martyrs. When the blessed martyr's body was pierced through, this very place was full of wolves: one sheep, taken captive, has overcome all those wolves; slaughtered, one sheep has filled this place with sheep. Then the sea was raging with the mighty waves of the persecutor. It burst upon dry land that thirsted for God's heaven. But now through the sufferings of those which broke the attack, Christ's name is glorified: walking on the crests of the seething flows, He has taken possession even of those very forces. These are the accomplished facts. Do you then suppose that when those who do not share our faith witness our assemblies, our celebrations and solemnities, the manifest and public honors done to our God in these days, do you suppose they look calmly, do you suppose they do not quiver with rage? It is now that the prophecy spoken of them is fulfilled: The wicked shall see and be angry. What though he be angry? Sheep that you are, do not be afraid of the wolf.[44]

The triumphalism is tempered by caution for those who may not be able to "rage," but who, nevertheless, "rumble with a secret suppressed murmur." Yet Augustine becomes explicitly martial, encouraging his hearers by exhorting them as the Church personified. "Then let the Church go forth, let her march ahead; the road is prepared, our highway has been prepared by our Commander in chief. Let us be zealous in treading the paths of good works, for that is our manner of marching."[45] Augustine seems to be concerned that his hearers not become overconfident in

---

42. Ibid.

43. This debate is present in many of Augustine's anti-Donatist works. However, extended treatment can be found in *De Baptismo*. In this work, Augustine deals extensively with the legacy of Cyprian. For discussion of this work, and these issues as they relate to Latin ecclesiological traditions, see Evans, 65–91.

44. Augustine, *Ennarationes in Ps.* 32.II.2:9.

45. Ibid., 2:10.

their triumph because "distress of trials from unexpected quarters" may be sent by the Lord to "train" the Catholic Christian.[46]

In bringing the sermon to a close, Augustine distinguishes the Donatists from the other religious rivals, the pagans and the Jews, in a way that is consistent with the initiatives called for at the August 25 Council of Carthage. Augustine invites his hearers to exercise charity "not only among yourselves, but also towards those who are without, whether they be still pagans . . . or whether they be separated from us, acknowledging the same Head as ourselves and separated from our body."[47] For Augustine, these "separated from our body," and not the pagans or the Jews, can be called "brothers." He implores his hearers with impassioned rhetoric to be fervent in seeking to bring them back to unity. Beginning with a quotation from Isaiah 66:5 of his Septuagint-based text, Augustine says:

> *To those who say to you: Ye are not our brethren, say ye: Ye are our brethren.* Look round and see of whom he could have spoken thus: was it the pagans? No, for according to the Scriptures and ecclesiastical usage we do not call them our brethren. Was it of the Jews who did not believe in Christ? Consult the Apostle, and you will see that when he speaks of brethren without any qualification, he means to refer only to Christians: *For a brother or sister,* says he, *is not under servitude in such cases:* in speaking of matrimony, he has given the title of brother and sister to a Christian man and woman. Again he says: *But thou, why judgest thou thy brother, or thou, why dost thou despise thy brother?* And in another place, *But you do* wrong *and defraud,* he says, *and that to your brethren.* Hence those who tell us: You are not our brethren, call us pagans. For that reason indeed they want to rebaptize us, saying that we do not possess what they give. From this follows their error in denying that we are their brethren. But why did the prophet tell us: *Say ye to them: Ye are our brethren,* if not because we recognize they have something we do not repeat? They, by refusing to recognize our baptism, deny that we are their brethren; we, on the other hand, by not repeating theirs but recognizing it for our own, say to them: *Ye are our brethren. . . .* I adjure you, therefore, brethren, through the very heart of charity, by whose milk we are nourished, by whose bread we are strengthened, through Christ our Lord, through His Meekness—for it is time for us to pour forth upon them great charity and abundant mercy, beseeching God on their behalf that now at last He may give them sound understanding, to come to their senses again and see themselves, and realize that they have no argument whatsoever against the truth; nothing is left to them but sickly spite, all the more feeble in proportion as it fancies itself formal. I adjure you on behalf of the weak, of those who mind earthly things, of the brutish and carnal-minded, who are yet our brethren, who celebrate the same holy mysteries, identical though not in our company; who make answer with the same Amen, identical though not in our company: pour forth to God the quintessence of your charity on their behalf. I have indeed done something for

46. Ibid.
47. Ibid., 2:29.

their welfare in the council, which time does not allow me to explain to you today. Hence I exhort you to assemble more promptly and in larger numbers, and I count on you to warn the brethren who are not here present to assemble tomorrow at the Church of the Tricliae.[48]

Sermon 32

Sadly, the sermon that he promised at the Tricliae has been lost. But it should be clear that Augustine had in mind the mobilization of the total Catholic body in the strategic city of Carthage in an effort to bring about reunion. Instead we have *Sermon* 32, which Edmund Hill and Eric Rebillard place on the following day. This placement is based on a reference in section 23 of the sermon that seems to refer to *Ennarationes in Ps.* 32.II.2. Hill, however, notes that aside from not fulfilling the promise Augustine made in that sermon, *Sermon* 32 "makes not the slightest reference to the Donatists."[49] Certainly we might expect something. What could account for the absence? What do we do with the sermon? If we find the lack of Donatists troubling enough, we do not place it here in Carthage in September 403. I am not going to take that option, though. I think that it is fine to leave it, and I believe that I have a possible reason why Augustine might not have an obvious Donatist polemic here.

I believe that Augustine uses Tyconius in this sermon, and he sought to avoid explicit discussion of Donatism because he was using the famous Donatist exegete. Here, Augustine seems to make reference at a number of places to Tyconius's rules. For example, in section 5, as he interprets the story of David and Goliath, Augustine says: "In the whole scene you can observe two kinds of life sparring with each other, the old one among the Philistines, the new one among the Israelites. On that side the body of the devil, on this a prefiguration of the Lord Jesus Christ."[50] This distinction between the devil's body and Christ is probably a use, on Augustine's part, of the first, second, and seventh rules of Tyconius, which are: "The Lord, and His Body," "the Lord's Bipartite Body," and "the Devil and His Body," respectively.[51] Further confirmation of this is found in section 6, where Augustine says: "Your holinesses should know this too, besides other rules, in order to be able to learn things easily when you listen to the reader." But the question may remain, even if

---

48. Ibid.
49. He speaks on this theme for some time, 10–13.
50. Augustine, *Sermon* 32:5.
51. See Tyconius, *Tyconius: The Book of Rules,* translated by William S. Babcock, edited by Robert L. Wilken and William R. Schoedel, SBL Texts and Translations Series 31, Early Christian Literature Series 7 (Atlanta: Scholars Press, 1989), chaps. 3.8, 4.3.2.

he used Tyconius, why not criticize the Donatists as well? In *Against the Letter of Parmenian*, praise for Tyconius is prominently featured, as well as condemnation of the Donatist movement as a whole. Augustine can be surprising in what he says and does not say. Why, for example, is there no mention of the Donatists in the *Confessions*?

Nevertheless, in this sermon, there is no clear, explicit critique of Donatism; instead, Augustine seems preoccupied with an anti-Jewish and anti-pagan polemic. And, as always, he exhorts his hearers to take up the Christian life consistent with Catholic morals. Thus, he still manages to present his twofold agenda of Catholicization. A particularly interesting point of *Sermon* 32 is the way Augustine foregrounds his self-understanding in the opening of the sermon:

> Our Lord and God takes care of and heals every ailment of the soul, and so he produced many medicines from the holy scriptures (which you could call the shelves of his pharmacy or drugstore) when the divine readings were being read. It is my ministry to apply these medicines to our wounds. For while I indeed own to being the doctor's assistant, whom he is happy to employ in the treatment of others, it is not as though I myself had no need of his care. If we present ourselves to him unreservedly for treatment, we shall all be cured.[52]

In the spirit of the *Confessions*, Augustine presents himself, humbly, as a model of recovering humanity. He invites his hearers to follow his example of relating to God. This, according to Augustine, involves careful attention to the plain and hidden meanings of the Scriptures, and so his particular role, as "the doctor's assistant," is to draw out and apply these medicines, as Ambrose did for him and the rest of the hearers in Milan.[53]

In *Sermon* 32, the figures of David and Goliath are read as relating to Christ and the Devil, respectively. Focusing on David's taking of the "five pebbles" from the stream, Augustine interprets the stream as "a fluid, unstable people, given over to temporal concerns, in love with passing things, rushing down the rapids of greed to the sea of this age." These people are, for Augustine, "the Jews." Taking the stones from the stream and putting them into the shepherd's gourd symbolizes how "the Lord took the law . . . and transposed it into grace." The sermon then moves to contrasting law and grace, with Augustine admonishing his hearers that each person should not "rely on his own powers."[54] He cautions them to avoid opening to the devil "the doors of greed or fear," whereby "greed for temporal things and fear of temporal punishments, frequently draw people on to wickedness and give the devil a

52. Augustine, *Sermon* 32:1.
53. Augustine, *Confessions*, 6.
54. Augustine, *Sermon* 32:7–9.9.

foothold."[55] In the description of things for which people might be greedy, or have fear of, many examples are things that were characteristic of pagan elites.

Claude Lepelley, in his article "*Saint Augustin et la cité romano-africaine*," describes the late antique city of North Africa and gives us a possible description of pagan elites and why they were such a concern to Augustine.[56] Lepelley argues that some of the background for understanding Augustine's "two cities" theme that governs his *De Civitate Dei (DCD)* is Augustine's conflict with civic notables in the course of his life as a bishop.[57] In the cities of the empire in the late fourth and early fifth centuries, according to Lepelley, the civic notables clung to old forms of civic life that had clear ties to the paganism that was the foundation of their status and prestige in the city. These notables sponsored games, spectacles, the theater, and civic festivals, as well as building temples and monuments that they then gave to the masses. But, according to Augustine, these displays are motivated by pride rather than by love.[58]

Lepelley also points out that the surviving inscriptions from this period show that, in North Africa, civic building was continued in the pagan vein; there were public monuments and even pagan temples, but no Christian buildings.[59] Christian building projects, in contrast, were from private, not public, figures. In a very few cases, there was some overlap. But the point is that those who had wealth and were civic leaders were putting their wealth to use in very traditional and pagan ways, even in the face of "Christianization" by legislation.

Thus, in this sermon, and as we shall see in others, Augustine seeks to have his Catholic hearers distinguish themselves from the mind-set and influence of pagan elites. He cautions against "fraud in order to make some money," threats from "a powerful man in town, powerful in the world," and greed to acquire money to "waste it all on luxuries, on trifles, on crazy monstrous spectacles."[60] He continues with such comments while directing people to stand firm in their humble Christian commitment that is content with God, whether God gives material prosperity or takes it away. "Thus the Christian people, brothers, who say in its heart, 'Let him take away whatever he likes, provided he doesn't deprive me of himself,'" are "*the blessed people whose God is the Lord*" (Ps. 144:15).[61]

55. Ibid., 32:13.

56. Lepelley, "Saint Augustin et la cité romano-africaine," 13–39.

57. Dolbeau notes that the material of *Sermon* 198/ D 26/ M 62:17–24 gets recapitulated in *DCD*.

58. *Sermon* M 62:2.

59. Lepelley, "Saint Augustin," and Lepelley, *Les cités de L'afrique romaine au bas-empire*, Tome I: *La permananence d'une civilisation municipale* (Paris: Études Augustiniennes, 1979), 331–369.

60. Augustine, *Sermon* 32:15–19.

61. Ibid., 32:28.

Autumn 403 *En. in Ps.* 36.I, II, and III

Against Zarb and others, Pierre-Marie Hombert dates these three sermons to September 403. This is done by first recognizing that they fit together as a series, and then, second, seeing that the second sermon begins to address positions taken by the Donatist bishop Primian of Carthage against the Catholics in general and Augustine in particular.[62] More will be said about this after giving a brief overview of the series.

In the first sermon, Augustine covers Psalm 36 (37) in its entirety. None of the themes of Catholicization are strongly represented. There are only general moral exhortations in light of the text. Augustine links Matt. 24:40, "one will be taken, the other left," with the psalm's own eschatological focus, and argues that God is instructing the faithful that there are two kinds of people, somewhat indistinguishable now because some know how to be impostors in many arenas including the Church. Augustine could have in mind some of the issues associated with the Donatist Church, but the sermon lacks clear polemic.

In contrast, the next sermon in the series explicitly takes on the Donatists. Augustine opens by saying:

> We have been ordered to speak to you about this psalm, dearest friends, and we have no option but to obey, for the Lord has seen fit to delay our departure by the heavy rains. It is our bounden duty not to let our tongue remain idle in your regard, since you are always the chief preoccupation of our heart, as we also are of yours.

By 36.II.11, the discussion of the eschatological nature of the good and the bad turns towards contemporary cases. In 36.II.10, Augustine had taken Psalm 36 (37):10, "sinners will perish," and claimed that: "For sinners there is no place to rest in anything outside themselves, because there they endure afflictions; nor does their conscience offer them any consolation, because they are not comfortable with themselves." He then goes on in 36.II.11 to tell of two Donatists. One had been excommunicated, and, according to Augustine,

> [b]ecause he could not have what he wanted there—empty honors, trumpery rank he came to look among us for what he had lost there, and he did not find it. So he perished. He was wounded and groaning, and refused consolation; for horrible thorns, unacknowledged, were fixed in his conscience. We tried to comfort him with the word of God, but he was not one of the prudent ants that have laid in supplies in summertime to live on during the winter. It is when things are peaceful that people should harvest the word of God for themselves, and store it in the inner recesses of their hearts, as the ant stores the results of summer's labor in the cavities of its nest.

62. Hombert, 12–13.

There is time to do this in the summer months, but winter will overtake us—the time of trouble, I mean—and unless we can find resources within ourselves we shall inevitably starve to death. This man of whom I was speaking had not gathered the word of God for his own sustenance, and winter came upon him. He did not find among us the adulation he craved, and nothing else could console him: he derived no comfort whatever from the word of God.

Augustine gives no indication of what actually happened to this person. The other, by contrast, Augustine describes as follows:

For a subdeacon of theirs, against whom no charge stood, chose the peace and unity of our Catholic Church, and leaving the Donatists came over to us. He truly came as one making his choice of the good not as repudiated by evil persons. He was accepted among us and his conversion brought us joy. This reminds me to recommend him to your prayers, for God is powerful enough to make him better and better.

So it seems that the policy of conditional acceptance of Donatist clergy achieved some results—positive and negative—that Augustine shares with his hearers as a fitting illustration of the points that he had sketched in the first sermon. From this part of the sermon on, Augustine takes on the Donatists directly.

In section 18, the sermon takes a particularly interesting turn as Augustine likens the Donatists to "lying witnesses" against the resurrected Christ who were paid by the "Jews."[63]

So now, though Christ's body is extended throughout the world, it is never free from those who will taunt it, "Traitors' brood." Your charge is untrue. I can show you up as a lying witness by examining a few of your words. You fling against me the accusation, "You are a traitor." I reply, "You are a liar." But you will never and nowhere make any charge of treachery stick against me, whereas I will here and now prove you are lying from your own words. Undeniably you said that we have sharpened our swords; I read out from your Acts what your Circumcellions have done.

He proceeds to give other Donatist charges against Catholics, countering with what he says is found in various documents. Aside from the aforementioned "Acts" dealing with Circumcellions, he refers to documents of the Maximianist controversy and a petition made by the Donatists to Emperor Julian.[64] This moves beyond mere "hearsay" when, by section 19, he reminds people of the

---

63. Section 17.

64. Clemens Weidmann, *Augustinus und das Maximinianistenkonzil von Cebarsussi, Zur historischen und textgeschichtlichen Bedeutung von Enarratio in Psalmum* 36, 2, 18–23 (Wien: Verlag der Österreichischen Akademie der Wissenschaften, 1998), 9–10.

beginning and continuing drama of the controversy within the Donatist camp between the Primianists and the Maximianists by quoting verbatim from the Council of Cebarsussi.[65] He introduces this material by framing it as a fitting parallel to the events that divided the African Church over the election of Caecilian.

> Keep before your eyes the unity of the whole world at that time, brothers and sisters, from which unity they split off in their opposition to Caecilian. Keep also in view the Donatist sect today, from which the Maximianists have split off in their opposition to Primian. What the Donatists did to Caecilian at that earlier date, the Maximianists have now done to Primian. This is why the Maximianists claim to be more authentic than the Donatists, because they have given a better imitation of the actions of their forebears! They have raised up Maximian to Primian, just as the Donatists then raised up Majorinus against Caecilian and they have complained about Primian in the same terms as those others did about Caecilian.

Maximian had been a deacon under Parmenian of Carthage, and then under Primian, whom he opposed. Primian was challenged by elders of the Donatist Church of Carthage and by four of its deacons, Maximian among them. Discussing the proceedings of the council, Augustine is admittedly enthused.

> We have, then, an amazing and incontrovertible example of history repeating itself: the Maximianists are bringing the same complaints against Primian as those others brought against Caecilian. I can hardly express to you, brothers and sisters, how moved I am, and how thankful to God, that his mercy toward them has provided an example that should illuminate their darkness, if they have the wit to see it. Now, if you will bear with me a little while, brothers and sisters, listen while I read to you the proceedings of the Maximianist council, for God has put the document into our hands.

Augustine had mentioned the Maximianist schism in *On Baptism* (400), but this sermon in the autumn of 403 seems to indicate that only recently had he received the proceedings of the council. In the rest of the sermon, he hammers home the inconsistency in the Donatists' charges against the Catholics in light of the actions taken by Primian against the Maximianists. These proceedings would be used by Augustine to help justify the increasingly hard line they were taking against the Donatists, particularly in the use of the coercive power of the state.

---

65. The assembled bishops of Cebarsussi censured and deposed Primian and elected Maximian in his stead. Primian, however, had strong support in Carthage as well as in Numidia. He was able to rally at least three hundred bishops to his side at a council in Bagai in April 394. They condemned the Maximianists but gave them until Christmas 394 to reunite with the main body of Donatists. See Weidmann, 5–17.

In the third sermon on Psalm 36, the guiding theme that Augustine addresses is the problem raised by verse 25. Augustine wonders, given experience and biblical examples like Abraham,[66] "How can it be true, then that *'never have I seen seen a just person destitute, or a child of righteous parents begging for bread?'*" Augustine answers this question through allegorizing and discovering the spiritual meaning of the text in connection with other texts. Bringing in Matthew 4:3–4, he tells his hearers that "the word of God" is the truly sustaining bread for the righteous. In the rest of the sermon, pursuit of righteousness, along with how the righteous are fed and cared for, is further explained. In discussing God's care, from verse 33, "*[t]he sinner spies on the just and seeks to kill him, but the Lord will not leave the just in his hands,*" Augustine focuses on the persecution of the just. The examples he uses are Job, Jesus, and Cyprian. It is odd that, especially given his emphasis expressed further on in commenting on verses 34–36, where it says "the godless" will perish, he would spend time on this at all.

Augustine seems to be working from an eschatology that is not very imminent. After describing the ultimate vindication of the martyred Cyprian, Augustine quotes: "Nor will God condemn him, when the time comes for him to be judged." Then he asks rhetorically, "[b]ut when will that be?" He responds:

> Do not imagine that it will happen quickly, this is the time for hard work, the time for sowing, the season when the weather is still cold. Sow your seed then, even if the winds are howling round you and then rain pouring down. Do not be lazy; summer will come to gladden you, and then you will be happy that you sowed. "So what must I do now?" "*Wait for the Lord.*"

Thus, we have a sense of tension in this sermon between the "now" and the "what is to come." Augustine tries to produce resources for his hearers, as well as himself, to live in that tension. Key resources are found in the instructions contained in the Scriptures. Reading the text prophetically consistent with the strategies of Tyconius enabled the faithful to find in the texts God's promises of what is to come. Consistent with his self-understanding and bidden by Aurelius, Augustine sees his duty as being a teacher of the text. He lifts up for his hearers the promise of a Catholic Church that embraces the whole world. This Catholic Church is where the believer will be ultimately vindicated and delivered from all suffering and persecution. To further encourage his hearers, he can point to the progress, not only since the time of Christ, but, perhaps most strikingly, since the time of the great martyr Cyprian.

66. Exposition 3 on Psalm 36.1. Referring to Abraham in Genesis 12:10 and Genesis 26:1.

In the autumn of 403, to these hearers, it seems that Augustine recognizes the Donatists as the great seducers and "liars" who would try to convince Christians not to lay hold of God's promises of a Catholicized world. Yes "the pagans" of this time were real competition, as were others like Jews and Manichees. But Augustine does not refer to them overtly, and the implied message is that the Donatists are "the ungodly" about whom Augustine says:

> [Y]ou will not see the ungodly anywhere; you will need to search for his place. What is this place of his? It is his present station, where he wields power, enjoys wealth, and has his proper rank in human society, so that many people bend to his whims, and he gives orders and is obeyed. This place of his will not exist any longer; it will pass away, so that you will be able to say, *I passed on further, and look! he was not there.* Passed on further—in what sense? I made progress, I arrived at spiritual understanding, I entered God's holy place to see what would happen at the end. *And look! he was not there; I searched for him, but his place was not to be seen.*[67]

As Augustine draws his sermon to a close, he takes up a number of personal charges raised by Primian against Augustine. Primian apparently raised questions about Augustine's past sins and whether he had truly been baptized.[68] Augustine replied that his past sins are just that, past, and that since the Donatist communion barely reaches beyond Africa, Primian has no basis to challenge the validity of his baptism in Milan. Ultimately, however, Augustine does not want to get mired in a defense of his role as a valid bishop. He falls back on his self-understanding of his role as being subordinate to Christ. He encourages his hearers not to see him as a "mediator" in any way, but to place their faith in Christ.

> Well now, brothers and sisters, we are about to go forth in Christ's name, and they will have plenty to say. How shall we conclude? Take care to dismiss my case summarily. Say nothing to them except this: "Keep to the point, friends. Augustine is a bishop in the Catholic Church, he has his own burden to bear and he will have to render an account to God. I have known some good of him. If he is bad, he knows it himself, but if he is good, he is not the foundation of my hope for all that. This above all I have learned in the Catholic Church, not to set my hope on any human being. It is understandable that you reproach us for the human faults among us, because you do set your hope on human beings."

67. Augustine, *Sermon* 36.3.15.
68. Ibid., 36.3.18–20.

Be clear about this, brothers and sisters. When they criticize us, you can be as dismissive as they are. We know what a place we have in your hearts, because we know the place you have in ours. Do not engage in battle against them to defend us. Whatever they say about us, pass over it briskly, lest you become so embroiled in defending our cause that you lose your own. This is part of their cunning. They are afraid we will discuss the real issue, and they want to prevent it; so they batter us with irrelevancies, hoping to keep us so busy exonerating ourselves that we stop trying to convict them of error.

Given the serious defense of the aspect of the Catholics' plan of Catholicization that called for opposing the Donatists, and given Augustine's own strength of conviction defending himself against Primian's personal attacks, one wonders why Augustine would go after the Donatists right away in the first sermon on Psalm 36.

On certain occasions, when Augustine did not speak about the Donatists around this time, late in 403 and into 404, some wondered whether he might have been afraid to speak openly against them.[69] The plot of the Circumcellions to attack him was foiled by Augustine taking a wrong turn on a road.[70] Other Catholics were suffering violence at the hands of the Circumcellions, including his friend and disciple Possidius. Augustine was indeed shaken by these events. His comments on the subject can be interjected into his train of thought and speech at unexpected moments. Thoughts of the violence of the Circumcellions, in fact, helped move him from his earlier position, which was to persuade the Donatists into unity, to a position of compelling them into unity. He even, on occasion, protests that the Circumcellions have not cowed him into silence on the Donatist issue. Does he protest too much? Perhaps. From this series in the autumn, it seems that Augustine was soft on the issue in the first sermon, and clearer and firmer in the next two. From what he says at the beginning of the second sermon about Aurelius having required him to preach, and given the rains, seemingly by God as well, we might reconstruct the events as follows.

The council meets in August. Augustine wants to get back to the safely of Hippo as soon as possible. Aurelius tells him to preach. He is weary, he hates traveling, but he preaches. He "soft-sells" the party line, however, and tries to leave. The rains come; Aurelius says to him, in effect now, go up there and really preach. So Augustine lets loose an unrestrained attack with the most powerful weapon he has come upon to date, the documents from the Maximianist-Donatist Council of Cebarsussi.

---

69. We shall see this issue raised in *Sermon* 299A/ M 9/ D 4:3.
70. Augustine, *Sermon* 198/ M 62/ D 26:45.

The December–June Group[71]
Sermon 114B/ M 12/ D 5 (Carthage)[72]

Hombert, following Dolbeau, argues that the sermon on Psalm 47 was displaced by *Sermon* 114B/ M 12/ D 5 due to an accident of the lector, who read out the gospel passage from Lk. 17:27, "just as in the days of Noah they were eating and drinking, marrying husbands and wives, buying and selling, when the ark was being built by Noah, and the flood came and destroyed them all," instead of the psalm. In spite of the accidental reading, Augustine takes it as "the good management of the Lord" and preaches on the gospel passage.[73] Following a tradition in Africa going back at least to Cyprian, Augustine talks in section 2 of the ark as a figure of the Church. The ark is also "a sort of herald crying out, Be converted to God," as he adds in the same section. Thus, the Church has been, and is still, prophesying of judgments to come, and warning people to change their way of life so that they can be safe aboard the ark.

The metaphor of the journey is introduced in sections 4 and 5, and Jesus, whom Augustine identifies as "God-made-man-for-the-sake-of-men," guides us on the path to take in order to come to "a vast field of joys" so as to avoid the road that "leads to doom." By section 6, the "blessed seed" is used again to show how reliable the guide is to show how prophecy is already being fulfilled in that the Church is spread

---

71. All the sermons to be treated in depth in this group are part of a relatively recently discovered collection of sermons. In 1990 François Dolbeau discovered twenty-six "new" sermons of Augustine. Dolbeau's *Vingt-Six Sermons au Peuple D'Afrique* is a compilation of the various articles wherein Dolbeau previously published editions of the Latin text of the sermons with commentary in French. These articles can be found in *Revue Bénédictine* 101–104 and in *Revue des Études Augustiniennes* 37–40. This compilation adds a preface, pages 5–7; and also addenda, corrigenda, and indexes of selected subjects; works of Augustine; and works of other ancient writers. For a brief description of the collection in English, see Henry Chadwick "New Sermons of St Augustine," *Journal of Theological Studies* 47 (April 1996), 69–91. A collection of papers on the new sermons has been published and will be very helpful: *Augustin Prédicateur (395–411): Actes du Colloque International de Chantilly (5–7 septembre 1996)*, edited by Goulven Madec (Paris: Institut d'Études Augustiniennes, 1998). There is a translation into English by Edmund Hill in *The Works of Saint Augustine: A Translation for the 21st Century*. This volume is part of an ongoing series in which scholars present, for the first time, an English translation of the complete extant works of Augustine. So far more than three hundred of Augustine's sermons have been published. Volume 1 provides an extensive introduction to Augustine as a preacher, with an extremely helpful chronological table that gives the standard numbering of the sermon; its theme or biblical text(s); the dating, noting scholarly disputes; and the edition that is the current standard. This volume was published without taking account of Dolbeau's discovery.

72. Hombert, 565–566.

73. Section 1.

throughout the world and people are forsaking the worship of idols. To further illustrate the manner of following the guide, Jesus is later described as the camel that squeezes through the eye of the needle. Rich and poor alike must humble themselves and endure suffering, for Christ's sake, to come to the field of joys.

Sermon 114B/ M 12/ D 5 is followed the next Sunday by *En. in Ps.* 103. Hombert places the group of sermons on the Psalms in the following order: *Ennarationes in Ps.* 103; 80; 146; 2; 57; and 66, all in Carthage during December. His reasoning for doing so comes from numerous parallels that he is able to show between the Psalms sermons and the Dolbeau sermons.

We now will turn to a discussion of the rest of the sermons datable to the period of 404 before the African Catholic Bishops' Council of June 404.

Sermons 198/ M 62/ D 26 in 403 and On the Kalends in 404

The longest surviving sermon of Augustine's, at 1,546 lines, is *Sermon* 198/ Mayence 62/ Dolbeau 26.[74] It is a sermon given on the Kalends of January (January 1) 404 in Carthage.[75] Augustine gives an extended examination and criticism of the festival of the Kalends.[76] Perhaps, still conscious of the criticisms of Faustus the Manichee[77], Augustine presents it as a celebration of which Christians can have no part because of its associations with paganism. According to Robert Markus, the celebrations were rooted in a religious past, but "articulated a corporate civic and municipal consensus."[78] The reason for its extraordinary length is Augustine's desire to keep the congregation in church and away from the festivities that he is preaching against for as long as possible.[79] What emerges as the key point on which Augustine attacks pagans is mediation.[80] Augustine presents all pagan rites and

---

74. Dolbeau, *Vingt-Six Sermons*, 5–7.

75. Ibid., 356.

76. The Kalends of January was the day new consuls were sworn in. It was a time of celebration with drinking, gift giving, and masquerades. Sacrifices were also performed. For an extended study of this festival in late antiquity, see M. Meslin, *La fête des Kalendes de janvier dans l'empire romain* (Brussels: Latomus, 1971). For a briefer discussion in English based on Meslin, see Robert Markus. *The End of Ancient Christianity* (Cambridge: Cambridge University Press, 1990), 103ff.

77. Markus notes that in *Contra Faustum* 20.4, Augustine responds to a wide range of criticism from Faustus. One of these is the claim that Christians celebrate the Kalends and Solstices (Markus, *The End of Ancient Christianity*, 102).

78. Ibid.

79. Dolbeau, *Vingt-Six Sermons*, 75.

80. For more on Augustine's understanding of Christ as mediator, see Brian Daley, "A Humble Mediator: The Distinctive Elements in St. Augustine's Christology," in *Word and*

practices as attempts at mediation between humans and God that will ultimately be unsuccessful. They will be unsuccessful because a false mediator, the devil, carries them out. The devil presents various paths that are distinguished by pride, whereas the true path is the way of Christ, which is the way of humility. Although the chief objects of Augustine's criticism are pagans, the Donatists are also criticized under the same charge of establishing false ways of mediation.

Mediation is significant for Catholicization because it is only the Catholic Church that provides true mediation, since it alone has a correct understanding of the mediator and the full power of the sacramental rituals energized by the bond of love in the Holy Spirit. This bond provides for the unity of the Catholic Church not only over its worldwide extension, but also it provides for unity across time and, metaphysically, to God, all because of the work of Jesus Christ, the true mediator.

Augustine begins the sermon by using the liturgy of the service to aid in making his point. "Admonishing their charity" (*S* 198/ M 62/ D 26:1), he calls them to remember that they have just chanted "*save us, O Lord our God, and gather us from among the nations, that we may give thanks to thy holy name*" Psalm 105:46 (106:47). He then proposes that if they really believe this, they must not celebrate the Kalends as the pagans do. The "three dispositions of the heart, believing, hoping and loving," must be the distinguishing lines between Augustine's hearers and the pagans. "If," he says to the faithful singer of the psalm, "you do not believe what the heathen believe in, you do not hope what the heathen hope, you do not love what the heathen love, gather away from the heathen" (*S* 198/ M 62/ D 26:2). Whereas the pagans believe in a plurality of false gods, Christians believe in the one true God that makes them a distinct gathered community.

> If then you wish to mingle with the heathen, you do not wish to follow him who redeemed us. You are mingled then in your life, in your deeds, in your heart by hoping such things, believing such things, and loving such things. You are ungrateful to your redemptor, nor do you acknowledge the price he paid, the blood of the immaculate lamb. In order to follow the one who redeemed you, who redeemed you with his blood, do not mingle with the heathen in likeness of the morality and the deeds. They give New Year's gifts, you give charity. For we are not saying to you, brothers, "They give, you refuse to give"; but rather give more than they, but like people who believe in different things, hope something else, love something else, we are not telling you: "They believe, you refuse to believe; they hope, you refuse to hope; they love, you

refuse to love"; but we are saying to you: "They believe in that, you believe in this, they hope that, you hope this, they love that, you love this, they give that or to those, you give this or to them." Therefore if they give gifts for the celebration of the New Year's day, you give charity. If they commit themselves to earthly events, you commit yourselves to the words of the divine scriptures. If they run to the theatre, you run to the church. If they get drunk, you fast. If truly you do these things, then truly you chanted: *Save us, O Lord our God, and gather us from among the nations.* Now let those who listened eagerly to what I said stand with those whom did not listen eagerly, and yet these are congregated from the heathen, and those mingled with them.[81]

Above, drawing on the traditional biblical language, Christ is presented as Redeemer.[82] He is the one who frees Christians from captivity to sin. This redemption, thus, places the redeemed in a kind of debt service to the redeemer. The contrast and the challenge set, Augustine carries it through the entire sermon, while bringing into sharper relief the role of Christ in distinguishing true Christians from the pagans.

Augustine, in fact, sees at least two general categories of pagans that he must critique. The first are the "party pagans," those referred to in the above passage and discussed in *S* 198/ M 62/ D 26:1–9. They tempt Christians to join with them in their merriments. These, Augustine says, can be defeated and won over with fasting and prayers and by the example of a holy life. The other general class, that of the learned or "philosophical pagan," is picked up in *S* 198/ M 62/ D 26:10, and discussed from them on. These pagans also deplore the excess of celebrations such as the Kalends: "For certain of them condemn those people as being devoted to the evil of pleasures and drunkenness, with the following words: 'Just as you have bad Christians, so we have bad pagans. Take a look and see what good pagans are like.' And so they name people as wise men and philosophers of the world, as if they were imbued with excellent doctrine"(*S* 198/ M 62/ D 26:10). In addition to fasting, prayers, and the example of a holy life, these pagans need to be addressed with rational argument.

Christians need to beware, for although these are sober, intellectual pagans, they are nevertheless in error and following a false religion.

Don't let them frighten you. Grandeur is one thing, puffery quite another. For that also appears to be grand which is puffed up, but it is not healthy. Listen to the apostle when he says (Col. 2:8–10): *See to it that nobody makes a prey of you by philosophy and empty deceit, according to human tradition, according to the elemental spirits of the universe, and not according to Christ. For in him the whole fullness of deity dwells bodily and you have come to fullness of life in him, who is the head of all rule and authority.* They make for the principles

---

81. *S* 198/ M 62/ D 26:2.
82. See, for example, Rom. 3:24; 1 Cor. 1:30; Eph. 1:7; and Heb. 9:12.

of the world so that their idols can be understood learnedly and wisely. You criticize someone because he worships an idol and because it is clear that he worships the idol: he is convicted because by that fact alone he places his emotion there—in that very idol—, there he places his whole understanding, but what does the pagan say to you as if he were more sophisticated and learned? "Unsophisticated pagans do this, I mean worshiping an idol as an idol, just as your people do when they worship pillars in the church."[83]

Essentially their fault is pride,[84] which is a form of idolatry. Augustine argues that all pagan religion is worship of idols. It does not matter whether it is worship through rowdy celebrations, like the Kalends, or through intellectual attunement, like with the learned pagans. Further, he charges his hearers to not give cause for the pagans to criticize the Christians because of their own seemingly idolatrous worship (*S* 198/ M 62/ D 26:11). Thus, they must change the focus of their worship. They must not "worship" pillars and paintings, and engage in unseemly activity on martyrs' feasts and at their tombs.[85] These exterior foci must be shifted inward (*S* 198/ M 62/ D 26:11). The true Christian temple is interior and it must be purified with holy living. Besides, the martyrs know that they are but servants in the household, and they do not claim the honor or worship owed to the Lord of the household (*S* 198/ M 62/ D 26:11–12).

Augustine next begins a lengthy criticism of the philosophical pagan justification of the place of statues in pagan worship (*S* 198/ M 62/ D 26:17–24). The distance between the creator and the creatures is subsequently discussed. Here Augustine argues that some philosophers raise themselves through contemplation to attain vision or knowledge of God, as Paul claimed in Romans 1.[86] This is knowledge to which they do not hold fasts, but fall from because of their pride (*S* 198/ M 62/ D 26:25–37).

Then Augustine comes to the discussion of mediation proper. God is just and immortal; humans are unjust because of sin and are therefore mortal because

---

83. *S* 198/ M 62/ D 26:10.

84. For more on the idea of pride versus humility with respect to mediation, see Daley. He notes the longevity of this idea in Augustine's writings appearing as early as 394 in *Epistolae ad Galatas expositio* (394/5) 24. See also *De catechizandis rudibus* (399) 4.8.

85. *S* 198/ M 62/ D 26:10. Augustine held these sober opinions for years given that *Ep.* 22 of 392 was written while he was still a priest; see also *Ep.* 29 of 395. And see Peter Brown, "Augustine and a Practice of the *imperiti*," in *Augustin Prédicateur (395–411)*, edited by Madec, 367–375.

86. Augustine returns to this passage again and again when criticizing the pagans, in this sermon and elsewhere. TeSelle claims that this reflects the influence of Ambrosiater's Romans commentary on Augustine (Eugene TeSelle, *Augustine the Theologian* [New York: Herder, 1970], 247).

of the resultant punishment for sin (*S* 198/ M 62/ D 26:39). Humans, consequently, need the help of a mediator to be reconciled with God. Jesus is the only being capable of mediating because he alone shares the proper qualities of God and humans (*S* 198/ M 62/ D 26:40). Jesus is just and mortal because he humbled himself to accept death. His sacrifice and example provide the way for reconciliation. The devil, who is fallen because of his pride, seeks to deceive those seeking a mediator. He is unjust and immortal, deceiving those who follow him into believing that he can bestow immortality, but he cannot. The only way to achieve immortality is by the one true mediator, the one true way, Jesus Christ (*S* 198/ M 62/ D 26:41–43).

Changing to another image, Augustine claims that Christians must be a part of the right family. God is the Father/Bridegroom and the Church is the Mother/ Bride (*S* 198/ M 62/ D 26:42–43). This shift leads to discussion of the Donatists. They are not pagans, but they are not true Christians in Augustine's eyes because they "prefer Donatus to Christ." I suspect Augustine realized that this was somewhat of an exaggeration. However, Augustine moves to a related claim made with greater seriousness. Referring to a letter of Parmenian's,[87] Augustine says that the Donatists claim that the bishops are mediators for the people. Augustine rejects this position, and claims that Jesus Christ is the one and only true mediator between God and humans (*S* 198/ M 62/ D 26:45–46).

Although Augustine speaks of pagans in a general way, it is the second class of pagans that he spends the majority of his time critiquing in *S* 198/ M 62/ D 26, where they are again subdivided into two groups. There are first those who claim to be like Pythagorus, and need no mediation because they ascend to God by contemplation (*S* 198/ M 62/ D 26:36). Then there are those who use rites ministered to idols or magic as forms of mediation (*S* 198/ M 62/ D 26:36–37). Interestingly, although the Pythagorean group, let's call them 2A, are seen by Augustine as also proud, he seems to leave room for some of them to actually be saved.[88]

---

87. This is presumably the same letter to which Augustine replies in his *Contra Epistulam Parmeniani* of 400/401. In this work, Augustine sought to defend Tyconius the Donatist, also dead by this time, against the criticism he received in a letter from Parmenian. Parmenian, or Parmenianus, became Bishop of Carthage in 363 following Donatus. He died some time before Augustine wrote against him. Augustine's reply after Parmenian's death (391) is a testimony to the influence of his life.

88. He says in *S* 198/ M 62/ D 26:36: "But for those who do not worship any idols or tie themselves up in any other chaldaic or magical rites, we should not condemn them in anything, lest perhaps it escapes our notice that to them in some way was revealed that savior without whom no one can be saved." Let us not overlook the fact that even here Augustine is consistent in the position that salvation is brought about by Christ's mediation.

With the group of pagans that uses rites and magic, let's call them 2B, Augustine repeatedly claims that they are proudly ignoring the true mediator and following the false mediator, the devil (*S* 198/ M 62/ D 26:38). They do not want to follow a humble way that would have them participate in rites with a lower class of people.

> My brethren, you who perhaps cannot see with their clarity of vision and are not yet ready by your mental processes to rise above creation's totality (both bodily and spiritual), and to see the unchanging God, by whom and through whom all things were made,—you brethren, don't fear, don't despair, because he made himself our path by coming right down to us, lowly and weak people. What good does it do arrogant people to see their hometown from afar? They don't find the path, because the path to their high-up hometown begins low down. They see their hometown as if from the mountain of arrogance, they see it from the opposite peak. But nobody reaches it without descending first. They don't want to descend for the sake of ascending, that means they don't want to be humble in order to be Christians. When they say to themselves, "So I'll be a concierge rather than a Plato or a Pythagoras?" puffing themselves up with arrogant words, they don't want to descend and they can't ascend. For our Lord descended to us from the height of his majesty, and yet they don't want to descend from the puffery of their presumption. He descended to elevate the lowly of the world and to confound the strong–minded and vain of the world and to confound the wise; *God chose what is low and despised in the world, even things that are not, to bring to nothing things that are* (I Cor. 1:28).[89]

Again we may have a hint of Lepelley's picture of Augustine's conflict with civic notables. The pagans whom Augustine criticizes are status conscious and want a religion that confirms their elite status. The accessibility of Christianity to the unlearned masses is definitely not a selling point.

It is interesting to note that the sentiments that Augustine puts in the mouths of these pagans carry a slight echo of an opinion he expressed at the beginning of the famous conversion scene in the *Confessions*.

---

89. *S* 198/ M 62/ D 26:59. For a treatment of Augustine's emphasis on Christ as the Homeland and the Way, see Goulven Madec, *Le Patrie et La Voie: Le Christ dans la vie et la pensée de saint Augustin* (Paris: Desclée, 1989). Madec's work brings into sharp relief the centrality of Christology in Augustine's thought. This Christology, for Madec, is summed up in Augustine's statement from *Sermon* 123.3.3: "God Christ is our Homeland where we must go, the man Christ is the Way we must go. To him we must go. By him we must go." So, for our purposes here, we note that Christ the Way is another way to express his mediatoral action. In Chapter 9, Madec presents a diagram that illustrates Christ's mediatorial role in relation to the median position of the soul.

Then in the middle of that grand struggle in my inner house, which I had vehe-mently stirred up with my soul in the intimate chamber of my heart, distressed not only in mind but in appearance, I turned on Alypius. "What is wrong with us? What is it that you have heard?" Uneducated people are rising and capturing heaven (Matt. 11:12) and we with our high culture without any heart—see where we roll in the mud of flesh and blood. Is it because they are ahead of us that we are ashamed to follow?[90]

Perhaps Augustine began to see, in the philosophical pagans, the person he was and the person he feared to become, content in the pursuit of the lusts of the flesh, the eyes, and the pride of life.[91]

Sermons 359B/ M 5/ D 2 (at Carthage) and On Obedience, January 22, 404

A particularly interesting aspect of this sermon is that it is preached the day after a failed sermon. Augustine is doing the textbook spin doctor role. The day before was Saint Vincent's Day, and we learn in this sermon that Augustine had come to Carthage to preach for Aurelius. The crowd apparently got out of hand and Augustine refused to preach while the crowd was so rowdy, and the Mass had to continue without a sermon. It seems that some had the impression that there was some rift between Augustine and Aurelius that caused him not to preach. Augustine's sermon On Obedience turns the issue from being about what he did to what the congregation did. The problem was one of their obedience. Augustine tells those assembled that they are the model church for Africa, and if they do not obey the authorities set over them, they are setting a poor example. He is, in this manner, appealing to their investment in being leaders. They can lead other congregations by showing how well they follow.

---

90. See Augustine, *Confessions* 10.30.41–10.36.59. Augustine was, as he said in the *Confessiones*, "restless" (*Confessions*, 1.1.1); and on Brown's reading of him ambitious as well, Brown, *Augustine of Hippo*, 61. This desire to be successful and peacefully happy can account for Augustine's need to move beyond the constraining provincialism of Thagaste. His ticket out was his intellect. Augustine was exceedingly bright and his parents pushed him to excel. They spent beyond their means to give Augustine an opportunity for upward mobility.

91. As Brown elaborates in *Power and Persuasion,* this education, *paideia*, was the key to social status and the exercise and maintenance of power (35ff). Being introduced to this fast track life was not enough for Augustine, however; he questioned. This questioning led him eventually to Christ the mediator as presented in the teaching of the Catholic Church. We can thus envision Augustine's criticism of these philosophical pagans as contempt from familiarity with fellow men of *paideia*.

In the course of this sermon, Augustine does not use the terms associated with mediation, and the humble and prideful mediators and their respective ways of mediation, but implicitly the themes are there. We can easily see that pride and disobedience would be akin for Augustine. They both have to do with a disordering of proper relationships in the human and divine communities. In this sermon, Augustine even links the false gods with false martyrs in a fashion similar to the way he linked false schemes of mediation through false gods and bishops in his critiques of various forms of non-Christian religion and Donatism. It is only in the Catholic Church that there is the opportunity to participate in the right ordering of relationships so as to receive salvation.

We have here an unusually exaggerated example of an attempt at social order. Augustine says to his hearers at one point: "This place where we sit gives the impression that we bishops are set over you; yet so heavy is the burden of anxious solicitude and care for you that it presses us down under your feet" (S 359B/ M 5/ D 2:12). Augustine wants to communicate that he believes and practices the servant life of the bishop. Thus, obedience of a congregation to a bishop implies mutual subjugation. However, appeals from pulpits for obedience can be seen to be merely reinscribing already established social hierarchies. Ecclesiastical authority is then seen as taking up power roles formally exclusively held by civic notables.[92]

Sermon 360A/Mainz 60/ Dolbeau 24

This sermon is of moderate length. At just under than 300 lines of Latin text in Dolbeau's edition, it would have taken about thirty minutes to deliver. In section 1, Augustine begins by asserting that "God's promises were the foundation of faith for our ancestors, and God's gifts are the fulfillment of faith for us." Faith comes, he says, by hearing and sight. "Hear, daughter and see. Hear, he says, and see and forget your own people and your father's house, since the king has desired your beauty."[93] This daughter he takes to be the Church, with the King being God (S 360A/ M 60/ D 24:1). This introduces the central themes and images of the sermon related to marriage and faithfulness.

---

92. A haunting issue for Augustine, and for some Church leaders but not all, is the degree to which accommodation to the use of coercive, violent force is acceptable. As Augustine deals with particularly Donatists and pagans from August 403 to June 404, he will become increasingly comfortable with the state's use of force for protection and for a coerced establishment of Catholicism. "Compel them to come in" from Luke will come to be seen as justification for such coercion.

93. *Sermon* 360A/ Mainz 60/ Dolbeau 24:1:7–10; Psalm 45:10–11/ Vulgate Psalm 44:11–12.

The content of the promises mentioned in section 1 is what Augustine reveals in section 2. Augustine takes Genesis 22:18, "[i]n your seed shall all the nations of the earth be blessed," and Is. 11:10 LXX; Romans 15:12, "[t]here will be a root of Jesse, and one who will arise to reign among the nations; in him shall all the nations hope,"[94] as prophecies of Christ and the spread of Christianity to all nations. These texts are woven back into his themes and images from Psalm 45. He finds in verses 45:13–14 the queen robed in a garment of many colors, and he claims that this represents the many nations of the world. Using a rhetorical question, he asks:

> What are the many colors of her gown? The great number of languages. Latin speakers talk in one way, Greeks in another, Punic speakers in another, in another Hebrews, in anther Syrians, in another Indians, in another Cappadocians, in another Egyptians. Variety in color, unity in weave. Many colors I mean to say, all included in one woven cloth, they embroider, they don't tear apart. Variety of languages, but not variety of doctrine. Variety of speaking, but unity of love.[95]

Shifting texts and imagery, Augustine introduces the story of Gideon and the fleece from Judges 6. In that chapter of Judges, Gideon asked God for a sign of favor. First, he asks that God make a fleece that he lays out on the threshing floor wet while leaving the rest of the floor dry. After God gives this sign, Gideon troubles God for another. This time, he asks that the reverse be done. That is, he wants the fleece dry and the floor wet. God does this also. Augustine interprets this as a prophecy of how the world, for a time, will be dry of God's grace while the people of Israel were wet with grace, and how, by his time, the world is overflowing with God's grace through the spread of Christianity, while the Jews had become dry. He asserts that the dry Jews are dry in that they "killed him," citing Mk. 12:7–8. Killing him, "the fleece is now dry," for "Christ has been wrung out of it." Further Augustine says:

> Having wrung out the fleece, they tossed the water away outside. From it, however, to spread further afield the humility of the one who had been wrung out, he took whom he would and went to the nations, to fulfill the second sign; the fleece being now dry, he watered the threshing floor. And this faith is not concealed in the woolly cloud of the fleece, but openly manifest; it is proclaimed to all, it is known by all. It celebrates its sacrament in secret, its word in public. All these things are seen now, exactly as they were foretold; exactly as promised has payment now been made. *As we have heard, so too have we seen* (Psalm 48:8), because it was we who in the unity of the Church were foretold, *Hear, daughter, and see* (Ps. 45:10).[96]

---

94. *Sermon* 360A/ Mainz 60/ Dolbeau 24:2.
95. Ibid.
96. Ibid., 24:3.

In contrast to this unity, which Augustine sees as Catholic unity, he places the heretics. About them he says:

> But now the heretics on the other hand, having cut themselves off from any links with this global reality, neither wish to hear what they read nor to see what they know. We have been invited to the wedding, we have been praising the bride, and presenting her divine testimonials from the scriptures.

Augustine then explicitly names the heretics of present concern as Donatists and compares their treatment of the scriptures with the pagans and finds more guilty because they profess to love Jesus Christ and the scriptures yet they have broken the bond of unity in the body of Christ. Regarding the pagans Augustine asks his hearers:

> The pagan wanted to consign this volume of mine to the flames, he detested the scriptures themselves, he persecuted them. Small wonder, wouldn't you say, if it pains him to live according to what he wanted to burn?[97]

Augustine then uses direct address to rhetorically draw his hearers into sharing his sharp criticism of the Donatists.

> You, however, you heretic, say that you saved this volume from the flames. As you didn't want it burnt, acknowledge it when it's produced, listen to it when it's read. This volume certainly contains the words: *In your seed shall all the nations be blessed* (Gen. 22:18). You certainly didn't want these words to go up in flames. Why have you gone up in flames yourself over them, in your lust for dissension? (*Quare in eis cupiditate dissensionis arsisti?*) Why, I beg you, if not because you're lying, because you say that you saved what you have in fact handed over and betrayed?

> The pagan, if he doesn't believe, hates what I read out; you, though you don't want to appear to have been led by a pagan into committing an impious act, have surpassed the pagan in impiety. He hates the object and chucked it away; you hold on to it and deny it. You say that I burnt the will and testament, while you can see I hold the inheritance; you say that you preserved the will and testament, though you have disinherited yourself.[98]

Augustine next introduces his passages of scripture that "foretold that sooner or later the time would come when idols would be done away with, and this has been fulfilled, just as they foretold that the time would come when the Church would spread through the whole world, and this too has been fulfilled in the same way" (*S* 360A/ M 60/ D 24:5). The pagans and heretics both, for Augustine, stand under the judgment of prophecy, but the heretics are guiltier because "[t]he pagan's

97. Ibid., 24:4.
98. Ibid.

crime of not believing what he pays no attention to is not as great as the heretic's of not believing what he reads so attentively."[99]

The first passage in section 6 is from Wisdom 14:11–13: "Notice will be taken, of the idols of the nations, since creatures of God were made hateful, and into temptations for the souls of men, and into a mousetrap for the feet of fools. For the beginning of fornication is the devising of idols, and the invention of them the corruption of life. For neither were they there from the beginning, nor will they be there forever."[100] For Augustine it is clear that those who are idolaters are fornicators and they will not be around forever.

Next, in section 7, from Zechariah, he cites 13:1–2: "There will be an open place for the house of David. And it shall come to pass on that day, the Lord will banish the names of the idols from the earth and no mention will be made of them at all." Noting that the Wisdom passage does not give a time frame, Augustine interprets the "open place for the house of David" to be the threshing floor, which is the period of the publicly manifest church.

In section 8, he turns to the subject of the hiding of idols.

> And the wrongdoings of men shall be humbled and fall, and the Lord alone shall be exalted on that day, and they will hide all things made by their hands. The Lord shall be exalted on that day, and they will hide all things made by their hands, taking them into the dens and into the caverns of the rocks, and the crevasses of the earth, from the face of the fear of the Lord, from the splendor of his might, when he rises up to crush the earth. For on that day men will throw away their abominations of silver and gold that they have made.

In this passage, Augustine sees a prophecy of the retreat of idolatry. He sees in this passage two categories of people "one sort of them in the church, the other in the neighborhood of the Church." Some are hiding their idols in caves, others have thrown them away. "In either case, the abomination is done away with. Yes, let it be done away with—and if only it could be done away with from the hearts of earthly men, as it has been from these earthly places! May God do away with these things from the places through the hands of his servants, through his hands from people's hearts."[101] The idolaters, he says, even today are hiding their images. But, he says, "wherever they hide one, it's dragged out of there when it's overthrown in their hearts."[102]

99. Ibid., 24:5.

100. Ibid., 24:6.

101. Ibid., 24:9. "Per manus servorum suorum deus de locis tollat haec, per manum suam de cordibus."

102. Ibid., 24:8. "Ubilibet abscondant, inde eruitur, cum in corde euertitur."

Next, Augustine presents two passages from Jeremiah. With the first discussed in section 9, Jeremiah 16:19, he contrasts the hope of those who say that the Lord is their "strength," "help and refuge in the day of evils" with those who, like "our fathers," possess lies in that they had idols. In the second, Jeremiah 10:2, discussed in section 10, Augustine says: "Do not walk in the way of the nations" who are characterized by their attention to "signs of the heavens" and creation of, and devotion to, idols of wood, silver, and gold. To these things and the people that make them, from Jeremiah, Augustine says that Christians have clear instructions: "You're Christians, listen to the prophet; thus shall you say to them, don't keep quiet: Gods which did not make heaven and earth, let them vanish from the earth and from under heaven. Not from heaven surely, where they never were. . . . Let the false gods vanish; as for you, hold on to the true one."[103]

Concluding, in section 11, he says: "We have heard the predictions, what was going to happen to the idols; now let us hear the precepts, what is to be done with the idols."[104] In this final section, Augustine uses two passages from Exodus to call for radical commitment from his hearers in sharply defining their particular kind of Christianity.

> Certainly it was said that the idols were going to vanish; may he abolish them, as for you, what are you breaking? But God wished to abolish them by means of people whom he did not wish to see perishing. *And he will lead you in,* he says, *to the Amorite and the Hittite and the Perizitte and the Canaanite and the Girgashite and the Hivite and the Jebusite, and I will rub them out. You shall not adore their gods or serve them. You shall not act according to their works, but overthrowing you shall overthrow them and smashing you shall smash their idols* (Ex. 23:23–24).

> And, *Behold, I myself will cast out before your face Amorite, Canaanite and Hittite and Perizzite and Hivite and Girgashite and Jebusite. You shall not make a covenant with those occupying the land into which you will enter to them, lest it become a trip-wire for you among you all. You shall overthrow their altars and smash their monuments and cut down their groves. For you shall not worship foreign gods. For the Lord is a jealous God, his name is God the Jealous* (Ex. 34:11–14).[105]

The sermon concludes with the words: "Listen brothers and sisters; you're shaken to the core because it said 'The Lord is jealous' O soul of the Church, O that wife of his, you're afraid of your husband's jealousy; guard and preserve your chastity."[106]

---

103. Ibid., 24:10.
104. Ibid., 24:11.
105. Ibid.
106. Ibid., 24:11:294–296. "Audite, fratres, exhorrescitis quia dictum est: Deus zelans est. O anima ecclesiae, o illa coniux, times virum zelantem: serva castitatem."

Sermon 360B/ Mainz 61/ Dolbeau 25 (Boseth)

Particularly in *Sermon* 360B/ M 61/ D 25, we see parallels to Augustine's arguments given in *S* 198/ D 26/ M 62.[107] *Sermon* 360B/ M 61/ D 25 was given at Boseth in 404, some weeks after *Sermon* 198/ D 26/ M 62,[108] to the congregation there and some visiting pagans, which helps to explain the title given to the sermon—*Cum pagani ingrederentur*. In both *S* 360B/ M 61/ D 25 and *S* 198/ D 26/ M 62, the chief criticism of the pagans is that they are proud. Unlike *S* 198/ D 26/ M 62, in *S* 360B/ M 61/ D 25 Christ as mediator is not discussed using the term "mediation." But the theme is present and emphasized throughout. In *S* 360B/ M 61/ D 25, Christ is the "medicus,"[109] the doctor; Augustine says to these pagans, "the humility of Christ is medicine for your pride."[110] The comments of Lepelley regarding pagan elites mentioned above, can also be useful here in understanding Augustine's critiques of pagan pride. The manner of Augustine's dealing with the pagans seems to have hardened over time. Robert Markus notes that early in his career, in 393, Augustine, preaching to his hearers, tells them to abstain from participation in the festivals of the pagans and to tolerate them. This position changes in 399 when imperial officers come to North Africa to enforce laws closing pagan temples. In *Epistle* 50, from 399, he addresses the notables of the town of Sufes where sixty Christians have been killed after, given occasion by the laws, they proceeded to destroy a statue of Hercules.

> Earth reels and heaven trembles at the report of the enormous crime and unprecedented cruelty which has made your streets and temples run red with blood, and ring with the shouts of murderers. You have buried the laws of Rome, in a dishonoured grave, and trampled in scorn the reverence due to equitable enactments. The authority of emperors you neither respect nor fear. In your city there has been shed the innocent blood of sixty of our brethren; and whoever approved himself most active in the massacre, was rewarded with your applause, and with a high place in your Council. Come now, let us arrive at the chief pretext for this outrage. If you say that Hercules belonged to you, by all means we will make good your loss: we have metals at hand, and there is no lack of stone; nay, we have several varieties of

---

107. For Dolbeau on the parallels of *Sermon* 198/ D 26/ M 62 and other works of Augustine, see 356–357. On *S* 360B/ M 61/ D 25, see Dolbeau, 227–268 (*RE Aug.*, 37–77).

108. Dolbeau takes the reference to an imperial visit to Rome to be that of Honorius on January 1, 404. And even though the exact location of Boseth is uncertain, it is thought to be in the countryside of Proconsular Africa. From Perler, 405–406, he places Augustine in the area at about this time (Dolbeau, *Vingt-Six Sermons au Peuple D'Afrique*, 245–247).

109. For a brief description of the connection between Christ as *medicus* and Christ as *mediator*, see Madec, *La Patrie et La Voie*, 142–145.

110. *Sermon* 360B/ M 61/ D 25:17.

marble, and a host of artisans. Fear not, your god is in the hands of his makers, and shall be with all diligence hewn out and polished and ornamented. We will give in addition some red ochre, to make him blush in such a way as may well harmonize with your devotions. Or if you say that the Hercules must be of your own making, we will raise a subscription in pennies, and buy a god from a workman of your own for you. Only do you at the same time make restitution to us; and as your god Hercules is given back to you, let the lives of the many men whom your violence has destroyed be given back to us.[111]

Given the conflict with pagans in Sufes, it is possible to imagine that Christians might have even invited Augustine to stave off such violence in Boseth.

Although there is no direct reference to Christ as mediator by use of the term, Augustine addresses the idea in his extended consideration of the Neoplatonic assent of the soul.[112] As in *Sermon* 198/ D 26/ M 62, the key problem with the pagan way is that it is prideful.[113] They reject the humble way of Christ and are, as a result, then rejected by God.

Sermons 159B/ M 54/ D 21 *On the Words of the Apostle: "Oh the Depths"* 404 (Thignica)

Thignica is on the southerly route from Carthage. It seems as if Augustine stopped here on his way from spending several weeks in Carthage, during which time he preached the Kalends sermon, and failed in his attempt to preach St. Vincent's, which led to the Obedience sermon the day after. The sermon begins with some interesting exegesis, but I want to draw attention to the ending. Towards the end of the sermon, Augustine comes around to presenting the party line. That is, he emphasizes the importance of the way of humility as found with Jesus the one true humble mediator in opposition to Manichean views of Jesus. He, subsequently, brings in a critique of Donatist views and a criticism of the prideful ways of Jews and gentiles.

The last sections of the sermon are full of exhortations and encouragements, such as: "Hold firmly onto this, that tunic, though, which *is woven from the top*, cannot be put in division. Rejoice that you belong to it, you that are the sprigs of

---

111. Augustine, *Epistula* 50 (*NPNF* Series 1, vol. 1, edited by Philip Schaff. This text is available at http://www.ccel.wheaton.edu/fathers/.

112. In both sermons 1 Cor 2:9 plays a key role. We need to transcend what the eye can see, what the ear can hear, and what the mind can conceive in order to attain God. This is the major theme of *S* 360B/ M 61/ D 25 and is found throughout.

113. See, for example, *S* 360B/ M 61/ D 25:6; and *S* 360B/ M 61/ D 25:9, which have elements directed against pride in works of the city from government to monuments.

the Catholic Church."[114] The tone by the end of the sermon is, in the same way, like that of a campaign rally.

Council of June 16, 404

Affirming their posture of "episcopal peace," and citing "horrible acts of violence such as laying ambushes for numerous bishops and clergy (not to speak of laity) and the seizure or attempted seizure of various churches," the council asks

> that protection be provided openly for the various orders in the Catholic Churches in individual cities and various areas on certain neighbouring estates. At the same time one must ask that they confirm the law originating from their father of pious memory, Theodosius, by which a penalty of ten pounds of gold is laid upon those heretics who ordain or are ordained, or upon landowners on whose property heretical congregations assemble. The object of its confirmation is to bring it to bear on whose against whom on account of their ambushes, exasperated Catholics have entered a suit, so that by fear at least of legal action they may refrain themselves from heretical or schismatical wickedness, who fail to be amended or corrected by the thoughts of everlasting punishment. [Similarly we request the law about inheritances be reconfirmed with safeguards against those who become Catholics merely to secure an inheritance.][115]

The Catholics are essentially reflecting on the actions taken at the council of August 403, where they put forward a "pacific commonitory coming of love."[116] They, in June, are saying, in effect, "[W]e tried peaceful discussion, but the Donatists, particularly the Circumcellions, replied with violence." In this shift, reflecting on Augustine's preaching between the two councils, we can hear, in what is called for by the June 404 council, testimony of Augustine's personal experience. Augustine tried to meet with bishops, and where this was not possible, he carried out discussion through correspondence, as in *Against the Letter of Petilianus*. In numerous places, and particularly in *Ennarationes in Ps.* 2 and 3, he takes on Donatist positions in his sermons. Though the council only asks for protection against the Donatists, this, because as the Catholics were pushing their program of Catholicization, the Donatists were violently pushing back. We have seen Augustine consistently address the external aspects of Catholicization by engaging in polemics against the Donatists, other heretics, pagans, and Jews. Augustine did not encourage legislation against the Jews; he did, however, against

---

114. *Sermon* 159B/ M 54/ D 21:18.
115. Canon 93 (*NPNF*, vol. 14).
116. Council of August 25, 403.

the Donatists and the pagans.[117] We have also seen him consistently address the internal aspects of Catholicization by emphasizing how Catholics are to be morally distinct from pagans, heretical Christians, and Jews by the objects of their faith, hope, and love. Augustine's Catholicism is not just geographically universal, it is universal in its social reach, the educated and the uneducated, the rich and poor all have access to God because of the mediation of Jesus Christ found through the Catholic Church. Augustine's preaching between the two councils can be seen as a campaign to persuade various hearers to accept this message.

Sermon 299A / M 9 / D 4 (Carthage or Utica)

There is a final sermon to discuss that reflects the points above. Dolbeau argues, for a number of reasons, that this sermon most likely occurs in Carthage in 404.[118] Accepting the year, but because of "a veiled allusion to the martyrs of the *Massa Candida*, the White Mass, who were martyrs of Utica," Hill places the sermon in Utica.[119] However, because the date, June 29, is certain, since it is a sermon on the martyrdoms of Peter and Paul, it would have to have been given on the way from the Council of Carthage June 16, 404.[120] Location in Carthage or Utica makes little difference for this study. Coming just after the council, the sermon provides an early spin on the new Catholic position.

Peter and Paul are lauded as Catholic martyrs on whom heretics have no claim. Peter is said to have fed the Lord's sheep, not his own, in contrast to the heretics. In response to those who think that he has been silent on the Donatist question, Augustine responds:

> A few of the brethren and sisters were very possibly surprised that in the earlier ser-
> mons I preached I said nothing about the heretics, although I am certainly very keen
> to win back and take in our brothers and sisters from the dead end of their error. And
> it has come to my ears that those pitiable and ever to be pitied people have been saying
> that it was dread of the Circumcellions which imposed silence upon me. It is indeed
> very true that they never stop trying to deter me by terror tactics from preaching the
> word of peace; but if I am to be frightened off by wolves, what answer shall I give to
> the one who tells us, *Feed my sheep* (Jn. 21:15–17). They thrust forward their fangs for
> savaging the sheep, I my tongue for healing them. I speak openly, and I don't keep

---

117. In sermons like *Sermon* 360A/ M 60/ D24, we can see how he advocated the enforcement of repressive measures against the pagans.

118. See Dolbeau, *Vingt-Six Sermons*, 402–410.

119. See note 1 for this sermon in *The Works of St. Augustine: A Translation for the 21st Century*, translated and notes by Edmund Hill, 272.

120. See Chapter 3 and elsewhere in Chapter 5 for more on this council.

quiet, and I say the same things, and I say the same things very often; let them hear what they don't want to hear, let them do what they ought to do. Yes indeed, I make a nuisance of myself to those who are unwilling to hear; but if the reason I enjoy the love of those who hear willingly is that I should go on facing danger from the unwilling, I will put my trust in the name of Christ as I persevere in preaching the word of God, with your prayers helping me along.

I am convinced, you see, that when you hear of the perils I face, of how I have to spend my time among the furious assaults of men who are no better than bandits, then you do pray for me; what makes this clear to me is our mutual love for one another. Not, of course, that I have entered into your minds; but the one who is in you makes it clear to me, because he is also in me. I would urge upon you, though, that when you pray for me, what you should pray for is that God should above all take care of that safety of mine which is in his eyes eternal safety, or salvation. About this safety in time, let him do what he knows is best for me and his Church. After all, we have heard from the same master, the shepherd and chief and head of shepherds, that we shouldn't *fear those who kill the body, but cannot kill the soul* (Mt. 10:28).[121]

Moving from the John passage and discussion of Peter to a passage from 2 Timothy and the example of Paul, Augustine says:

> I adjure you before God and Christ Jesus, who is going to judge the living and the dead, and by his manifesting of himself and by his kingdom; he bound him by adjuring him like that, and then added, *preach the word; press on in season and out of season* (2 Tm. 4:1–2). When I hear this, I, too in my small measure am seasonable for you, unseasonable and a nuisance for them. All the same, I do not rest from publishing the word of God, from the preaching of peace, and from repeating it again and again in Christ's name, in *season, out of season.*
>
> You are seasonable for the hungry when you offer them bread, unseasonable for the sick when you force them to eat. Food is offered the first, rammed into the second; refreshment is pleasing to the one, distasteful to the other, but loving concern neglects neither. So let us take the merits of the apostles as examples for ourselves, while as for their sufferings, let us not only not be afraid of them, but also, should it be necessary, share them.[122]

Concluding this sermon in which he defends his service as a bishop, Augustine, as he has done numerous times, he turns to the prophecy of the blessed seed.

> What did he [God] promise to us? In your seed shall all the nations be blessed (Gn. 22:18). How did this come about through them? Their sound has gone forth into all

---

121. *Sermon* 299A/ M 9/ D 4:3.
122. *Sermon* 299A/ M 9/ D 4:4.

the earth, and their words to the ends of the whole wide world (Ps. 19:4). What will the heretics chant against this? I imagine that they too are celebrating the birthday of the apostles today; they pretend, indeed, to celebrate this day, but they certainly daren't sing this psalm.

Conclusion: Council of June 16, 404, and the Embassy to Honorius

In these sermons, we have seen Augustine advance his vision of Catholicization in both its internal and external aspects. Key to both is the development of his understanding of Christ as mediator. As mediator and as doctor, he serves all, providing for the soul's ultimate good. In these sermons, we also begin to see Augustine carrying forward a rhetorical assault on paganism in coordination with the legal attack. As Peter Brown notes, in "Religious Coercion in the Later Roman Empire: The Case of North Africa,"[123] during this time period we see the Catholic bishop playing a key role in the process of Christianization. The Catholic bishops lobbied for legislation against their rivals and lobbied to have it enforced. They were the ones who determined what in fact right belief and practice were, and they were the ones who would denounce those who were not in accord, or in communion, with the state, as were sacrilegious[124] pagans or heretics. Sometimes the bishops, or as was common in the east, the monks, took the repression of the heterodox into their own hands, as with the destruction of the Serapion or the murder of Hypatia. In *Sermon 198/ M 62/ D 26*, Augustine is not calling for such violence; he is merely leveling a verbal attack. Augustine will, eventually, come to support the use of physical violence by the state to repress pagans and Donatists and other dissenters.[125]

123. Peter Brown, "Religious Coercion in the Later Roman Empire: The Case of North Africa," *History* 48 (1963): 283–305, and in *Religion and Society in the Age of Saint Augustine* (London: Faber and Faber, 1972), 301–331.

124. David Hunt argues that in imperial laws sacrilege had both a political and religious meaning. Going against the imperial in a sense meant going against divine commands. Thus we can see that religion that was dissenting from what was official threatened religious purity and political stability (Hunt, 147).

125. For example, there is Calama. The events, c. 408, can be pieced together from the correspondence between Nectarius, a pagan notable of Calama, and Augustine (*Epp.* 90; 91; 103; 104). Apparently there was a pagan festival in the aftermath of which Christians were attacked. Fearing harsh reprisals from the government, Nectarius asks Augustine to intercede. Augustine replies that the pagans were in opposition to the laws by merely having their festival in the first place. He goes on to say that there are no innocents to be spared among the pagans, for they all

In *S* 198/ M 62/ D 26, and elsewhere, we receive a clearer picture of the arguments that Augustine raises against paganism before his elaboration of them in *De Civitate Dei*. Furthermore, we see how these sermons support Lepelley's contention that those later elaborations are possibly grounded in Augustine's ongoing conflict with civic notables who are proudly clinging to a civic paganism.

Given the repetition of the laws, and Augustine's preoccupation with pagans, it seems that paganism was still a viable religious option, especially among the intellectual elite. The Catholics of North Africa were probably somewhat nervous about their relative position in society. Being a numerical minority in relation to the Donatists, who had their strongest constituency amongst the less educated, perhaps Augustine felt the need to assert the Catholic position on both fronts. It would seem that Aurelius also had this mind-set, for it is from his *cathedra* that Augustine preaches *S* 198/ M 62/ D 26. In this reconstruction, Augustine is the spin doctor on the campaign trail, or the "hired gun" who is brought in to "clean up the town." Interestingly, it would seem that Augustine is a busy marshal, because these sermons, particularly the new sermons of the December–June group, put him in a number of towns preaching against pagans, Donatists, and Jews.

---

were complicit in the celebration and in the violence against Christians. Augustine lays particular blame at the feet of the civic leaders who allowed both the celebration and the violence.

CHAPTER SIX

The Edict of Unity and Its Aftermath

The Edict and *Decreta* and Fallout

From the imperial court at Ravenna between February and March 405, an edict and three *decreta* were dispatched to Africa. The edict declared:

> No one shall recall to memory a Manichee, no one a Donatist, who especially, as we have learned, do not cease their madness. There shall be one Catholic worship, one salvation; equal sanctity within the Trinity, harmonious within itself, shall be sought. But if any persons should dare to participate in practices that are interdicted and unlawful, he shall not escape the toils of innumerable previous constitutions and of the law that was recently issued by Our Clemency. If perchance seditious mobs should assemble, he shall not doubt that the sharp goads of a more severe punishment will be applied to him.[1]

1. *Codex Theodosianus (CT)* 16.5.38. CTh.16.5.38. "Idem aa. et theodosius a. edictum. nemo manichaeum, nemo donatistam, qui praecipue, ut comperimus, furere non desistunt, in memoriam revocet. una sit catholica veneratio, una salus sit, trinitatis par sibique congruens sanctitas expetatur. quod si quis audeat interdictis sese illicitisque miscere, et praeteritorum innumerabilium constitutorum et legis nuper a mansuetudine nostra prolatae laqueos non evadat et si turbae forte convenerint seditionis, concitatos aculeos acrioris conmotionis non dubitet exserendos. dat. prid. id. feb. ravennae stilichone ii et anthemio conss (405 febr. 12)."
   See *The Theodosian Code [Codex Theodosianus] and Novels and the Sirmondian Constitutions*, translated, with commentary, glossary, and bibliography, by Clyde Pharr in collaboration with

Following the instructions of the Catholic council of June 404, Evodius and Theasius had presented the African Catholic bishops' cause at court in Ravenna. "But," as Augustine says to a Donatist in a letter, "by the time that the deputation came to Rome, the wounds of the Catholic bishop of Bagae [Bagai], who had just then been dreadfully injured, had moved the Emperor to send such edicts as were actually sent."[2] The one whose words and wounds predisposed the court to act against the Donatists was a former Donatist bishop, Maximian of Bagai.[3] Maximian had converted from the Donatist camp to the Catholic camp, and was later the victim of an attack by Circumcellions.[4] Having been beaten, but escaping to take his story straight to Ravenna, Maximian had already started the legislative machinery when Evodius arrived.

Although laws do not a Christian make, and although the understanding of the Catholicization of the late Roman Empire, "whatever it may be, was not achieved simply by making paganism and heresy illegal,"[5] we, nevertheless, have a significant moment in the process of Christianization in Africa in the issuance of the Edict of Unity in 405.[6] With these laws, the Donatists were brought under the same kinds of repression ordered against pagans and heretics, and, thus, cast outside the orbit of "true religion." The Edict of Unity and accompanying decrees (*CT* 16.5.37–38; 16.6.4–5; and 16.11.2) were major triumphs of Augustine's and his colleagues' plan of Catholicization. Catholics advanced against the Donatists and other rivals armed with this legislation and supported by governmental authorities

---

Theresa Sherrer Davidson and Mary Brown Pharr, introduction by C. Dickerman Williams (Princeton: Princeton University Press, 1952).

2. Augustine, *Ep.* 88.7.

3. Maximian of Bagai was one of the success stories of some of the earlier initiatives of the African Catholic bishops to recruit clergy from the Donatist camp.

4. In the *Contra Cresconium,* which I shall discuss in greater detail below, Augustine tells us that Maximian hid under the altar, had it broken over the top of him, and was dragged out to be beaten (*Contra Cresconium* 3.47).

5. David Hunt, "Christianising the Roman Empire: The evidence of the Code," in *The Theodosian Code: Studies in the Imperial Law of Late Antiquity,* edited by Jill Harries and Ian Wood (London: Duckworth, 1993), 143–144.

6. The Donatists did not slink away when Africa received these laws, nor were the Catholics able immediately to eliminate them as competition. With this edict and its accompanying sanctions, the Catholic bishops of Africa acquired a useful weapon in their war against the Donatists, but the war would not really be won until the Council of Carthage in 411. Even then the Donatists did not completely vanish. In the meantime, the Catholics' use of force yielded some notable gains, but on the whole only limited success. See Frend, *The Donatist Church* (Oxford: Oxford University Press, 1985), 261–299; and Geoffrey Grimshaw Willis, *Saint Augustine and the Donatist Controversy* (London: SPCK, 1950), 60–92.

from Ravenna to the vicar of Africa in Carthage and all the way down to the local town council level.[7] In fact, the laws put into place penalties against civil officials who refused to enforce the measures.

> Thus, if the governors of the provinces, in contempt of this sanction, should suppose that their consent ought to be given, they shall know that they will be punished with a fine of twenty pounds of gold, and their office staffs shall be subject to like condemnation. The chief decurions and defenders of the municipalities shall know that they will be held subject to the same fine unless they execute what We command, or if in their presence violence should be done to the Catholic Church.[8]

There had been growing cooperation between the Catholics, led by Aurelius, and the government since the restoration of the western imperial order in the squashing of the revolt of Gildo.[9] But now these bonds were being cemented under the renewed attention of Honorius's government, led by Stilicho, to see order maintained in Africa. The Catholics were thus able to have old and new legislation enforced to their advantage, making material and numerical gains. In Carthage and in Hippo, for example, Aurelius and Augustine were able to push out their Donatist rivals and take over those congregations and basilicas.[10] Success was dramatic, but not uniform or universal. If it cannot be clearly established that hearts and minds were won, it can be shown that Catholics gained buildings and bodies. In general, the Catholics gained and consolidated power in the northern urban areas. In the southern and rural areas, however, Donatists found refuge and became entrenched. In those areas, the Circumcellions still provided violent resistance. Aside from the Circumcellions, there were bishops, priests, and laypersons who resisted the Catholic pressure; however, most did not display the militancy of the Circumcellions.[11]

---

7. See Frend, *The Donatist Church*, 262ff.

8. *CT* 16.6.4.2. "Ac ne forsitan sit liberum conscientiam piacularis flagitii perpetrati intra domesticos parietes silentio celare, servis, si qui forsitan ad rebaptizandum cogentur, refugiendi ad ecclesiam catholicam sit facultas, ut eius praesidio adversus huius criminis et societatis auctores adtributae libertatis praesidio defendantur liceatque his sub hac condicione fidem tueri, quam extorquere ab invitis domini temptaverint, nec adsertores dogmatis catholici ea, qua ceteros, qui in potestate sunt positi, oportet ad facinus lege constringi, et maxime convenit omnes homines sine ullo discrimine condicionis aut status infusae caelitus sanctitatis esse custodes" (February 12, 405).

9. Frend, *The Donatist Church*, 249ff.

10. Ibid., 264–265.

11. Ibid., 265ff. See also Remi Crespin, *Ministère et sainteté: Pastorale du clergé et solution de la crise donatiste dans la vie et la doctrine de saint Augustin* (Paris: Études Augustiniennes, 1965), 74.

Nevertheless, from the promulgation of the edict in 405 till around 408, the Catholics were in the ascendancy. By June 26, 405, the law was promulgated at Carthage and Aurelius took full advantage of it.[12] In many places, the Catholics who faced Donatist bishops were able to force their opposing bishop into exile and take over their congregations with the help of civil officials and little violence. Many of these forced converts did not seem to mind the change. This fact was recognized by Augustine and emboldened him in the use of coercive measures.[13] Thus, this is a period of important change in Augustine's thoughts and actions. The relative smoothness of the advancement of Catholicization went on until the execution of Stilicho in 408. Stilicho's fall from the graces of Honorius led to a purge of Stilicho's supporters, a chill in the political climate, and, accordingly, a freeze on the cooperation from the civil authorities who had worked so well in the favor of the Catholics.[14]

Contra Cresconium: Overview

In the rest of this chapter, we shall turn our attention to a somewhat surprising critic of the Catholics' cooperation with the civil authorities as it was led by Augustine. That critic was the Donatist grammarian Cresconius. While it is not surprising that a Donatist would be critical of Augustine, his colleagues, or their tactics, it is surprising that this critic was a layman. As a lay grammarian of the Donatist camp, Cresconius wrote in defense of a Donatist bishop. It is also surprising that, while it is probably the case that Cresconius wrote against Augustine in 403, well in advance of the Edict of Unity of February 405, the criticisms of Catholic collusion with the government had real bite in the period of Catholic use of the edict in a very prophetic way. Augustine claims to have published his reply to Cresconius after the recent laws of Honorius, having only received Cresconius's letter "a long time after it had been written."[15] We do not have Cresconius's original work; all that remains are the fragments recorded by Augustine in his work *Contra Cresconium*. This work from Augustine is perhaps the conclusion of a long, tangled cord of letters and treatises weaving back and forth across the Donatist-Catholic divide.

---

12. Both Crespin and Frend refer to the *Liber Genealogus*, 627 (cited in Monceaux, 4:379; Crespin, 74; Frend, 266).

13. Frend, *The Donatist Church*, 266; Augustine, *Ep.* 93.

14. Frend, *The Donatist Church*, 270ff.

15. Augustine, *Contra Cresconium grammaticum* (*CC*) 1.1. "[L]onge postea quam scripsisti." Also see Augustine's self-reflective comments some years later in *Retractations* 2.52.

To unravel this tangle, we must trace the story back to Petilianus, Bishop of Cirta/Constantine, who wrote a letter attacking the Catholic position. Around the year 400, Augustine came into possession of a fragment of a letter of Petilianus's, written to his presbyters against the Catholic Church. Petilianus was the most prominent Donatist bishop of his time, even exceeding the prestige of Primianus, the Donatist bishop of Carthage. Petilianus had a reputation of being quite learned, so Augustine was astonished by the position that Petilianus took in his letter. Augustine felt that in his arguments, Petilianus made the Donatist position obviously vulnerable (*Contra litteras Petiliani*, 1.1). Augustine's reply to these letters elicited further response from Petilianus. The work that comes down to us as *Contra litteras Petiliani* captures this back and forth correspondence, which probably ranged over two or three years.[16] Thus, the exact dating of the work is difficult. But according to Pierre-Marie Hombert, Books 1 and 2 were completed by 402, while Book 3 was not completed until at least 403, and most likely not until 405.[17] This correspondence and its preservation by Augustine, in published form as *Contra litteras Petiliani,* are important for our understanding of the *Contra Cresconium.*

16. See Chapter 3. The composition of *Contra litteras Petiliani* (*CLP*) is very interesting. As I said above, in Book 1 Augustine tells us that he had been presented with a portion of a letter that Petilianus had written to his Donatist followers. Augustine writes with at least three audiences in mind. He probably had in mind the encouragement of Catholics, lest the fragments of the Petilianus letter poison their faith; second, he was trying to be persuasive to Petilianus himself; and third, to Donatists in general. Book 1 was put in circulation and Augustine set himself to further refutation as he acquired the complete text of Petilianus's letter; this is the content of Book 2. Here Augustine begins a point by point refutation, quoting Petilianus with the formula "Petilianus said . . ." followed by "Augustine answered . . . ." While Augustine was working on Book 2, Petilianus received a copy of Book 1 and issued a letter in response to Augustine. Augustine acquired this letter and issued a response that became Book 3. That seemed to be the end of that exchange, for there is no record of further responses from either Petilianus or Augustine.

See Augustine's comments and Sister Mary Inez Bogan's notes in Saint Augustine, *Retractations* 2.51, translated by Sister Mary Inez Bogan (Washington, D.C.: Catholic University of America Press, 1968). See also Pierre-Marie Hombert's comments in his *Nouvelles Recherhcesde Chronologie Augustinienne*, Collection des Études Augustiniennes, Séries Antiquité 163 (Paris: Institut d'Études Augustiniennes, 2000), 189–193; and Chester D. Hartranft, "Introductory Essay: Writings in Connection with the Donatist Controversy," in *The Nicene and Post-Nicene Fathers*, First Series, vol. 4: *St. Augustine Writings Against the Manichees and Against the Donatists*, translated by J. R. King, and revised with additional notes by Chester D. Hartranft (Reprint, Grand Rapids, MI: Eerdmanns, 1983).

17. Hombert, *Nouvelle Recherches*, 189–194.

Contra Cresconium is a treatise written by Augustine in response to the letter written to Augustine by Cresconius in defense of Petilianus. From the contents of *CC*, it seems that Cresconius was familiar with at least Book 1 of Augustine's writing against Petilianus.[18] The *CC* is a work in four books and, from Augustine's description in the *Retractations*, and from what he says in the work itself, we know that Augustine initially conceived the refutation as a project in three books.[19] After discussing material regarding the Maximianist schism[20] in Book 3, however, Augustine says:

> I saw that all his [Cresconius's] arguments could be answered by dealing with the sole case of the Maximianists whom the Donatists condemned as schismatics and despite this, admitted some of them with their honors and did not repeat baptism administered to them outside their own communion, I further added a fourth book in which, to the best of my ability, I demonstrated this carefully and clearly.[21]

From what can be reconstructed, Cresconius puts forward arguments that can be understood as challenging Augustine's self-understanding, rhetoric, and plan for social order. Clearly, in large measure, Cresconius is not original; he explicitly built on the criticisms of Petilianus. However, he seems to go beyond Petilianus, particularly in calling into question Augustine's self-understanding. And this compels Augustine to defend himself on these three points in a much more thorough fashion than he had with Petilianus. Before moving to a discussion of these points, I will give a brief overview of the contents of the *Contra Cresconium*.

As mentioned, the *Contra Cresconium* is a work in four books originally conceived as three with the fourth added later. As noted by A. C. De Veer, the two sections of the work are, in fact, two different responses to Cresconius bound into one book.[22] The fact that Cresconius's attack on Augustine was the motivating factor in writing is made clear in the first section of the *CC*. Augustine addresses Cresconius directly. He acknowledges the delayed receipt of Cresconius's letter and trusts that his own work will reach him also. Augustine notes, with some annoyance, that Cresconius is writing in defense of Petilianus. He seems to feel that Cresconius has no business bothering Augustine for at least three reasons.

18. No citations in *Contra Cresconius* refer to any part of *CLP* beyond Book 1.

19. *Retractations* 2.52; *CC* 4.1.

20. See *Encyclopedia of the Early Church*, 1992 ed., s.v. "Maximian the Donatist-Maximianist," by F. Scorza Barcellona. This is the same controversy that is mentioned in *En. in Ps.* 36.II.

21. *Retractations* 2.52.

22. See A. C. De Veer's introduction to *Oeuvres de saint Augustin: Bibliotheque Augustinienne* 31, 4th series: *Traites Anti-Donatistes*, Vol. IV: *Contra Cresconium Libri IV and De Unico Baptismo*, edited and translated into French by G. Finaert, introduction and notes by A. C. De Veer (Paris: Desclée de Brouwer, 1968), 27–43.

First, the initial controversy was with Petilianus. Second, Cresconius, a mere lay-men, "bound by no clerical obligation," dared to write to Augustine, a bishop. Third, not only is Augustine a bishop, he is a busy bishop. In spite of these reasons, Augustine sees himself as duty bound to reply to Cresconius.[23]

Augustine then begins responding to specific criticisms raised by Cresconius. It is evident throughout the work that the topics for discussion were generally determined by points that were raised by Cresconius. For example, in Book 1, two main concerns can be noted. First, Augustine defends his eloquence and use of dialectic.[24] Then he contrasts the Donatist and Catholic views of baptism.[25] Both of these points are elaborations of themes found initially in Petilianus's work.

Thus Augustine argues for the unity of the Catholic Church under one baptism, supported by statements regarding divisions in Corinthians (1 Cor. 1.12). For Augustine, Paul's refusal to be mired in the factionalism of some who supported him against those who were supporters of Apollos and others is a clear example of how to maintain unity by affirming the primacy of Christ. The Donatists and the Catholics can both have valid baptisms because Christ is the guarantor of the baptism's validity. Thus, there is no need to be rebaptized when moving from one group to another.[26] He argues his point at length from numerous scriptures, and even the case of Cyprian that Cresconius raised is not a valid counterexample for Augustine.[27]

The discussion of baptism continues in Book 2 and is handled from a number of perspectives. By 2.21, Augustine starts to discuss baptism in light of Petilianus's claims about the conscience of the minister. Petilianus had said that "the holiness of the conscience of the one giving is attended to that it may cleanse the receiver."[28] Augustine rejects Petilianus's claim and Cresconius's defense of it by counter claim-ing first, that the minister's and every individual's conscience is unknowable, and second, that it is in fact Jesus Christ and the Holy Spirit, and not the minister, that are the ultimate guarantors of the validity of baptism. If this is not the case and the Donatists are right about the minister's role, then, Augustine argues, no one can be certain of the validity of sacramental acts because, although a minister may have a good or bad reputation, the state of his conscience, good or bad, will really remain unknown. This issue of conscience Augustine extends to all believers, and he claims

---

23. Augustine, *CC* 1.1. A fourth reason that is not explicitly stated but that can be inferred is that Augustine has some irritation at having to repeat himself.

24. Ibid., 1.2ff.

25. Ibid., 1.27ff.

26. Ibid., 1.32.

27. Ibid., 1.38.

28. See *CC* 2.21, which is referring to *CLP* 1.1.2 and/or 2.3.6.

that there will always be secret sinners, and that true Christians in the true Catholic Church must tolerate them. Cresconius, following Petilianus, however, argues that purity can be achieved in the church only by separation. In the case of baptism, a sinner cannot validly baptize. In response, Augustine makes a sharp reply:

> You say, you even write that no sinner in the least way should usurp the right to baptize. If this is so you are not baptized. Then retract your vain statement or seek angels to baptize you.[29]

In the latter part of Book 2, he makes a strategic appeal to Cyprian in an effort to delegitimize the claims of the Donatists that they stand in the tradition of Cyprian. Augustine concedes that Cyprian was both rebaptized and taught rebaptism, but argues that Cyprian's authority was not equal to that of scripture. Augustine, subsequently, has no qualms with saying that, while Cyprian was in error on that subject, at the core of Cyprian's life and work was an emphasis on unity.

> You inserted in your letter his [Cyprian's] words from the letter to Jubaianus. You wanted to show that one must baptize in the Catholic Church those who were baptized in the heresy or the schism. I do not accept the authority of this letter, because they do not have the authority of the canonical books. Rather, I judge them using the canonical books, and all that is congruent with the authority of divine Scripture with praise I accept. But what does not agree with Scripture I reject with peace. And by this if that which you recall from Cyprian in that which he wrote to Jubaianus was taken from the canonical books of the Apostles or the Prophets I would not have any opposition to that. But since the quotations that you make me are not canonical, I use of all the freedom to which the Lord calls us, to reject the contrary opinions of this man, whose excellence I feel powerless to attain, whose many writings mine cannot compare with, whose genius delights me, whose eloquence I enjoy, whose love I marvel at, whose martyrdom I venerate. That which I would otherwise recommend I do not accept. I do not accept, I say, that which the blessed Cyprian thought concerning baptism of heretics and schismatics, since the Church for which the blessed Cyprian has poured its blood, does not accept it.[30]

29. Augustine, *CC* 2.35. "Tu enim dixisti, tu etiam minime scribere timuisti: 'Ut quisquis peccator inter omnes homines fuerit, ius sibi Baptismatis non usurpet.' Si autem nondum baptizatus es, aut hanc vanissimam sententiam corrige, aut a quibus baptizeris angelos quaere."

30. Ibid., 2.32.40. "Verba eius ex epistola ad Iubaianum inseruisti litteris tuis, quibus ei placuisse monstrares, baptizandos eos esse in Ecclesia catholica, qui fuerint in haeresi vel schismate baptizati. Ego huius epistolae auctoritate non teneor; quia litteras Cypriani non ut canonicas habeo, sed eas ex canonicis considero, et quod in eis divinarum Scripturarum auctoritati congruit, cum laude eius accipio; quod autem non congruit, cum pace eius respuo. Ac per hoc, si ea

We even get an occasion where Augustine invokes the "blessed seed" to support his cause. He attacks Donatist claims that they are the only pure and, thus, true Christians. Augustine responded that, in the world, the Church, which contains "wheat and chaff," is like

> a city set on a hill that cannot be hidden and like the seed of Abraham multiplied like the stars of heaven and as the grains of sand on the sea shore and in which all the nations will be blessed.[31]

Cyprian leads off Augustine's comments in Book 3 as Augustine continues to argue against claims that Cyprian supports the Donatist cause. In his letter to Augustine, Cresconius argued that, contrary to Catholic claims, Donatists did have fellowship with some churches outside Africa. The evidence he cited was a letter from the Council of Serdica addressed to African bishops.[32] Among those named was Donatus. Augustine has two lines of attack in response. First, he argues that the Donatus of the letter was not necessarily Donatus the "heretical" bishop of Carthage. Augustine, second, claims that even if it was Cresconius's Donatus, the Council of Sardica is rejected by Catholics because it ended up supporting Arian doctrine.[33] Augustine seems to relish showing this connection because it further paints the Donatists as heretics. In addition to these prominent subjects, Augustine, in continuing to refer to the events related to the Maximianist controversy, shows the inconsistency of the Donatists' position.

Aside from documents related to the Maximianist controversy in support of his claims, Augustine quotes at length from ecclesiastical and civil documents,

---

quae commemorasti ab illo ad Iubaianum scripta, de aliquo libro Apostolorum vel Prophetarum canonico recitares, quod omnino contradicerem non haberem. Nunc vero quoniam canonicum non est quod recitas, ea libertate ad quam nos vocavit Dominus, eius viri cuius laudem assequi non valeo, cuius multis litteris mea scripta non comparo, cuius ingenium diligo, cuius ore delector, cuius caritatem miror, cuius martyrium veneror, hoc quod aliter sapuit, non accipio. Non accipio, inquam, quod de baptizandis haereticis et schismaticis beatus Cyprianus sensit; quia hoc Ecclesia non accipit, pro qua beatus Cyprianus sanguinem fudit."

31. Ibid., 2.36.45. "[Q]uippe civitas quae abscondi non potest super montem constituta, per quam dominatur Christus a mari usque ad mare, et a flumine usque ad terminos orbis terrae, tamquam semen Abrahae multiplicatum sicut stellae coeli, et sicut arena maris, in quo benedicuntur omnes gentes."

32. Ibid., 3.34.38; 4.44.52. This argument came to Augustine's attention in 396/397 when Augustine, Alypius, and others had a meeting with Fortunius, the Donatist bishop of Thiave. See *Ep.* 44 for the record of the meeting in Thiave. On the use of the Council of Sardica and Augustine's rejection of it, see A. C. De Veer's notes in *Oeuvres de saint Augustin*, 805–809.

33. For discussion of the council, events leading up to it, and its aftermath, see W. H. C. Frend, *The Rise of Christianity* (Philadelphia: Fortress Press, 1984), 528–532.

going all the way back to the original controversy over the ordination of Caecilian as Bishop of Carthage. Augustine is careful to point out that the Donatist claims against Caecilian and the Catholics rest mostly on oral testimony passed down over the years, not on clear textual evidence. Donatist claims that Caecilian's ordination was tainted by the hands of Felix of Apthungi, a *traditor*; that Caecilian was exiled by Constantine; and that the Catholics have been constantly and consistently persecutors of the Donatists are challenged by Augustine. From Augustine's evidence, he argues that it should be concluded that the Donatists were tainted by the crimes of apostasy and *traditio,* that Caecilian was exonerated by Constantine and bishops overseas, and that Donatists as well as Catholics appealed to the government for support of their positions. Augustine goes on to argue that it is not suffering that makes one the victim of persecution, and, thus, a potential martyr; it is, rather, suffering for the right cause. For Augustine, the Donatists' theology of purity over unity is the wrong cause.

By his own admission, Augustine initially thought to end his response to Cresconius with the conclusion of Book 3, but decided that he had not done justice to the material related to the Maximianist controversy. Beginning with Book 1, Augustine has alluded to these materials in support of various points, but in Book 4, he attempts to systematically refute the charges of Cresconius and Petilianus in particular, as well as all Donatists in general.[34]

Beginning with the criticism of his eloquence, Augustine recapitulates the previously discussed arguments of Cresconius. In response to the issue of eloquence, Augustine argues that the condemnation of the Maximianists was put forth in the most eloquent language by the majority group of Donatists. Most of the points Augustine makes are substantial repetitions of what he has said in earlier books. Book 4 could in fact stand on its own as a more condensed, polished, and direct refutation of Cresconius, using the powerful evidence of the Maximinanist controversy against the Donatist mainstream. Now having exposed the reader to the general landscape of *Contra Cresconium*, I shall now look at the work as Augustine's response to Cresconius's challenge to his self-understanding, rhetoric, and social order.

Cresconius's Attack on Augustine's Self-Understanding

Though there are many places that Cresconius's challenge to Augustine briefly appear, it can be found most explicitly at the end of Book 3. Augustine addresses

---

34. Actually, we have seen that Augustine began to use these materials as early as the fall of 403 with his sermon in Carthage.

three issues, which Cresconius raised, that were attempts to undercut Augustine's authority by tarnishing his reputation and invalidating his claim to be a bishop. First, Cresconius claims that Augustine did not practice the leniency that he promised. Second, Cresconius claimed that this related to the fact that Augustine was no true Christian—but a Manichee who had not really converted. Third, Cresconius pointed out that Augustine's ordination was questionable in that his own primate opposed it.[35] Augustine not only does not shy away from defending himself from these charges but, consistent with his self-understanding as a servant of God and the Church, Augustine spins these issues back to the core Catholic message: Christ is the true foundation of faith and ministry. Referring to personal attacks against him, Augustine says to Cresconius: "Give up such arguments; I am only one man. The Church is the case before us, not me. It is the Church I say which has learned from its Redeemer to put its hope on no man."[36] Thus, from Augustine's perspective, although what Cresconius says about him distorts the facts, it would not matter if the allegations were completely true, as the substance of what Augustine had been arguing remains true. The validity of the Catholic sacraments and its claims to universality all rest on Christ and his promises and not on the minister.

Cresconius's Aattack on Augustine's Rhetoric

Eloquence (or rhetoric) and dialectic are the two main headings under which Cresconius's criticism of Augustine's rhetoric falls. Both of these are first mentioned by Augustine in Book 1 and recur at points throughout the work, most notably in Book 4. As mentioned above, in Book 1, the use of scripture is a key aspect of the criticism and a key part of the debate. Cresconius's attack on Augustine's use of rhetoric and dialectic is twofold. One of Cresconius's claims is that it is not fitting for a "supposed" bishop to use dialectic, polished rhetoric, and pagan and legal sources the way Augustine does. Cresconius argues that a bishop ought to be simple in his style, use the Bible, and avoid the craft of rhetoric. As a grammarian, Cresconius uses his training to criticize Augustine's use of words. These attacks range from criticizing Augustine's use of the term "Donatist"[37] to his challenging Augustine's designation of the Donatists as "heretics." Instead of "Donatist," Cresconius argues that Augustine should use the term "schismatic."

---

35. Augustine, *CC* 3.78.90–3.80.92.

36. Ibid., 3.80.92. "Desine talibus: unus homo sum. Ecclesiae inter nos agitur causa, non mea, Ecclesiae, inquam, quae in nullo homine spem ponere a suo didicit redemptore."

37. According to Cresconius, this is an improper declension of the noun.

Augustine responds that dialectic allows one to defend the truth and expose error; therefore, it is a valuable tool for a bishop.[38] Key to understanding the debate on these points is recognizing the way in which scripture is used on both sides. For example, with reference to eloquence and dialectic, Cresconius contends that eloquence is a cause of sin according to Proverbs 10:19, and dialectic is quarreling that leads to the same end. Augustine takes care to show how eloquence and dialectic have scriptural support in considering the prophets, Paul, and even Jesus.[39]

Further, Augustine defends his designation of Donatism as heresy. Cresconius asked, referring to a comment by Augustine in *CLP* 1.1 where he spoke of "the sacriligeous error of the Donatists," "how can you say [that], for heresy is only between those who follow different doctrines?" He goes on to note that the Manicheans, Arians, Marcionites, Novatians, and others are heretics because

> among them stand doctrines contrary to the Christian faith but since among us [Donatists and Catholics] we have the same Christ born, died and resurrected, one religion, the same sacraments, with no difference in Christian observance, this makes it schism; it should not be called heresy.[40]

For Cresconius, Augustine's use of the term "heresy" against the Donatists can only be understood as "criminal zeal"[41] on Augustine's part. Accepting these definitions used by Cresconius, Augustine argues that the Catholics and Donatists do in fact have a different doctrine. He asks, "If we have one religion, the same sacraments, no difference in Christian observance, why, then, do you rebaptize a Christian?"[42] Then Augustine asserts, "If you rebaptize a Christian and I do not, yes, truly we follow different doctrines."[43] So, for Augustine, by the practice of rebaptism and the theology behind it, Cresconius and the Donatists show themselves to have a different, and thus heretical, religion.[44]

38. Augustine, *CC* 1.16.17.

39. I will discuss these criticisms in more detail below in the section on Cresconius's attack on Augustine's rhetoric.

40. Augustine, *CC* 2.4. "Quid sibi vult + inquis + quod ais haereticorum sacrilegum errorem? Nam haereses nonnisi inter diversa sequentes fieri solent, nec haereticus nisi contrariae vel aliter interpretatae religionis est cultor, ut sunt Manichaei, Ariani, Marcionitae, Novatiani, caeterique quorum inter se contra fidem christianam diversa sententia stat. Inter nos, quibus idem Christus natus, mortuus et resurgens, una religio, eadem Sacramenta, nihil in christiana observatione diversum, schisma factum, non haeresis dicitur."

41. Ibid., 2.4. "[S]tudio criminandi."

42. Ibid., 2.6. "Si una religio est, eadem sacramenta, nihil in christiana observatione diversum, quare ergo rebaptizas christianum? Si autem in eo quod tu rebaptizas christianum, ego non rebaptizo? Diversa utique sequimur."

43. Ibid.

44. Ibid.

Cresconius's Attack on Augustine's Sense of Social Order

In *Epistle* 22, Augustine presented a plan to reform the morals of the Catholics in Africa and form strategies to address its opponents. This plan we have called Catholicization. Cresconius's criticisms of Augustine address his plan for social order in its internal and external forms. Cresconius argues that the Catholics lack a sense of holiness and purity in the life of the Church. He also argues that the Catholics are persecutors. Thus, in defense of the Donatist tradition of Christianity, Cresconius essentially argues that Catholicization has produced something that is in fact not Christian on two counts.

In response to the charges against the internal aspects of Catholicization, Augustine argues that the Catholics are indeed concerned about holiness and purity, but their view differs from the Donatists' view in two important ways. First, Catholics view holiness at a deeper level. Holiness is essentially about interior purity that may or may not be clearly reflected in reputation. Second, sacramental purity does not and cannot rely on the purity of the minister. This is because only God knows the interior state of a person, and because the object of the believer's faith and guarantor of the validity of the sacrament is Christ.

Responding to the charge of being persecutors, Augustine argues that the Donatists can only be blessed according to Jesus if they suffer for justice. Augustine exploits this distinction in his spin. He argues that Donatists, as obstinate schismatics, were not just when they suffered persecution in the early years in the time of Macarius and in contemporary times. By the end of Book 3, Augustine saw further opportunity to take the offensive by using examples from the Maximianist controversy. Using these materials, Augustine argues, as he had done many times before, that the main body of Donatists were the persecutors of the party of Maximian.

Augustine's *Epistle* 93: An Apology for Coercive Catholicization

Augustine now sees punishment from God as an educational principle, and defends his tactics accordingly. Writing to Vincentius of Cartenna in 407 or 408,[45] Augustine describes a change of mind that he had.

---

45. Vincentius, an old acquaintance of Augustine's from Carthage, was the Rogatist bishop of Cartenna in Mauretania Caesariensis. The Rogastists were yet another group that broke away from the main Donatist body.

17. I have therefore yielded to the evidence afforded by these instances which my colleagues have laid before me. For originally my opinion was, that no one should be coerced into the unity of Christ, that we must act only by words, fight only by arguments, and prevail by force of reason, lest we should have those whom we knew as avowed heretics feigning themselves to be Catholics. But this opinion of mine was overcome not by the words of those who controverted it, but by the conclusive instances to which they could point. For, in the first place, there was set over against my opinion my own town, which, although it was once wholly on the side of Donatus, was brought over to the Catholic unity by fear of the imperial edicts, but which we now see filled with such detestation of your ruinous perversity, that it would scarcely be believed that it had ever been involved in your error. There were so many others which were mentioned to me by name, that, from facts themselves, I was, made to own that to this matter the word of Scripture might be understood as applying: "Give opportunity to a wise man, and he will be yet wiser" (Prv. 9:9). For how many were already, as we assuredly know, willing to be Catholics, being I moved by the indisputable plainness of truth, but daily putting off their avowal of this through fear of offending their own party! How many were bound, not by truth—for you never pretended to that as yours—but by the heavy chains of inveterate custom, so that in them was fulfilled the divine saying: "A servant (who is hardened) will not be corrected by words; for though he understand, he will not answer" (Prv. 29:19)! How many supposed the sect of Donatus to be the true Church, merely because ease had made them too listless, or conceited, or sluggish, to take pains to examine Catholic truth! How many would have entered earlier had not the calumnies of slanderers, who declared that we offered something else than we do upon the altar of God, shut them out! How many, believing that it mattered not to which party a Christian might belong, remained in the schism of Donatus only because they had been born in it, and no one was compelling them to forsake it and pass over into the Catholic Church![46]

In this letter Augustine again found opportunity to use the "blessed seed" as a prophetic polemic.[47] Augustine also, once again, finds room for anti-pagan and anti-Jewish polemic. In the post–Edict of Unity world, however, there is a more chilling quality to his attacks. Seeing the results of compelling[48] Donatists to come

---

46. Augustine, *Ep.* 93.17.

47. Ibid., 93.15; 93.19; and 93.20.

48. A favorite passage of Augstine's for justifying coercion was Lk. 14:23, "compel them to come in." See *"compelle intrare,"* in Augustinus-Lexikon 1 (1986–1994): 1084–1085. See also Peter Brown, "St. Augustine's Attitude to Religious Coercion," in his *Religion and Society in the Age of Saint Augustine* (London: Faber and Faber, 1972), 260–278, esp. 271, 278; also in *JRS* 54 (1964): 107–116. Brown rightly notes that only heretics like Donatists were at this point forced into the Catholic Church. However, legislation supported by the Catholics sought to end public paganism. Although Augustine's language against the Jews can be harsh, he held to the "preservation of the Jews" doctrine that we heard in a number of the sermons in Chapter 5.

in, Augustine has been converted completely to the value of coercion.[49] Consider the following passage:

> For he whose aim is to kill is not careful how he wounds, but he whose aim is to cure is cautious with his lancet; for the one seeks to destroy what is sound, the other that which is decaying. The wicked put prophets to death; prophets also put the wicked to death. The Jews scourged Christ; Christ also scourged the Jews. The apostles were given up by men to the civil powers; the apostles themselves gave men up to the power of Satan. In all these cases, what is important to attend to but this: who were on the side of truth, and who on the side of iniquity; who acted from a desire to injure, and who from a desire to correct what was amiss?[50]

To Vincentius, Augustine links his often used medical imagery with the radical measures taken against the enemies of the Catholic Church. If *Epistle* 22 was the charter of Catholicization giving it incipient shape, then *Epistle* 93 was the apology for its hardened development, at least for its external aspect. And yet, Augustine still had reservations like those expressed to Paulinus of Nola in this letter written in 408.

> 3. What shall I say as to the infliction or remission of punishment, in cases in which we have no other desire than to forward the spiritual welfare of those in regard to whom we judge that they ought or ought not to be punished? Also, if we consider not only the nature and magnitude of faults, but also what each may be able or unable to bear according to his strength of mind, how deep and dark a question it is to adjust the amount of punishment so as to prevent the person who receives it not only from getting no good, but also from suffering loss thereby! Besides, I know not whether a greater number have been improved or made worse when alarmed under threats of such punishment! at the hands of men as is an object of fear. What, then, is the path of duty, seeing that it often happens that if you inflict punishment on one he goes to destruction; whereas, if you leave him unpunished, another is destroyed? I confess that I make mistakes daily in regard to this, and that I know not when and how to observe the rule of Scripture: "Them that sin rebuke before all, that others may fear" (1 Timothy 5:20); and that other rule, "Tell him his fault between thee and him alone" (Matt. xviii. 15); and the rule, "Judge nothing before the time" (1 Cor. iv. 5). "Judge not, that ye be not judged" (Matt. vii. 1) (in which command the Lord has not added the words, "before the time"); and this saying of Scripture, "Who art thou that judgest another man's servant? to his own master he standeth or falleth: yea, he shall be holden up, for God is able to make him stand" (Rom. xiv. 4.); by which words he makes it

---

49. I am in agreement with Brown against Willis that Augustine's change was not just a product of the Edict of Unity (Brown, "St. Augustine's Attitude to Religious Coercion," 263–264).

50. Augustine, *Ep.* 93.8.

plain that he is speaking of those who are within the Church; yet, on the other hand, he commands them to be judged when he says, "What have I to do to judge them also that are without? do not ye judge them that are within? therefore put away from among yourselves that wicked person" (1 Cor. v. 12, 13). But when this is necessary, how much care and fear is occasioned by the question to what extent it should be done, lest that happen which, in his second epistle to them, the apostle is found admonishing these persons to beware of in that very example, saying, "lest, perhaps, such an one should be swallowed up with overmuch sorrow"; adding, in order to prevent men from thinking this a thing not calling for anxious care, "lest Satan should get an advantage of us; for we are not ignorant of his devices" (2 Cor. ii. 7, 11). What trembling we feel in all these things, my brother Paulinus, O holy man of God! what trembling, what darkness! May we not think that with reference to these things it was said, "Fearfulness and trembling are come upon me, and horror hath overwhelmed me. And I said, Oh that I had wings like a dove! for then would I fly away, and be at rest. Lo, then would I wander far off, and remain in the wilderness." And yet even in the wilderness perchance he still experienced it; for he adds, "I waited for Him who should deliver me from weakness and from tempest" (Ps. lv. 5–8, as given in the LXX). Truly, therefore, is the life of man upon the earth a life of temptation (Job vii. 1).[51]

Indeed, Augustine would like to be away, apart from these things. But, as he reveals later in life with the story of the judge who must use torture,[52] he had the sense that his place was inescapable. He was given by God the dreaded responsibility to act, and he acted.

Conclusion

A. C. De Veer has argued that *Contra Cresconium* was innovative in the method of argument that Augustine used. In addition to his well used arguments from scripture like the "blessed seed," Augustine uses numerous historical documents and dialectic. De Veer states that the use of dialectic in particular was perhaps spurred by the "liberal culture"[53] of Cresconius and the manner in which he attacked Augustine specifically on the use of dialectic and rhetoric. Cresconius was a lay grammarian, unlike Augustine's earlier Donatist interlocutors, such as Fortunius, Petilianus, Parmenian, and Primian, who were all bishops. Against the bishops, Augustine tended to put greater emphasis on scripture, although he used, to varying degrees, dialectic and history. Against Cresconius, however, in

---

51. Ibid., 95.3. See Brown, *Augustine of Hippo*, for discussion of Augustine's ambivalence, 239.

52. Augustine, *DCD*, 19.6.

53. See De Veer's introduction to *CC*, 45.

response to the direct challenge of the use of dialectic and rhetoric, Augustine adjusts his rhetorical strategy and meets his opponent's arguments, which were grounded in dialectical distinctions that were part of the grammarian's skills, with the use of dialectic.[54]

Furthermore, Augustine cites at least ten documents to refute various Donatist claims. With these documents, Augustine argued that Caecilian was innocent of the charges against him, and so were those who ordained him. Augustine also made his most sustained and extensive use of the documents from the Maximianist controversy to show that the Donatists were inconsistent in their application of the doctrine of baptism and use of the coercive power of the state.[55]

I am in agreement with Brown, who says: "Some profound and ominous changes had taken place in Augustine's attitude to the church and society in the first ten years as a bishop."[56] Noting particularly Augustine's ideas on grace and predestination, Brown observes that there is increasing rigidity and rigorism in these ideas. We remember that in Augustine's early days as a priest his hope was to hang on to his optimistic view of human nature, human society, and free will. He hoped to be able to persuade his opponents to become good spiritual Catholics. Over time, however, he saw that this could not be the case. As Augustine became convinced of the need for strong measures, according to Brown, he summed up this idea in the word "*disciplina*" meaning "an essentially active process of corrective punishment, a 'softening-up process,' a 'teaching by inconvenience'—*a per molestias eruditio.*" Brown goes on to show that Augustine, reflecting on God's process of discipline exercised against Israel in the Old Testament through disasters, would come to see the actions taken against the Donatists as "a 'controlled catastrophe' imposed by God, mediated by the laws of Christian Emperors."[57]

Augustine looks to powers outside of the measures he could affect as a spiritual leader, and speaks of the responsibilities of Christian clergy and rulers, the prophecies of the end of paganism, and the spread of the Catholic Church. Brown speaks of this saying:

> Augustine by contrast, had as much as admitted that man, in his fallen state, required more than purely spiritual pressures to keep him from evil. A part of his power as a bishop to "warn" wayward sheep among the Christians of Africa had been devolved

---

54. Ibid., 44–46.

55. Ibid., 45–46; 47–48.

56. Brown, *Augustine of Hippo*, 231.

57. Ibid., 236, and Brown, "St. Augustine's Attitude to Religious Coercion," 260–278, esp. 270ff.

on the "terror" of Imperial laws; and the "Apostolic discipline" of the bishop had been diffused throughout society, from Emperors issuing laws, to heads of families flogging their Donatist dependents into submission to the Catholic Church.[58]

Contra Cresconium and *Epistle* 93 are two important windows into the hardened external aspect of Catholicization after the Edict of Unity and before the impact of the death of Stilicho. His death would weaken state support for the Catholics' coercive measures against their opponents. Augustine would go on to press Catholicization, his agenda of social order, in cooperation with his colleagues, in spite of this and other setbacks until his death in 430.

58. Brown, *Augustine of Hippo*, 235236.

CHAPTER SEVEN

Conclusion

In this book, I have drawn attention to the way in which the much written about Christianization of the Roman Empire needs to be seen with a much more attentive eye, at least in the case of Roman Africa of the late fourth and early fifth centuries. Catholicization, rather than Christianization, is the name I assign to the process that comes into view when considering the role of Augustine in the changes during the period under investigation. From his *Epistle* 22, we heard Augustine speaking from a Catholic consciousness birthed less than a decade earlier. What he envisions with his friend Aurelius of Carthage, Primate Bishop of Africa, is a revitalized, morally and theologically sound clergy and laity that can not only stand against its opponents but also thrive against them. Augustine, as he went from being a servant of God to a servant of the servants of God, became increasingly convinced of the certainty of God's promises to see the Church be that "blessed seed of Abraham," and multiply over the earth as numerous as the stars and grains of sand on the seashore.

There was success achieved in the aftermath of the promulgation of the Edict of Unity in 405 till the death of Stilicho three years later. Afterward, there was Donatist resurgence until the council at Carthage in June 411, which brought to a climax the Donatist controversy. Augustine would never have the Donatists completely gone from his jurisdiction. The Circumcellions would still commit sporadic acts of violence against Catholics, and Augustine would write against them from time to time; however, in the years after the Council of Carthage, he would be increasingly occupied with the Pelagian controversy, and his *magnum opus, City of God Against the Pagans* (*De Civitate Dei*), which responded to claims that forsaking the old gods was the cause of the sack of Rome by Alaric.

Lest we conclude that Augustine was a "lone ranger" who, prompted only by developing predestination out of the writings of Paul, became the first Inquisitor, let us remember some important details. Violence was a fact of the times.[1] Brown points out in *Power and Persuasion in Late Antiquity* that the latter Roman Empire was daily growing more violent. The Donatists were far from being merely innocent martyrs; their side also had blood on their hands, the Circumcellions saw to that. Augustine had many fellow bishops who were on the avant garde of using force against the Donatists. And Augustine himself was only later persuaded to see the application of force as desirable. Outside the Church, emperors, like Theodosius, and officers, like Marcellinus, were zealous to establish a religiously and politically orthodox empire. These things are said not to excuse Augustine, but, rather, they are put forth to place him in his proper context.

Augustine's preaching in 403 and 404 provides us with interesting information to help make this shift in Augustine intelligible. Quite intriguing are the points where we see issues with the Donatists bubbling hot beneath the surface, only to erupt at unexpected moments. When speaking of humble angels and humans, and proud angels and humans, in *Sermon* 198/ M 62/ D 26, Augustine says:

> See, brothers, above all, to which angels the humble men are similar and to which the proud men are similar. For those, who create schisms and heresies, wish their name to be glorified and the name of Christ to lie in darkness and they also choose their seat in the north. Nor, once they leave the church, would the men follow them as if they were Christ, unless their intelligence was darkened and they were alienated from the warmth of love. . . . (What other did Simon want than to be praised through his miracles, to be lifted up in pride? For that very pride compelled him to believe that the gift of the holy intelligence could be bought with money. Contrary to his pride, the apostle in humility, remaining in the south, being warm in intelligence, glowing with prudence, said: *Neither he who plants is anything, nor he who waters, but God who gives the increase [I Cor. 3:7].* And again: *Was Paul crucified for you, or were you baptized in the name of Paul [I Cor. 1:13]?* How did he despise to be worshipped instead of Christ, how fervent was he on behalf of the bridegroom and did not wish by an unfaithful fornicating soul to show off himself instead of the bridegroom?) Such were those saints within their limits.[2]

---

1. See Gaddis, chaps. 3 and 4. I am very thankful to the author for allowing me to see the chapters before publication.

2. *S* 198/ M 62/ D26:53.

S 198/ M 62/ D 26 gives us a glimpse of how Augustine was seeking to shape the religious culture of North Africa. From his personal conviction of the significance of the universal extension of the Church, and Christ as mediator between humans and God, which he developed while in Milan, he fleshed out a polemic and apologetic argument for use against heretics (especially Donatists), pagans, and Jews. We glimpse in this sermon the endurance of civic paganism and the rhetorical lengths, literally, Augustine goes to in order to galvanize the Catholics as a cohesive body with Christ as its head. We glimpse also the significance that this has for the North African Church as a whole. For in *S* 198/ M 62/ D 26, we see Augustine preaching in Carthage for his friend Aurelius, Primate of the African Church. Augustine makes known in *S* 359B/ M 5/ D 2 the significance of the actions of *this* Church for the other churches of the province. It, the Catholic Church at Carthage, set the pace. Augustine wants them to be separate and distinct, over and against those with whom they had much in common. Augustine wants to see a radical change in the relationships that would prohibit common frolicking on the Kalends, with the pagans, and common devotion at the tombs of the martyrs, with the Donatists.

In this period of the early fifth century, Augustine is changing his rhetoric from persuasion to coercion. Particularly in this Kalends sermon, we have preliminary articulations of the lines of argument of which Augustine elaborates in the *De Civitate Dei*. Christ is the only source of mediation, and, save for a curious exception,[3] mediation must be obtained in the Body of Christ that is the visible Church. We must accept God as the Father and the Catholic Church as our mother, Augustine argues. What the Church offers is a new family and a new society parallel to, mixed with, but yet distinct from, the worldly city and its pride.

3. Recall *Sermon* 198/ M 62/ D 26:36.

Bibliography

Primary Sources[1]

Augustine

Augustin D'Hippone *Vingt-Six Sermons au Peuple D'Afrique: Retrouve a Mayence*, edites et commentes par François Dolbeau. Collection des Études Augustiniennes, Series Antiquite 147. Paris: Institut d'Études Augustiniennes 1996.

| agon. de | agone christiano (396) | CSEL 4 |
| c. acad. | contra academicos (386) | CCSL 29 |

1. I list below the main critical editions of the texts below. I have used the editions of the texts found on the CETEDOC database. I have also used the *Patralogiae Latinae* editions found at. I will use various translations of these texts into English and French. As necessary, I will provide my own translation or adapt an existing one. I will note which translation at the place of citation. The CETEDOC database references texts from the following collections:

> *CC: Corpus Christianorum, Series Latin* (c) Brepols
> *PL: Patralogiae Latinae Supplementum* (c) Brepols
> *CSEL: Corpus Scriptorum Ecclesiaticorum Latinorum* (c) Hoelder, Pichler, Tempsky
> *SC: Sources Chrétiennes*
> *S. Bernadi Opera Omnia* (c) Edizioni Cistercensi
> *BSV: Bibla Sacra juxta vulgatam versionem* (c) W. Württembergische Bibelenstalt

c. Cresc.	contra Cresconium grammaticum (405/6)	CSEL 52
c. ep. Parm.	contra epistulam Parmeniani (400)	CSEL 51
c. Faust.	contra Faustum manichaeum (397/9)	CSEL 25.·1
c. Fort.	acta contra Forunatum manichaeum (392)	CSEL 25.·1
c. litt. Pet.	contra litteras Petiliani (400/3)	CSEL 52
cat. rud.	de catechizandis rudibus (399)	CCSL 46
civ.	de civitate dei (413, 426/7)	CCSL 47, 48
cons. ev.	de consensu evangelistarum (399/400 2D ?)	CSEL 43
div. qu. Simp.	de diversis quaestionibus VII ad Simplicianum (396)	CCSL 44
divin. daem.	de divinatione daemonum (407)	CSEL 41
doctr. chr.	de doctrina christiana (396 [completed 427])	CCSL 32
En. Ps.	enarrationes in Psalmos (392/417)	CCSL 38, 39, 40
ep (epp.)	epistula (epistulae) (386/430)	CSEL 34, 44,
ep. cath.	epistula ad catholicos de secta donatistarum (405)	CSEL 52
exp. prop. Rom.	expositio quarumdam propositionum ex epistola ad Romanos (394)	CSEL 84
f. et symb.	de fide et symbolo (393)	CSEL 41
Gal. exp.	epistolae ad Galatas expositio (394/5)	CSEL 84
Gn. c. man.	de Genesi contra manichaeos (388/90)	PL 34
Gn. litt.	de Genesi ad litteram (401/15)	BA 48, 49
Gn. litt. imp.	de Genesi ad litteram imperfectus liber (393/4–426/7)	CSEL 28.·1
gramm.	de grammatica (387)	PL 32
haer.	de haeresibus (428)	CCSL 46
imm. an.	de immortalitate animae (387)	CSEL 89
lib. arb.	de libero arbitrio (387/8–391/5)	CCSL 29
mag.	de magistro (389/90)	CCSL 29
mor.	de moribus ecclesiae catholicae et de moribus manichaeorum (388)	PL 32
mus.	de musica (388/90)	PL 32
nat. b.	de natura boni (398)	CSEL 25.·2
ps. c. Don.	psalmus contra partem Donati (394)	CSEL 51
Rom. inch. exp.	epistolae ad Romanos inchoata expositio (394/5)	CSEL 84
s (ss.)	sermones (392/430)	PL 38, 39, MA I, etc.
trin.	de trinitate (399, 422/6)	CCSL 50, 50A
vera rel.	de vera religione (390/1)	CCSL 32

Baxter, J. H., trans. *Augustine: Select Letters*. Loeb Series. Cambridge, MA: Harvard University Press, 1953.

Bogan, Mary Inez., *Retractations* Fathers of the Church Series, vol. 60. Washington: Catholic University of America Press, 1968.

Boulding, Maria, trans. and notes. *Expositions of the Psalms 1–32: The Works of Saint Augustine, A Translation for the 21st Century*, III/15. Hyde Park, NY: New City Press, 2000.

———, trans. and notes. *Expositions of the Psalms 51–72: The Works of Saint Augustine, A Translation for the 21st Century*, III/17. Hyde Park, NY: New City Press, 2001.

————, trans. and notes. *Expositions of the Psalms 73–98: The Works of Saint Augustine, A Translation for the 21st Century*, III/18. Hyde Park, NY: New City Press, 2002.

Burleigh, J. H. S., ed. *Augustine: Earlier Writings*. Library of Christian Classics. Philadelphia: Westminster, 1953.

De Veer, A. C., intro. and notes. *Oeuvres de saint Augustin: Bibliotheque Augustinienne*, 31, 4th series. *Traites Anti-Donatistes*, Vol. IV: *Contra Cresconium Libri IV and De Unico Baptismo*. Edited and with a French translation by G. Finaert. Paris: Desclée de Brouwer, 1968.

Augustine, Scholastica Hebgin, and Felicitas Corrigan. *St. Augustine on the Psalms 1, Psalms 1–29*, Ancient Christian writers, no. 29. Westminster, Md: Newman Press, 1960.

Augustine, Scholastica Hebgin, and Felicitas Corrigan. *St. Augustine on the Psalms 2, Psalms 30–37. Ancient Christian writers*, 30. Westminster, Md: Newman Press, 1961.

Plumer, Eric, intro., text, trans., and notes. *Augustine's Commentary on Galatians*. Oxford Early Christian Studies. New York: Oxford University Press, 2003.

Rotelle, John E., ed. *The Works of St. Augustine: A Translation for the 21st Century*, III/11. *Newly Discovered Sermons*. Translated by Edmund Hill. Hyde Park, NY: New City Press, 1998.

S. Aureli Augustini Hipponiensis Episcopi De Doctrina Christiana Liber Quartus: A Commentary, with a Revised Text, Introduction, and Translation by Thérèse Sullivan. Washington, D.C., 1930.

Teske, Roland, trans. and notes. *Letters 1–99: The Works of Saint Augustine, A Translation for the 21st Century*, II/1. Hyde Park, NY: New City Press, 2001.

Other Primary Sources

Actes de la Conference de Carthage en 411. Edited by Serge Lancel. SC 194, 195, 224, and 373. Paris: Cerf, 1972–1979.

The Book of Rules of Tyconius. Edited by F. C. Burkitt. Cambridge: Cambridge University Press, 1894.

Claudian. 2 vols. Edited and translated by Maurice Platnauer. Cambridge: Loeb, 1963.

Concilia Africae A. 345–525. Vol. 149 of *Corpus Christianorum: Series Latina*. Edited by Charles Munier. Turnhout, Belgium: Brepols, 1974.

Gesta Conlationis Carthaginiensis, anno 411. Accedit Sancti Augstin *Brevicvlvvs conlationis cvm Dona*. Tvrnholti: Corpus Christianorvm, Series Latina, 1974.

Optatus. *Optatus: Against the Donatists*. Translation and introduction by Mark Edwards. Liverpool: Liverpool University Press, 1997.

Greenslade, S. L. *Early Latin Theology Selections from Tertullian, Cyprian, Ambrose, and Jerome*. The Library of Christian classics, v. 5. London: SCM Press, 1956.

Possidius. *Life of Saint Augustine*. Introduction by Michele Pellegrino. Villanova, PA: Augustinian Press, 1988.

The Theodosian Code and Novels and the Sirmondian Constitutions. Translation with commentary, glossary, and bibliography by Clyde Pharr in collaboration with Theresa Sherrer Davidson and Mary Brown Pharr. Introduction by C. Dickerman Williams. Princeton: Princeton University Press, 1952.

Tyconius: The Book of Rules. Translated by William S. Babcock. SBL Texts and Translations Series 31, Early Christian Literature Series 7. Edited by Robert L. Wilken and William R. Schoedel. Atlanta: Scholars Press, 1989.

Translations

ACW: *Ancient Christian Writers*
BA: *Bibliothèque Augustinienne*
FC: *Fathers of the Church*
NPNF: *Select Library of Nicene and Post-Nicene Fathers*
WSA: *The Works of Saint Augustine: A Translation for the 21st Century*

Reference Works

Augustine Through the Ages: An Encyclopedia. Edited by Allan Fitzgerald. *Sermones*, 789. Grand Rapids, MI: Wm. B. Eerdmans, 1999.
Augustinus-Lexikon, Herausgegeben von Cornelius Mayer. Vol. 2, Fasc. 5/6: Donatistas (Contra-) Epistulae. col. 640–1057. Basel: Schwabe Co. AG, 2001.
Cambridge Ancient History. Vol. XIII: *The Late Empire A.D.* 3rd ed. Edited by Averil Cameron and Peter Garnsey, 337–425. Cambridge: Cambridge University Press, 1998.
Encyclopedia of Contemporary Literary Theory. Edited by Irena R. Makaryk. Toronto: University of Toronto Press, 1993.
Encyclopedia of the Early Church. Edited by Angelo Di Berardino. New York: Oxford University Press, 1992.
A Latin Dictionary. New York: Lewis and Short, 1879. New York: Oxford University Press, 1984.

Secondary Sources

Alexander, J. S. "Aspects of Donatist Scriptural Interpretation at the Conference of Carthage." T & U 128. *Studia Patristica* 15 (1984): 125–130.
———. "Tyconius' Influence on Augustine, A note on their use of the distinction *corporaliter' spiritualiter, Congresso internazionale su S. Agostino nel XVI centario della conversione."* In *Studia Ephemerides Augustinianum*, 2:205–212. 24 Vols. Rome, 1987.
Ando, Clifford. "Pagan Apologetics and Christian Intolerance in the Ages of Themistius and Augustine." *Journal of Early Christian Studies* 4 (1996).
Arbesmann, R. "The Concept of 'Christus medicus' in St. Augustine." *Traditio* 10 (1954): 1–28.
Arnold, Duane W. H., and Pamela Bright. *De doctrina Christina: A Classic of Western Culture.* Notre Dame, IN: University of Notre Dame Press, 1995.
Babcock, W. S. "Augustine and Tyconius: A Study in the Latin Appropriation of Paul." *Studia Patristica* 17.3 (1982): 1209–1215.

Babcock, William. "Patterns of Roman Selfhood: Marcus Aurelius and Augustine of Hippo." *The Perkins School of Theology Journal* 29.6 (Winter 1976): 19.

Bacchi, Lee F. "Augustine, Symmachus and Ambrose." In *Augustine from Rhetor to Theologian*, edited by Joanne McWilliams, 7–13. Waterloo, Ontario: Wilfred Laurier University Press, 1992.

———."A Ministry Characterized by and Exercised in Humility: The Theology of Ordained Ministry in the Letters of Augustine of Hippo." In *Presbyter Factus Sum,* edited by Joseph T. Lienhard S.J.; Earl C. Muller, S.J.; and Roland J. Teske, S.J. New York: Peter Lang, 1993.

Barnes, Timothy D. *Tertullian: A Historical and Literary Study.* Oxford: Clarendon Press, 1971.

Battenhouse, Roy W., ed. *A Companion to the Study of St. Augustine.* New York: Oxford, 1955.

Batiffol, Pierre. *Le Catholicisme de Saint Augustin.* 5th ed. Edited by J. Gabalda et Fils. Paris: Librairie Lecoffre, 1929.

Beddoe, Paul V. "*Contagio* in the Donatists and St. Augustine." *Studia Patristica* 27 (1993): 231–236

Berger, Peter L. *The Sacred Canopy: Elements of a Sociological Theory of Religion.* Garden City, NY: Doubleday, 1967. Reprint, New York: Anchor, 1969.

Berger, Peter L., and Thomas Luckmann. *The Social Construction of Reality.* Garden City, NY: Doubleday, 1966. Reprint, New York: Anchor, 1967.

Bloch, Renee. "Methodological Note for the Study of Rabbinic Literature." Translated by W. S. Green. *Approaches to Ancient Judaism.* Vol. 1. Edited by W. S. Green. Missoula, MT: Scholars Press, 1978.

———. "Midrash." Translated by Mary Callaway. *Approaches to Ancient Judaism.* Vol. I. Edited by W. S. Green. Missoula, MT: Scholars Press, 1978.

Bogan, Mary Inez. *The Vocabulary and Style of the Soliloquies and Dialogues of Saint Augustine.* Washington, D.C.: Catholic University of America, 1935.

Bogomeo, P. *L'Eglise de ces temps dans la predication de saint Augustin.* Paris, 1962.

Bonner, Gerald. *"Quid Imperatori cum Ecclesia?* St. Augustine on History and Society." *Augustinian Studies* 2 (1971): 231–251.

———. *St. Augustine of Hippo: Life and Controversies.* First Edition, London: SCM Press Ltd., 1963. Reissued and Revised 1986 by The Canterbury Press, Norwich.

Booth, Edward. *Saint Augustine and the Western Tradition of Self-Knowing.* Villanova, PA: Villanova University Press, 1989.

Boston, Ray. "Spinning for a Living." *History Today* 46.9 (Sept. 1996): 8–9.

Bowersock, G. W., Peter Brown, and Oleg Grabar, eds. *Late Antiquity: A Guide to the Postclassical World.* Cambridge: Belknap Press of Harvard University Press, 1999.

Bright, Pamela Mary. *Augustine and the Bible.* Notre Dame, IN: University of Notre Dame Press, 1999. Based on *Saint Augustin et la Bible,* edited by Anne-Marie La Bonnardière. Paris, 1986.

———. *"Liber Regularum Tyconii:* A Study of the Hermeneutical Theory of Tyconius-Theologian and Exegete of the North African Tradition." Ph.D. Diss., University of Notre Dame, 1987.

———. *The Rules of Tyconius: Its Purpose and Inner Logic.* Christianity and Judaism in Antiquity 2. Notre Dame, IN: University of Notre Dame Press, 1988.

———. "Tyconius and His Interpreters: A Study of the Epitomes of the Book of Rules." In Kannengiesser, Charles, Pamela Bright, and Wilhelm H. Wuellner. *A Conflict of Christian*

Hermeneutics in Roman Africa: Tyconius and Augustine. Berkeley, CA, USA: Center for Hermeneutical Studies in Hellenistic and Modern Culture, 1989.

Brisson, Jean-Paul. *Autonomisme et Christianisme dans l'Afrique romaine de Septime Severe a l'invasion vandal*. Paris: Boccard, 1958.

Brown, Peter. *Augustine of Hippo*. Berkeley: University of California Press, 1967. First paperbound edition, 1969. 2nd ed., 2000.

———. *Authority and the Sacred*. Cambridge: Cambridge University Press, 1995.

———. *The Body and Society: Men, Women and Sexual Renunciation in Early Christianity*. New York: Columbia University Press, 1988.

———. "Christianization and Religious Conflict." In *Cambridge Ancient History*. Vol. XIII: *The Late Empire, A.D.* 3rd ed. Edited by Averil Cameron and Peter Garnsey, 337–425. Cambridge: Cambridge University Press, 1998.

———. *The Cult of the Saints: Its Rise and Function in Latin Christianity*. Chicago: University of Chicago Press, 1981.

———. "Late Antiquity." In *A History of Private Life*. Vol. 1: *From Pagan Rome to Byzantium*, edited by Paul Veyne, translated by Arthur Goldhammer, 235–311. Cambridge, MA: Harvard University Press, 1987.

———. *Power and Persuasion in Late Antiquity: Towards a Christian Empire*. Madison: University of Wisconsin Press, 1992.

———. *Religion and Society in the Age of Saint Augustine*. London: Faber and Faber, 1972.

———. "St. Augustine's Attitude to Religious Coercion." In *Religion and Society in the Age of Saint Augustine*, 260–278. London: Faber and Faber, 1972. Also in *JRS* 54 (1964): 107–116.

———. *The World of Late Antiquity*. New York: Harcourt Brace Jovanovich, 1971.

Burnaby, John. *Amor Dei: A Study of the Religion of St. Augustine*. London, 1938. Reissued with corrections and new foreward 1991 in paperback by The Canterbury Press, Norwich.

Burns, Patout. "Ambrose Preaching to Augustine: The Shaping of Faith." In *Collectanea Augustiana*, edited by J. C. Schnaubelt and F. Van Fleteren, 373–386. New York: Peter Lang, 1990.

Cameron, Averil. *Christianity and the Rhetoric of Empire: The Development of Christian Discourse*. Berkeley: University of California Press, 1991.

Capps, Donald. "Parabolic Events in Augustine's Autobiography." *Theology Today* 40 (1983): 260–272.

Cary, Philip. *Augustine's Invention of the Inner Self*. New York: Oxford, 2000.

Casey, Damien. "Irenaeus: Touchstone of Catholicity." *Australian eJournal of Theology*. Available at http://dlibrary.acu.edu.au/research/theology/ejournal/aet_1/Casey.htm.

Chadwick, Henry. "New Sermons of St Augustine." *Journal of Theological Studies* 47 (April 1996): 69–91.

———. *The Role of the Christian Bishop in Ancient Society*. Colloquy 35. Berkeley, CA: Center for Hermeneutical Studies in Hellenistic and Modern Culture, 1979.

Chestnut, Glenn F. *The First Christian Histories: Eusebius, Socrates, Sozomen, Theodoret, and Evagrius*. 2nd ed. Macon, GA: Mercer University Press, 1986.

Clarke, M. L. *Rhetoric at Rome*. 3rd ed. New York: Routledge, 1996.

Cochrane, Charles Norris. *Christianity and Classical Culture*. Oxford: Oxford University Press, 1942.

Colish, Marcia L. *The Stoic Tradition from Antiquity to the Early Middle Ages*. Vol. 2 of *Stoicism in Christian Latin Thought through the Sixth Century*. Studies in the History of Christian Thought 35. Leiden: E. J. Brill, 1985.

Conte, Gian Biagio. *Latin Literature: A History*. Translated by Joseph B. Solodow. Revised by Don Fowler and Glenn W. Most. Baltimore: Johns Hopkins University Press, 1994.

Courcelle, Pierre. *Late Latin Writers and Their Greek Sources*. Translated by Harry E. Wedeck. Cambridge, MA: Harvard University Press, 1969.

———. *Les Confessions de S. Augustin dans la tradition litteraire*. Paris: Études Augustiniennes, 1962.

———. *Recherches sur les Confessions de S. Augustin*. Paris: Boccard, 1950. 2nd ed., 1968.

Cox, M. G. "Augustine, Jerome, Tyconius and the *Lingua Punica*." *Studia Orientalia* 64 (1988): 83–106.

Crespin, Remi. *Ministère et sainteté: Pastorale du clergé et solution de la crise donatiste dans la vie et la doctrine de saint Augustin*. Paris: Études Augustiniennes, 1965.

Cross, F. L. "History and Fiction in the African Canons." *Journal of Theological Studies Studies* 12 (Oct. 1961): 227–247.

Crouse, R. D. "'Recurrens in te unum': The Pattern of Saint Augustine's *Confessions*." *Studia Patristica* XIV (1976): 389–392.

Daley, B. "A Humble Mediator: The Distinctive Elements in St. Augustine's Christology." In *Word and Spirit: A Monastic Review 9*, 100–117. Petersham, MA: St. Bede's Publications, 1987.

Daly, Lawrence J. "Psychohistory and St. Augustine's Conversion Process: An Historiographical Critique." *Augustiniana* 28 (1978): 231–254.

D'Arcy, M., M. Blondel, and C. Dawson et al. *Augustine: His Age, Life and Thought*. New York: Meridian Books, 1957. Reprint of *A Monument to St. Augustine*. New York, 1930.

Dixon, Sandra Lee. *Augustine: The Gathered and the Scattered Self*. St. Louis: Chalice, 1999.

Dolbeau, François. Augustin D'Hippone *Vingt-Six Sermons au Peuple D'Afrique: Retrouvés à Mayence*, édités et commentés par François Dolbeau. Collection des Études Augustiniennes, Séries Antiquité 147. Paris: Institut d'Études Augustiniennes, 1996.

Drobner, Hubertus R. *Augustinus von Hippo: Sermones ad populum*, xx–226. Vol. 49: *Überlieferung & Bestand, Bibliographie, Indices*, Supplements to *Vigiliae Christianae*. Leiden: E. J. Brill, 2000.

Esser, Frank, Carrsten Reinemann, and David Fan. "Spin Doctors in the United States, Great Britain and Germany: Metacommunication about Media Manipulation." *Press/Politics* 6.1 (Winter 2001): 16–45.

Evans, Robert. *One and Holy: The Church in Latin Patristic Thought*. London: SPCK, 1972.

Fenn, Richard. *The End of Time: Religion, Ritual, and the Forging of the Soul*. Cleveland, OH: Pilgrim Press, 1997.

Fenton, Joseph Clifford. "A Note on the Berber Background in the Life of Augustine." *Journal of Theological Studies* XLIII, nos. 171/172 (July–October 1942).

————. "St. Augustine's Use of the Note of Catholicity." *The American Ecclesiastical Review*, January, 1948. 47-58.

Ferrari, Leo. "The Boyhood Beatings of Augustine." *Augustinian Studies* 5 (1974): 1–14.

————. *The Conversions of Saint Augustine*. Villanova, PA: Villanova University Press, 1984.

————. "From Pagan Literature to the Pages of the Holy Scriptures: Augustine's *Confessions* as Exemplary Propaedeutic." In *Kerygma und Logos: Beiträge zu den geistesgeschichtlichen Beziehungen zwischen Antike und Christentum: Festschrift für Carl Andresen zum 70. Geburtstag*. Göttingen: Herausgegeben von A.M. Ritter, 1979.

Foucault, Michel. *The Care of the Self*. Translated by Robert Hurley. New York: Random House, 1986.

————. *Discipline and Punish*. New York: Random House, 1995.

Fowden, Garth. "Polytheist Religion and Philosophy." In *Cambridge Ancient History*. Vol. XIII: *The Late Empire, A.D.* 3rd ed. Edited by Averil Cameron and Peter Garnsey, 538–560. Cambridge: Cambridge University Press, 1998.

Fox, Robin Lane. *Pagans and Christians*. London: Viking, 1986.

Fredriksen, Paula. "Augustine and His Analysts: The Possibility of a Psychohistory." *Soundings* 51 (1978): 206–227.

————. *Augustine on Romans*. Texts and Translations, 23: Early Christian Literature. Series 6, Society of Biblical Literature. Chico, CA, 1982.

————. "Beyond the Body/Sul Dichotomy: Augustine's Answer to Mani, Plotinus and Julian." *RA* 23 (1988): 87–114.

————. "Paul and Augustine: Conversion Narratives, Orthodox Traditions, and the Retrospective Self." *JThS N.S.* 37 (1986): 3–34.

Frend, W. H. C. *The Donatist Church*. Oxford: Oxford University Press, 1985.

————. "A note on the Berber Background in the Life of Augustine." *Journal of Theological Studies XLIII*, nos. 171/172 (July–October 1942).

————. *The Rise of Christianity*. New York: Fortress, 1984.

Fux, Pierre-Yves, Jean-Michel Rössli, and Otto Wermelinger, eds. Augustinus Afer: *Augustin Afer: Saint Augustin: Africanité et universalité: Actes du colloque international Alber-Annaba, 1–7 avril 2001*. Paradosis. Vols. 45/1 et 45/2. Fribourg, 2003.

Gaddis, Michael. *There Is No Crime for Those Who Have Christ: Religious Violence in the Christian Roman Empire*. Berkeley: University of California Press, 2005.

Geerlings, W. *Christus Exemplum: Studien zur Christologie und Christusverkündigung Augustins*. Mainz, 1978.

Geertz, Clifford. *The Interpretation of Cultures*. New York: Basic Books, 1973.

Gilson, Etienne. *The Christian Philosophy of Saint Augustine*. New York: Knopf, 1960.

Gorday, Peter. "Principles of Patristic Exegesis: Romans 9–11 in Origen, John Chrysostom, and Augustine." *Studies in the Bible and Early Christianity, 4*. New York, 1983.

Grabowski, Stanislaus. *The Church: An Introduction to the Theology of St. Augustine*. St. Louis: Herder, 1957.

Green, William M. "Augustine's Use of Punic." In *Semitic and Oriental Studies Presented to W. Popper*, 179–190. University of California Publications in Semitic Philology, XI. Berkeley: University of California Press, 1951.

Greenslade, S. L. *Schism in the Early Church.* London: SCM, 1953.

Hagendahl, Harald. *Augustine and the Latin Classics.* 2 Vols. Göteborg: Studia Graeca et Latina Gothoburgensia 20, 1967.

Hahn, T. *Tyconius-Studien.* Leipzig, 1900.

Hartranft, Chester D. "Introductory Essay: Writings in Connection with the Donatist Controversy." In *The Nicene and Post-Nicene Fathers,* First Series. Vol. 4: *St. Augustine Writings Against the Manichees and Against the Donatists.* Translated by J. R. King. Revised with additional notes by Chester D. Hartranft. Reprint, Grand Rapids, MI: Eerdmanns, 1983.

Harrison, Carol. *Augustine: Christian Truth and Fractured Humanity.* New York: Oxford University Press, 2000.

Hefele, Charles J. *A History of the Councils of the Church.* Vol. 2: *AD 326–AD 429.* Edinburgh, 1896.

Hendrix, Scott H. *Ecclesia in Via; Ecclesiological Developments in the Medieval Psalms Exegesis and the Dictata Super Psalterium (1513-1515) of Martin Luther.* Studies in medieval and Reformation thought, v. 8. Leiden: Brill, 1974.

Hombert, Pierre-Marie. *Nouvelle Recherches de Chronologie Augustinienne.* Collection des Études Augustiniennes, Séries Antiquité 163. Paris: Institut d'Études Augustiniennes, 2000.

Hunt, David. "Christianising the Roman Empire: The Evidence of the Code." In *The Theodosian Code: Studies in the Imperial Law of Late Antiquity,* edited by Jill Harries and Ian Wood, 143–157. London: Duckworth, 1993.

Johnson, Elizabeth. "A Study of Paul's Midrash on Abraham in Romans 4." Unpublished Seminar Paper NT958: Pauline Theology. Spring 1997. Princeton Theological Seminary.

Jones, A. H. M. *The Later Roman Empire, 284–602: A Social, Economic and Administrative Survey.* 2 Vols. Baltimore: Johns Hopkins University Press, 1992. Originally 3 Vols. Oxford: Basil Blackwell, 1964.

Juel, Donald. *Messianic Exegesis: Christological Interpretation of the Old Testament in Early Christianity.* Philadelphia: Fortress, 1988.

Kaster, Robert. *Guardians of Language: The Grammarian and Society in Late Antiquity.* Berkeley: University of California Press, 1988.

Kelehen, James P. *Saint Augustine's Notion of Schism in the Donatist Controversy.* Mundelein, IL: Saint Mary of the Lake Seminary, 1961.

Kennedy, George. *Classical Rhetoric and Its Christian and Secular Tradition from Ancient to Modern Times.* 2nd and Rev. ed. Chapel Hill: University of North Carolina Press, 1999.

Kriegbaum, Bernhard. *Kirche der Traditoren oder Kirche der Martyrer: Die Vorgeschichte des Donatismus.* Innsbrucker Theologische Studien, Bd. 16. Innsbruck: Tyrolia, 1986.

Kunzelmann, A. *Die Chronologie der Sermones des Hl. Augustinus.* Vaticana: Tipografia poliglotta Vaticana, 1931.

La Bonnardière, Anne-Marie. "Les *Ennarationes in Psalmos* prêchées par saint Augustin à Carthage en décembre 409." *Recherches Augustiniennes* 11 (1976): 52–90.

Ladner, Gerhard. *The Idea of Reform.* Cambridge: Harvard University Press, 1959.

Lamirande, Emilien. *Church, State and Toleration: An Intriguing Change of Mind in Augustine.* Villanova, PA: Villanova University Press, 1975.

Lawless, George. *Augustine of Hippo and His Monastic Rule.* Oxford: Oxford University Press, 1987.

Leigh, David J. "Augustine's Confessions as a Circular Journey." *Thought* 60 (1985): 73–87.

Lepelley, Claude. *Les Cites de L'afrique romaine au bas-empire.* Tomes I et II. Paris: Études Augustiniennes, 1979.

———. *"Saint Augustin et la cite romano-africaine."* In *Jean Chrysostome et Augustin,* edited by Charles Kannengiesser. Paris, 1975.

———. "Spes saeculi: Le milieu social d'Augustin et ses ambitions séculières avant sa conversion." In *Congresso internazionale su s. Agostino nel XVI centenario della conversione,* Roma, 15–20 settembre 1986, Atti, 1.99–118. Rome, 1987.

Levenson, Carl Avren. "Distance and Presence in **Augustine's Confessions**." *The Journal of Religion* 65 (1985): 500–512.

Lieu, Samuel N. C. *Manichaeism in the Later Roman Empire and Medieval China.* Manchester, 1985. 2nd and Rev. ed., Tübingen: J. C. B. Mohr, 1992.

Lim, Richard. *Public Disputation, Power, and Social Order in Late Antiquity.* Berkeley: University of California Press, 1995.

MacMullen, Ramsay. *Christianity and Paganism in the Fourth to Eighth Centuries.* New Haven: Yale University Press, 1997.

———. *Christianizing the Roman Empire A.D. 100–400.* New Haven: Yale University Press, 1984.

Madec, Goulven. "Augustin, disciple et adversaire de Porphyre." *REAug* 10 (1964): 365–369.

———. *Augustin Prédicateur (395–411): Actes du Colloque International de Chantilly (5–7 septembre 1996).* Paris: Institut d'Études Augustiniennes, 1998.

———. Le Christ des paiens d'apres le De consensu euangelistarum de saint Augustin. Recherches augustiniennes 26 (1994), pp. 3–67

———. "Le milieu Milanais: Philosophie et christianisme." in *Bulletin de littérature ecclésiastique* 88 (1987): 194–205.

———. *Le Patrie et La Voie: Le Christ dans la vie et la pensee de saint Augustin.* Paris: Desclée, 1989.

Mandouze, Andre. *Prosopographie Chrétienne du Bas-Empire.* Vol. 1: *Afrique (303–533).* Paris, 1982.

———. *Saint Augustin: L'Aventure de raison et de grace.* Paris: Études Augustiniennes, 1968.

Markus, Robert. *Conversion and Disenchantment in Augustine's Spiritual Career.* Villanova, PA: Villanova University Press, 1984.

———. *The End of Ancient Christianity.* Cambridge: Cambridge University Press, 1990.

———. *Saeculum: History and Society in the Theology of Saint Augustine.* Cambridge: Cambridge University Press, 1984.

Marrou, Henri Irénée. *A History of Education in Antiquity.* Translated by George Lamb. Madison, WI: University of Wisconsin Press, 1982.

———. *Saint Augustine and His Influence through the Ages.* Translated by P. Hepburne-Scott. London, 1957.

———. *Saint Augustin et la fin de la culture antique.* Paris: Boccard, 1938.

Martin, Thomas F. *"Clericatus sarcina* (ep.126.3): Augustine and the Care of the Clergy." Available at: http://divinity.library.vanderbilt.edu/burns/chroma/clergy/Martinorders.html

Matthews, John. "Augustine, Symmachus and Ambrose." In *Augustine from Rhetor to Theologian*, edited by Joanne McWilliams, 7–13. Waterloo, Ontario: Wilfred Laurier University Press, 1992.

———. *Laying Down the Law: A Study of the Theodosian Code*. New Haven: Yale University Press, 2000.

———. *The Roman Empire of Ammianus*. Baltimore: Johns Hopkins University Press, 1989.

———. *Western Aristocracies and Imperial Court A.D. 364–425*. Oxford: Clarendon Press, 1975.

Matthews, John, and Tim Cornell. *Atlas of the Roman World*. Oxford: Phaidon, 1982.

McLynn, Neil B. *Ambrose of Milan: Church and Court in a Christian Capital*. Berkeley: University of California Press, 1994.

McMahon, Robert. *Augustine's Prayerful Ascent: An Essay on the Literary Form of the Confessions*. Athens, GA: Georgia University Press, 1989.

McNamara, Marie Aquinas. *Friends and Friendship for Saint Augustine*. Staten Island, NY: Alba House, 1964.

Meijering, E. P. *Augustine: De Fide et Symbolo*. Amsterdam: J. C. Gieben Publisher, 1987.

Merdinger, J. E. *Rome and the African Church in the Time of Augustine*. New Haven: Yale University Press, 1997.

Meslin, M. *La fete des Kalends de janvier dans l'empire romain*. Brussels: Latomus, 1971.

Monceaux, Paul. *Histoire Littéraire de L'Afrique Chretienne*. Vols. 1–6. Paris: Ernest Leroux, 1901.

Oberhelman, Steven M. *Rhetoric and Homiletics in Fourth-Century Christian Literature*. Atlanta: Scholars Press, 1991.

O'Connell, Robert J. "The Plotinian Fall of the Soul in St. Augustine." *Traditio* 19 (1963): 1–35.

———. *St. Augustine's Early Theory of Man, AD 386–391*. Cambridge: Belknap Press of Harvard University Press, 1968.

O'Daly, Gerard J. P. "Time as Distentio and St. Augustine's Exegesis of Philippians 3:12–14." *REAug* 23 (1977): 265–271.

O'Donnell, James. "Augustine's Classical Readings." *Recherché Augustiniennes* 15 (1980): 144–175.

———, ed. *Augustine: Confessions*. 3 Vols. New York: Oxford University Press, 1992. Special edition for Sandpiper Books Ltd., 2000.

O'Meara, John J. "Parting from Porphyry." In *Congresso internazionale su s. Agostino nel XVI centenario della conversione*, Roma, 15–20 settembre 1986, Atti, 2.357–369. Rome, 1987,

———. *Porphyry's Philosophy from Oracles in Augustine*. Paris, 1959.

———. *The Young Augustine*. London: Longmans, 1954. Reprint, Staten Island, NY: Alba House, 1965.

Pagels, Elaine. *Adam, Eve, and the Serpent*. New York: Random House, 1988.

Pelikan, Jaroslav. *The Christian Tradition: A History of the Development of Doctrine*. Vol. 1: *The Emergence of the Catholic Tradition* (100–600). Chicago: University of Chicago Press, 1971.

Pellegrino, Cardinal Michele. *The True Priest: The Priesthood as Preached and Practiced by Saint Augustine*. Edited by John E. Rotelle, O.S.A. English translation by Brothers of the Order of Hermits of Saint Augustine, Inc. Villanova, PA: Augustian Press, 1988.

Perler, Othmar, with J.-L. Maier. *Les Voyages de saint Augustin*. Paris: Institut d'Études Augustiniennes, 1969.

Pincherle, A. "Da Ticonio A Sant' Agostino." *Ricerche Rel.* 1 (1925): 443–466.

———. "L'ecclesiologia nella controversia donatista." *Ricerche Rel.* 1 (1925): 34–48.

Pollmann, Karla. *Doctrina Christiana: Untersuchungen zu den Anfängen der christlichen Hermeneutik unter besonderer Berücksichtigung von Augustinus, De doctrina Christiana*. Freiburg, Schweiz: Universitätsverlag, 1996.

Pontet, Maurice. *L'exégèse de S. Augustin prédicateur*. Paris, 1944.

Pope, H. *St. Augustine of Hippo: Essays Dealing with His Life and Times and Some Features of His Work*. New York, 1937.

Portalie, E. *A Guide to the Study of St. Augustine*. Tranlated by R. J. Bastian, S.J. Chicago, 1960.

Porter, Stanley. *Handbook of Classical Rhetoric in the Hellenistic Period 330B.C.–A.D.400*. Boston: Brill Academic Publishers, 2001.

Raby, F. J. E. *A History of Christian Latin Poetry From the Beginnings to the Close of the Middle Ages*. New York: Clarendon Press, 1927.

Ramsey, Boniface. *Ambrose. The Early Church Fathers* London: Routledge, 1997.

Ratzinger, Joseph. *Volk und Haus Gottes in Augustins Lehre von der Kirche*. München: K. Zink, 1954.

Raven, Susan. *Rome in Africa*. 3rd ed. New York: Routledge, 1993.

Remy, G. *Le Christ mediateur dans l'oeuvre de saint Augusin*. These de Strasbourg: Faculté de Thologie catholique, 1977. Reprint, Lille-Paris, 1979.

Rist, John M. *Augustine: Ancient Thought Rebaptized*. New York: Cambridge University Press, 1994.

Rondet, Henri, "Essais sur la chronologie des Enarationes in Psalmos de saint Augustin", Bulletin de litterature ecclesiastique 61 (1960) 111–127 et 258–286; 65 (1964), 110–136;68 (1967), 180–202.

Rousseau, Philip. *Ascetics, Authority and the Church in the Age of Jerome and Cassian*. Oxford: Oxford University Press, 1978.

———. "Augustine and Ambrose: The Loyalty and Single-mindednesss of a Disciple." *Augustiniana* 27 (1977): 151–165.

Sabah Ferdi, M. C. Cheriett, photographers. *Augustin de retour en Afrique 388–430: Reperes archeologiques dans le patrimoine algerien*. Fraibourg: Musee de Tipasa/Editions Unversitaires, 2001.

Saxer, Victor. *Morts, Martyrs, Reliques en Afrique Chrétienne*. Théologie Historique 55. Paris: Beauchesne 1980).

Schnaubelt, Joseph C., and Frederick Van Fleteren, eds. *Collectanea Augustiniana, Augustine, Biblical Exegete*. Peter Lang, 2001.

Semple, W. H. "Augustinus Rhetor: A Study from the Confessions of Saint Augustine's Secular Career in Education." *Journal of Ecclesiastical History* 1 (1950): 135–150.

Sharpe, A. B. "Tyconius and St. Augustine." *Dublin Review* 132 (1903): 64–72.

Shaw, Brent. "The Family in Late Antiquity: The Experience of Augustine." *Past and Present* 115 (May 1987): 3–51.

Siker, Jeffrey S. *Disinheriting the Jews: Abraham in Early Christian Controversy.* Louisville: Westminster/John Knox Press, 1991.

Simonetti, Manlio. "Tyconius." In *Patrology*, Vol 4. Edited by Angelo Di Berardino. Introduction by Johannes Quasten. Translated by Placid Solari. Westminster, MD: Christian Classics, 1994.

Starnes, C. J. "The Unity of the Confessions,"*Studia Patristica* XVIII.4 (1990): 105–111.

Stendahl, Krister. "The Apostle Paul and the Introspective Conscience of the West." *Harvard Theological Review* 56 (1963): 199–215.

Tengstrom, Emin. *Donatisten und Katholiken: Soziale, wirtschaftliche und politische Aspekte einer nordafrikanischen Kirchenspaltung.* Gotenborg, 1964.

TeSelle, Eugene. *Augustine the Theologian.* New York: Herder, 1970.

Tilley, Maureen. *The Bible in Christian North Africa: The Donatist World.* Minneapolis: Fortress Press, 1997.

———. *Donatist Martyr Stories.* Liverpool: Liverpool Univesrity Press, 1996.

Trapé, Agostino. In *Patrology*, Vol. 3. Edited by Angelo Di Berardino. Introduction by Johannes Quasten. Translated by Placid Solari. Westminster, MD: Christian Classics, 1994.

Van Der Meer, F. *Augustine the Bishop.* New York: Sheed and Ward, 1961.

Weidmann, Clemens. *Augustinus und das Maximianistenkonzil von Cebarsussi, Zur historichen und textgeschichtlichen Bedeutung von Enarratio in Psalmum 36, 2, 18–23,* Veröffentlichungen der Komission zur Herausgabe des Corpus der Lateinischen Kirchenväter. Heft XVI. Wien: Verlag der Österreichischen Akademie der Wissenschaften, 1998.

Wetter, Gillis Pison. "La catholicisation du Christianisme primitive." *Revue d'Histoire et de Philosophie Religieuses* (1927): 17–33.

Williams, Daniel H. *Ambrose and the End of the Nicene-Arian Conflicts.* New York: Oxford University Press, 1995.

Williams, Stephen, and Gerard Friell. *Theodosius the Empire at Bay.* New Haven: Yale University Press, 1994.

Willis, Geoffrey Grimshaw. *Saint Augustine and the Donatist Controversy.* London: SPCK, 1950.

Wuellner, William, ed. *A Conflict of Christian Hermeneutics in Roman North Africa: Tyconius and Augustine: Protocol of the Fifty-Eighth Colloquy: 16 October 1988.* Berkeley: University of California Press, 1989.

Young, Frances M. *Biblical Exegesis and the Formation of Christian Culture.* Peabody, Mass: Hendrickson, 2002.

Zarb, Seraphino M. *Chronologia Operum S. Augustini.* Romae: Apud Pont. Institutum "Angelicum, 1934.

———. *Chronologia Enarrationum S. Augustini in Psalmos.* Valetta-Malta , 1948.

Zmire, Paul. "Collegialité Episcopal." In *Recherche Augustiniennes*, Vol. 7, 3–71. Paris: Institut d'Études Augustiniennes, August 1971.

Index

PATRISTIC STUDIES

Gerald Bray, *General Editor*

This is a series of monographs designed to provide access to research at the cutting-edge of current Patristic Studies. Particular attention will be given to the development of Christian theology during the first five centuries of the Church and to the different types of Biblical interpretation which the Fathers used. Each study will engage with modern discussion of the theme being treated, but will also break new ground in original textual research. In exceptional cases, a volume may consist of the critical edition of a text, with notes and references, as well as translation. Revised doctoral dissertations may also be published, though the main focus of the series will be on more mature research and reflection. Each volume will be about 250–300 pages (100,000–120,000 words) long, with a full bibliography and index.

Inquiries and manuscripts should be directed to:

Acquisitions Department
Peter Lang Publishing, Inc.
P.O. Box 1246
Bel Air, MD 21014-1246

To order other books in this series, please contact our Customer Service Department at:

(800) 770-LANG (within the U.S.)
(212) 647-7706 (outside the U.S.)
(212) 647-7707 FAX

or browse online by series at:

www.peterlang.com